ALMOST THERE

First published 2022
© V.Behrens 2022

ISBN 978-0-6209871-4-1

All rights reserved. No part of this book may be reproduced by any means, without prior permission, in writing from the copyright owner.

Written and photographed by Dr Vivienne Behrens
Design and layout by Courtney Hodgson

 **FOLLOW THE VIV'S DAILY BREAD BLOG**

ISBN 978-0-6209871-4-1
9 780620 987141

Contents

ALMOST THERE

1	January	Page 9- 72
2	February	Page 73-130
3	March	Page 131-194
4	April	Page 195-256
5	May	Page 257-320
6	June	Page 321-382
7	July	Page 383-446
8	August	Page 447-510
9	September	Page 511-572
10	October	Page 573-636
11	November	Page 637-698
12	December	Page 699-762

DEDICATION

I dedicate this daily reading
to my precious sister.

Her faith, life and ultimately, her death, inspired me to examine my values, my purpose in life and my relationship with my Saviour. Her unfailing trust in Jesus and His love for her, despite many reasons to contradict that, epitomises the true child of the Living God. She died knowing that she is going to her heavenly home. She died without fear. She died looking at the face of her beloved Jesus.

I can only pray to be half
the woman she became.

ACKNOWLEDGEMENTS

The writing of this book was very much a lone wolf journey. However, during the four long years it took to reach completion, I used Blowfish Restaurant, located in the Dolphin Beach Hotel in Table View, Cape Town, as my work place. Monday and Tuesday evenings, with regularity, I was welcomed by management and staff alike as I took my regular spot at the bar counter. Oliver Seko and Rama Nkinze, the bar tenders, knew my favourite drink by heart and always greeted me with beaming faces and enquiries into my wellbeing. Occasionally, the manager on duty would waiver my bill – because I was such a loyal customer.

My heartfelt thanks to them all – in a very special way, they helped make this journey a joyous one. I hope to be back soon with renewed enthusiasm and a new lone wolf project.

THE LORD'S PRAYER

Our Father who art in heaven,
Hallowed be thy Name.
Thy kingdom come,
Thy will be done,
On earth as it is heaven.
Give us this day our daily bread.
And forgive us our trespasses,
As we forgive those who trespass against us.
And lead us not into temptation,
But deliver us from evil.
For thine is the kingdom,
and the power, and the glory,
for ever and ever.
Amen.

-Jesus of Nazareth

The Lord's Prayer may be committed to memory quickly, but it is slowly learnt by heart.

- Frederick Deniso Maurice

ALMOST THERE

DAY 1-31

January

DAY 1

January 01

In the beginning, was the Word and the Word was with God and the Word was God....... The Word became flesh and made his dwelling among us.

John 1:1

JOHN 1:1

The Word at the beginning of John 1 can be linked to the first words spoken by God at the beginning when he says, "Let there be light" and there was light (Genesis 1:3). Here the sending of light represents the creation. In the same way, January 1st represents the start of a new year and presents us with a chance to recreate ourselves and our lives.

Jesus is called the "Word" because he was the Son of God, sent to earth to reveal his Father's mind to the world. We are able to call on Jesus to help us to walk along the road that God has laid out for us. God is invisible and beyond our understanding. Yet, we can get to know him through reading the scriptures, praying, singing hymns and participating in the ritual of communion.

"Dost though love life? Then do not squander time, for that is the stuff life is made of."
- Benjamin Franklin

DAY 2

January 02

But you, Bethlehem Ephrathah, though you are small among the clans of Judah, out of you will come for me one who will be ruler over Israel whose origins are from old, from ancient times.

Micah 5:2

ALMOST THERE

MICAH 5:2

Micah 5:2 is believed by many to be a Messianic prophecy. This interpretation is strengthened by the fact that the Jewish religious leaders in the first century also identified it as such. Only Jesus Christ fits the Messianic claims made in Micah 5:2. He was born in Bethlehem Ephrathah. Jesus claimed to be the Messiah, the ruler of Israel (John 4:25-26). He also fits the description as being "from ancient times", or eternal (Colossians 1:16-17). No other ruler in Israel fits these requirements. Unlike this prediction of a Messiah who will come to save the world, we cannot predict our own future. Therefore the choices we make are paramount in determining our destiny. Deciding to follow Jesus is a personal commitment and a personal decision. But once the decision has been made we have to spend the rest of our lives choosing to follow Him.

Every day when we wake up we are faced with the decision of whom we will serve that day. As we drive to work, do our job, go grocery shopping or interact with friends and family, we are constantly choosing whether or not we will serve God. Our emotions and desires, as well as our anger and self-centredness, are all great barriers to living the life we were created to live – a life that looks like Jesus.

In 2 Corinthians 10:3-5, we are instructed to "take every thought captive". This must surely be one of the most difficult choices to make. It is relatively easy to make good choices when other people are watching. But, our innermost thoughts and desires are hidden from scrutiny. Somehow the fact that God knows our thoughts is not as bothersome to us as if our friends and family know them. The Bible teaches us that we should focus on things that are beautiful and pure (Philippians 4:8-9). When we fix our minds on God, our thoughts are naturally purer and less prone to sinful encroachment. However, if we spend our time filling our minds with worldly things, it becomes harder to avoid the attractions and allure of this world. The things we say, our thoughts and the actions we take, are all as a result of the choices we make. We don't live our lives by accident; we choose how we will conduct ourselves. If we want to follow Jesus we must make intentional and consistent choices to do so.

DAY 3

January 03

I will establish my covenant as an everlasting covenant between me and you and your descendants after you for generations to come, to be your God and the God of your descendants after you

Genesis 17:7

ALMOST THERE

GENESIS 17:7

Abraham was 99 years old when God appeared before him and made this covenant with him. The covenant was one of an exceedingly great and precious promise. God would be a God to him and his descendants. That meant God would provide the wisdom to guide and counsel them, the power to protect and support them, the goodness and kindness to comfort and feed them. But the covenant had to be mutual - "walk before me faithfully and be blameless". The token of this agreement was to be circumcision, which would be the outward sign that seals this covenant of grace.

This covenant extends to all God's people. Jesus, through His death and resurrection, established a new and everlasting one with all believers. Circumcision, as an outward sign of faith, has been replaced by baptism. Our covenant is twofold – "repent, believe and follow Jesus", and, "walk before God and be blameless". We must live our life with integrity. We must think, speak and act, in everything, according to God's word. But above all, we must "love the Lord our God with all our heart and with all our mind and love our neighbour as we love ourselves". (Matthew 22:37)

The New Year also represents new beginnings. It holds the promise of exciting possibilities and grants us the chance to start again with renewed hope and strength.

DAY 4

January 04

Jesus said, "A woman giving birth to a child has pain because her time has come; but when her baby is born she forgets the anguish because of her joy that a child is born into the world".

John 16:21

JOHN 16:21

In this part of Jesus' farewell discourse to his disciples, he directs their attention to the sorrow and grief that they are about to experience as a result of his crucifixion. But he assures them that this grief will soon be transformed into an enduring and abounding source of joy. The reason for this joy, Jesus explains, is "for I will see you again". (John 16:22) Jesus conquers sin and death on the cross, and, as a result of his resurrection, the disciples enter a new level of intimacy in their relationship with the Son and the Father.

In the same way, all the pain, sorrow, suffering and hardship that we encounter in this world are only temporary. The promise of enduring and abounding joy applies to us as well. When we acknowledge our sins and failings and ask God for His forgiveness, we experience a "rebirth". With the help of the Holy Spirit we too enter a new life and relationship with God.

"And God will wipe away every tear from their eyes; there shall be no more death, nor sorrow, nor crying. There shall be no more pain, for the former things have passed away". (Rev 21:4-5)

DAY 5

January 05

And God saw the light, that it was good; And God divided the light from the darkness. God called the light day, and the darkness He called night. So the evening and the morning were the first day.

Genesis 1:4-5

ALMOST THERE

GENESIS 1:4-5

Light not only reveals that which is hidden in darkness, it also provides the energy needed for the giving and sustaining of life. In the book of Genesis, we read that when the earth was dark and void, God provided light. This light, however, is not only necessary to give physical energy for the development of all life (including human beings). Through Jesus, it also serves as a spiritual light that guides us towards a life in obedience to God's word.

The apostle John wrote, "This is the message we have heard from him and declare to you; God is light; in him there is no darkness at all. If we claim to have fellowship with him yet walk in the darkness, we lie and do not live by the truth. But if we walk in the light, as he is light, we have fellowship with one another, and the blood of Jesus, his Son, purifies us from all sin". (1 John 1: 5-7) It is extremely easy to blur the line between light and darkness – white lies are deemed harmless, taking stationery from the office is commonplace and acceptable, unethical practice in the corporate world is the new norm and nobody even attempts to challenge it.

As Christians we cannot cross the boundary between the two, or remove the dividing line that God placed between them. "Woe to those who call evil good, and good evil; Who put darkness for light, and light for darkness; Who put bitter for sweet, and sweet for bitter!" (Isaiah 5:20)

DAY 6

January 06

So God created great sea creatures and every living thing that moves, with which the waters abounded, according to their kind, and every winged bird according to its kind and God saw that it was good.

Genesis 1:21

ALMOST THERE

GENESIS 1:21

Many of us have experienced God's presence in nature. Perhaps while standing next to a mountain range you felt awe at God's grandeur, or when sitting on a beach breathing in the salt spray coming off the ocean, you became aware of God's peace and felt his spirit enter your spirit.

In the same way that God communicates to us through beauty, grandeur, quiet and parable in the natural world, the bible is full of stories of people meeting God powerfully in natural surroundings – think of Moses and his burning bush in the wilderness, Elijah enduring an earthquake and fire on a mountain top and then, finally, hearing God in a gentle whisper of wind, and Jesus going up on a mountain to pray. Even Jesus met with God in nature! Something inside the soul comes alive when surrounded by the beauty of God's creation - be it the mountains, the desert, the plains, the beach, the woods or the forest. God's power and existence is evident through the work of his hands.

Albert Einstein was not a Christian believer, and yet, as he looked at the wonders of the universe, he knew there must be a God. When asked by an interviewer if he was an atheist, he had this to say: "I am not an atheist. The problem involved is too vast for our limited minds. We are in the position of a little child entering a huge library filled with books in many languages. The child knows someone must have written those books. It does not know how. It does not understand the languages in which they are written. The child dimly suspects a mysterious order in the arrangement of the books but doesn't know what it is. That, it seems to me, is the attitude of even the most intelligent human being toward God. We see the universe marvellously arranged and obeying certain laws but only dimly understand these laws."

DAY 7

January 07

Then God said "Let us create man in our image, according to our likeness; let them have dominion over the fish of the sea, over the birds of the air, and over the cattle, over all the earth and over every creeping thing that creeps on the earth".

Genesis 1:26

ALMOST THERE

GENESIS 1:26

From the beginning, we are told that we are made in the image and likeness of God. Theologians call it the "Imago Dei", the image of God – the idea that we are different from all of creation because we have been made in the image of God. The "Imago Dei" is God's investment in humanity – one of God-like glory, and with the moral capacity to reign and rule the earth as His God's Holy Church on earth teaches us that God has blessed us with characteristics that set us apart from the rest of creation.

When God created us he gave us the ability to learn about things and understand them by the use of our intellect. Our intellect guides our life as opposed to instinct that drives animals. We have been given the ability to choose between one action and another action. God gave us free will to choose what is true and good, not what is false or evil. When we choose what is false or evil we abuse our freedom, and contradict our intelligent nature. Because of our intelligence and freedom, we are capable of determining our own lives (self-determination). God wants us to decide for ourselves how to behave and not to blindly follow everyone else. Finally, God gave us a spiritual and immortal soul. It is precisely because of our spiritual nature that we are never completely satisfied with the world we live in. As Jesus said: "Man does not live by bread alone but by every word that comes from the mouth of God" (Matthew 4:4)

When we fully believe in, and accept, the "Imago Dei", we understand that not only am I created in the image and likeness of God, but every other person is as well, thus deserving dignity and respect. If only everyone realised his God given glory, there would be no more inequality or poverty or corruption or war. The world would be as God created, and intended, it to be.

DAY 8

January 08

Know that the Lord is God. It is he who made us, and we are his; we are his people, the sheep of his pasture... For the Lord is good and his love endures forever: His faithfulness continues through all generations.

Psalm 100:3 & 5

ALMOST THERE

PSALM 100:3&5

As Christians it is heart-warming to know that God is not only concerned about our safety and wellbeing, but also cares about the little things that happen in our lives. Although most of us, nowadays, are not acquainted with the concept of shepherding, the job of a shepherd is to protect and guide his sheep. Jesus considered himself the good shepherd. But, in fact, he is the ultimate shepherd! Luke 12:7 says, "Indeed, the very hairs of your head are numbered. Don't be afraid; you are worth more than many sparrows". Matthew 6:26 says, "Look at the birds of the air, they do not sow or reap or store away in barns, and yet your heavenly Father feeds them. Are you not more valuable than they?" And again, "Your father knows what you need before you ask him". (Matthew 6:8)

Jesus pays attention to the specifics of our lives. During his ministry on earth he demonstrated this when his compassion compelled him to feed the hungry multitudes. When he took time out from his busy schedule to talk to and bless the little children, he taught us a valuable lesson – "little things do not get in the way of more important things". No issue is too small or too irrelevant for God – God takes time to keep up with how many hairs we have – now that's a good shepherd!

Benny Hinn said that when you believe in God's power, "God can"….but when you believe in His love, "God will".

DAY 9

January 09

Good and bad, life and death, poverty and wealth, all come from the Lord.

Ecclesiasticus 11:14

ALMOST THERE

ECCLESIASTICUS 11:14

In the eyes of the Lord, all men are equal. This must surely be one of the hardest fundamentals of our faith to understand and to accept. We all have a cross to carry and we all need to search for the spiritual lesson that our allotted condition in life is trying to teach us.

There are probably few readers of the Bible not familiar with the parable of the Rich Man and Lazarus. And, although it is easy to jump to conclusions, we must not draw lessons from the parable that it was never meant to teach – the rich are not always bad and the poor are not always good. We must not believe that it is sinful to be rich. But, in the parable, the rich man had lived his life without God, without Christ, without faith, grace, pardon and holiness – he had his treasures vested in this life and had no "garments of righteousness". Lazarus, on the other hand, desperately poor and destitute, had to beg for crumbs that fell from the rich man's table. But, he was a child of God. He was an heir of glory. He possessed durable riches and treasures that accompanied him to the gates of heaven. In the words of Saint Paul – "He died for all, that they which live should not henceforth live unto themselves- but unto Him who died for them, and rose again". (2 Corinthians 5:15). So, if like the rich man, we live only for ourselves – we will ruin our souls forever. We can't just simply live a good life. We also have to pay attention to the "sins of omission".

"I was hungry – and you gave me nothing to eat;
I was thirsty – and you gave me nothing to drink;
I was a stranger – and you did not take me in;
I was naked – and you did not clothe me;
I was sick and in prison- and you did not take care of me".
(Matthew 25:42-43)

DAY 10

January 10

Then Mary said, "Behold the maidservant of the Lord! Let it be to me according to your word." and the angel departed from her.

Luke 1:38

ALMOST THERE

LUKE 1:38

According to Holman's Illustrated Bible Dictionary, a succinct definition of biblical obedience is "to hear God's word an act accordingly".

Mary, the mother of God, perfectly demonstrates this when she hears the words of the Angel, puts her trust in God, and then simply submits and surrenders to His will. As believers, we learn through her example, and from Jesus, that we are called to a life of obedience. Obedience to God is essential for our Christian growth. Jesus taught us that our motivation to obey his commands stems from love – "if you love me, you will obey what I command" (John 14:15). And in Matthew 22:36-38, he says that the greatest commandment of all is to "love the Lord your God with all your heart and with all your soul and with all your mind and to love your neighbour as yourself".

Being a Christian means more than participating in good works. It means striving to be more like Jesus. It means being obedient to God, knowing Him, loving Him, and having a personal, intimate relation with Him. To do this, we must be attentive to His laws. However, only Jesus is perfect and could walk in sinless obedience. We have to rely on the Holy Spirit to transform us from within so that we can grow in holiness.

"Joyful are people of integrity, who follow the instruction of the Lord. Joyful are those who obey his laws and search for him with all their hearts. They do not compromise with evil, and they walk only in his paths". (Psalm 119 1-8)

DAY 11

January 11

O Lord of hosts, God of Israel,
Enthroned above the cherubim,
you are the God, you alone, of all
the kingdoms of the earth; you
have made heaven and earth.

Isaiah 37:16

ISAIAH 37:16

"We may ignore, but we can nowhere evade, the presence of God. The world is crowded with Him. He walks everywhere incognito. And the incognito is not always hard to penetrate. The real labour is to remember, to attend. In fact, to come awake. Still more, to remain awake" C S Lewis

I strongly suspect that C S Lewis included nature in the places that God could be found incognito. The scriptures are clear that God's presence can be found in His Creation. For many, nature seems to be one of God's best hiding places. But for those of us who have ears to hear and eyes to see with, it is not hard to discover Him there. But, as C S Lewis points out – it takes great discipline to become and to "remain awake". We have to pay attention if we want God to reveal himself.

God created the world and all that is in it. Thomas Merton believed that God can be found everywhere, and when one comes to see Him in all places and spaces, then all the world becomes a prayer. It is through prayer and silent contemplation that we draw nearer to our Heavenly Father. "Let me seek, then, the gift of silence, and poverty, and solitude, where everything I touch is turned into prayer: where the sky is my prayer, the birds are my prayer, the wind in the trees is my prayer, for God is all in all".
- Thomas Merton

If we turn to the world in silence and solitude, with a poverty of spirit, it is impossible not to experience the presence of God.

DAY 12

January 12

It is He who made the earth by His power, who established the world by His wisdom and by His understanding, stretched out the heavens.

Jeremiah 10:12

JEREMIAH 10:12

The beauty of God's character is that each of his attributes compliments the other. His omnipotence – the infinite power of God –enables him to do anything he chooses. His omniscience – the infinite knowledge of God – allows him to know everything. His goodness motivates his every action, and results in his grace towards believers and unbelievers alike. But, it is his infinite wisdom that is the foundation of our lives and the basis upon which we build our spiritual "house" – "through wisdom a house is built…" (Proverbs 24:3)

In the scriptures wisdom always carries a strong moral connotation. It is seen as being pure, loving and good. Wisdom is the power to see, and the inclination to choose, the best and highest goal, together with the surest means of attaining it. In other words – it is the practical side of moral goodness. God's wisdom is vastly superior to ours – "For my thoughts are not your thoughts, neither are your ways my ways" (Isaiah 55:8). However, he has promised to give wisdom – the ability to put knowledge, understanding and discernment to good use – to those who sincerely seek it.

The Bible urges us to "acquire wisdom" (Proverbs 4:7). God's wisdom can be found in his written word, and through prayer and diligent study of the scriptures, we are able to "acquire" it. However, it is not possible without humility and modesty. With wisdom comes the ability to admit that we do not have all the answers, that our opinions are not always right, and that we need to seek God's advice on matters. But most of all we have to fear God – "The fear of Jehovah is the start of wisdom" (Proverbs 9:10). To fear God is to come before him with awe, trust and respect. This, in turn, brings our life in harmony with our knowledge of his will and ways.

"When I applied my mind to know wisdom and to observe man's labour on earth-his eyes not seeing sleep day or night-then I saw all that God has done. No one can comprehend what goes on under the sun. Despite all his efforts to search it out, man cannot discover its meaning. Even if a wise man claims he knows, he cannot really comprehend it". (Ecclesiastes 8:16-17)

DAY 13

January 13

"Worthy are you, our Lord and God, to receive glory and honour and power, for you created all things, and by your will they existed and were created."

Revelation 4:11

ALMOST THERE

REVELATION 4:11

It is fairly common to hear great sportsmen and women, famous actors, business people, or even politicians, claim some form of faith in God. Often they even contribute their victory or success to God. Sadly, more often than not, they talk, behave and live in a way that seems more about pursuing their own agenda than living under the authority of God and his Word.

"Nevertheless, many even of the authorities believed in him, but for fear of the Pharisees they did not confess it, so that they would not be put out of the synagogue; for they loved the glory that came from man more than the glory that comes from God". (John 12:42-43)

It is ironic that despite the fact that Jesus, the Son of God, was walking among them, the Authorities of the day were still blinded by their fear of, and love for, the glory of man. Tragically, it seems as if the majority of the world, to some extent, believe in God, but still live a life marked by pride, selfish gain, envy and malice.

As believers, our lives should express more of a love for the glory that comes from God than the glory that comes from man. However, while we live in the flesh, we still battle the desires of the flesh. Everyone wants to be successful, appreciated, liked and known to some degree. But sin distorts these desires, causing us to seek them for the advancement of our own name, rather than the Lord's. But, if we examine the motives of our heart and acknowledge our sinful nature, we receive God's grace. Through his forgiveness and the help of the Holy Spirit, we experience a change in heart and mind. And so, we can also be confident that "his sanctifying work will continue in my life until the day I am holy, perfect, and complete in his presence". (Philippians 1:6)

DAY 14

January 14

For by him all things were created, in heaven and on earth, visible and invisible, whether thrones or dominions or rulers or authorities– all things were created through him and for him.

Colossians 1:16

ALMOST THERE

COLOSSIANS 1:16

The Bible makes it abundantly clear that God created man, and that he created them for His glory: "Everyone who is called by my name, whom I created for my glory, whom I formed and made". (Isaiah 43:7)

But how do we, with our sinful, human nature, live a life that will glorify and please the Lord? In Psalm 100:2-3, we are told to worship God with gladness, and to "know that the Lord is God- it is he who made us, and we are his; we are his people, the sheep of his pasture". So, part of glorifying God is to acknowledge who he is and to praise and worship him as our creator.

The only worthwhile life is one of honour and obedience to God. Yet, our sinful nature and love of earthly pleasures, wealth and power, separates us from God and makes it difficult for us to glorify him on our own. When we understand and accept that we are sinners and "fall short of the glory of God", our relationship with God, through Jesus's sacrifice, is reconciled-our sins are forgiven and no longer create a barrier between God and us.

The more we get to know, understand and love our Creator, the better we understand who we are and what our purpose is. We were created to bring him glory. God has a unique plan for each of us, but whatever that is, it will, ultimately, result in his glory.

DAY 15

January 15

Ah, Lord God! It is you who have made the heavens and the earth by your great power and by your outstretched arm! Nothing is too hard for you.

Jeremiah 32:17

ALMOST THERE

JEREMIAH 32:17

Is anything too hard for God? He created the universe out of nothing (John 1:1). He turned Lot's wife into a pillar of salt (Genesis 19:26). He split the Red Sea (Exodus 14:22). He cleansed lepers (Luke 17:14). He gave sight to the blind (Matthew 9:30). He raised Lazarus from the dead (John 11:43).

Scripture abounds with examples of God's omnipotence. The word "omnipotence" refers to the fact that God is all-powerful. Power is a subject that is important to all of us on one level or another. Power structures rule almost every aspect of our life. There is political power, which plays an important part in, and, influences, our daily lives. In our schools, in our work place, in our family and in our relationships, the politics of power – who is in charge - runs all the way down the line.

To not get caught up in the power struggle, and to avoid corruption, we must be sensible enough to know that we don't know it all. We need to be willing to have business partners, best friends, and spouses, who are strong-willed enough to challenge us when we veer away from ethical behaviour and Godly principles.

God's omnipotence, like his other attributes – omniscience, goodness and wisdom – has a moral base. Unlike us, although he could use it anyway he chooses, he chooses to use it wisely and only for good purposes. When Jesus walked the earth he never used his power for convenience, for entertainment, or in order to "get back" at the people he disagreed with or who did him harm. God's power reflects his glory and helps to accomplish his sovereign will. As his disciples, we need to rise to the challenge to be "in the world but not of the world". We are called to resist the attractions of this world, and to use our talents and power for the glory of God.

DAY 16

January 16

For his invisible attributes, namely,
His eternal power and divine nature,
have been clearly perceived,
ever since the creation of the world,
in the things that have been made
so they are without excuse.

Romans 1:20

ALMOST THERE

ROMANS 1:20

Ultimately we trust that God is good, loving, just, and fair. The Bible teaches that, "the Lord is gracious and compassionate, slow to anger and rich in love" (Psalm 145:8). We have to believe that God is absolutely fair because the alternative just doesn't make any sense – why would God send His Son to come and die for our salvation if he was devious and unfair?

The Bible highlights two points that make it impossible for us to refute the existence of God. Firstly, we all have the light of creation. In Romans 1:19-20, Paul explains that people possess the light and knowledge of God because His invisible attributes are clearly seen in the magnificence of His creation. God's creation is a powerful revelation of our Creator. No one can say they have not been exposed to a glimpse of God through his creation.

Secondly, we all have the light of conscience. In Romans 2:11-15, Paul, a leader of the early church, explains that God will judge everyone on the basis of what they know. He explains that the Jew who knew the Jewish Law in the scriptures will be judged by that law. But for the Gentile who didn't have the Scriptures, God deals with him on the basis of his conscience. Since God knows the heart of man, he knows whether a man has obeyed his conscience or rejected its accusations. The conscience of man is proof that the law of God is written on every man's heart.

And so, if anyone, through the light of creation or the light of conscience, believes that God exists and searches for him, God will move heaven and earth to reveal himself and Jesus to them.

DAY 17

January 17

By faith we understand that the universe was created by the word of God, so that what is seen was not made out of things that are visible
Hebrews 11:3

Faith is being sure of what we hope for. it is being certain of what we do not see
Hebrews 11:1

HEBREWS 11:1&3

Christian hope "is not based on our word, but on God's Word" and on promises of salvation and eternal life. "Our hope is not based on human reasoning, predictions and assurances; real hope arises where there is no more hope, where there is nothing left to hope for."

True hope "is rooted in faith and precisely for this reason, it is able to go beyond all hope because it is built on faith in God and his promise". Pope Francis

Abraham's faith is held up as a model for everyone. Despite all logic – Abraham was old and his wife infertile – Abraham believed, hoping against hope, that he would become the "father of many nations".
Mary, too, believed in the unbelievable when the angel informed her that she would become the mother of God.

All we need to do is to believe in God's word and his love for us. When we open our hearts and surrender to God's will, his power will carry us forward and sustain us. He will do miraculous things and show us what hope is.

DAY 18

January 18

When I consider your heavens, the work of your fingers, the moon and the stars, which you have ordained, what is man that you are mindful of him and the son of man, that you visit him? For you have made him a little lower than the angels, and you have crowned him with glory and honour.

Psalm 8:3-5

PSALM 8:3-5

Then God said, "let us make man in our image, in our likeness…" So God created man in his own image, in the image of God he created him; male and female he created them". (Genesis 1:26-27)

Now what does it mean that man was created "in the image of God"? It does not mean that God is a physical being with two arms, two legs and a long flowing beard, as depicted on the ceiling of the Sistine Chapel. Rather, at a deeper level, it suggests that mans' basic characteristics are derived from the characteristics of God. Both God and people have intellect, emotions and will. In the Bible, God is sometimes portrayed as sad, hurt, angry or joyful – the same range of emotions that we humans experience.

Like God, man can think and reason. We appreciate beauty and language. And, unlike the animals, we have an inner sense of morality and the ability to grasp deep concepts. This enables us to commune with God, and that, most likely, is the very reason he created us "in his image". God wants a relationship with, and wants to have fellowship with, all mankind.

Being created in God's image is a huge responsibility. Another reason he made us in his image is so that we can take care of his creation. We are expected to be the custodians of this world and, as his intermediary, to take care of his handiwork. How can we manage this unless we stay close to God; unless we think like God; unless we are able to fulfill the will of God? Part of having a relationship with God is having the right relationship with his creation.

Being created in His image is an awesome gift, as well as a sacred responsibility.

DAY 19

January 19

Know that the Lord Himself is God; It is He who has made us, and not we ourselves; we are his people and the sheep of his pasture

Psalm 100:3

ALMOST THERE

PSALM 100:3

As David cared for his sheep, so God cares for us, "the sheep of his pasture". As sheep, we need to be cared for and we need to be led. But most importantly, we need a shepherd, and Jesus has taken that title upon himself.

As our shepherd, Jesus leads and cares for us in a number of ways. When it comes to wisdom, we either think we know it all, or we try to find it in all the wrong places. We look outward to our culture, or to other people, and inward to our emotions, for guidance. We like the idea of "following our heart". But wisdom is more than knowledge. It is taking the knowledge of God and applying it to our lives. We can't do this on our own – we need the help of the Shepherd. "For the Lord gives wisdom; from his mouth comes knowledge and understanding". (Proverbs 2:6)

The fact that God governs all things in the world, at all times, is a great source of peace and security. The Shepherd cares for us by his providence. Nothing that happens to us is a mistake – from the care of creation (Psalm 104) to the details of our life (Matthew 10:29). God knows what is best, and He knows all that needs to happen, in order to lead His sheep home.

And finally, we are fed by his pasture. The pasture refers to God's word. As we already know, it is in God's word that we find wisdom, but it is also in God's word that we find food for our souls – a spiritual feast that causes growth in faith and love for our Shepherd. To know the Lord as "shepherd" ultimately means that we know Jesus Christ, the "Great Shepherd" of the sheep (Hebrew 13:20). It means we recognize his voice and follow him. And, it means that as we follow Him, we learn to be content with where He leads us.

DAY 20

January 20

I will give thanks to you,
For I am fearfully and wonderfully
made; Wonderful are your works,
And my soul knows it very well

Psalm 139:14

ALMOST THERE

PSALM 139:14

"Gratitude unlocks the fullness of life. It turns what we have into enough, and more. It turns denial into acceptance, chaos to order, confusion to clarity. It can turn a meal into a feast, a house into a home, a stranger into a friend. Gratitude makes sense of our past, brings peace for today and creates a vision for tomorrow."
-Melody Beattie

We have so much to be thankful for. Yet when confronted with daily hardships, illness and death, financial strive, violence and war, it is easy to lose sight of the magnificence of God, our creator.

Isaac Watts' beautiful hymn puts it all back into perspective:

"When I survey the wondrous cross
On which the Prince of glory died,
My richest gain I count but loss,
And pour contempt on all my pride.
Forbid it, Lord, that I should boast,
Save in the death of Christ my God!
All the vain things that charm me most,
I sacrifice them to His blood.
See from His head, His hands, His feet,
Sorrow and love flow mingled down!
Did e'er such love and sorrow meet?
Or thorns compose so rich a crown?
Were the whole realm of nature mine,
That were a present far too small;
Love so amazing, so divine,
Demands my soul, my life, my all."

DAY 21

January 21

Then the Lord God formed man of dust from the ground, and breathed into his nostrils the breath of life; and man became a living being.

Genesis 2:7

GENESIS 2:7

What do you consider your reward in life - a fulfilling career, a satisfying relationships or being able to find joy in the simple things in life? What about success, notoriety, or financial security?

The problem with those "rewards" is that we often feel we are missing the mark when our expectations aren't met. But, if we adopt the mind-set of some of the great men of faith in the Bible, we can funnel every circumstance in life, every disappointment, and even every miserable failure, through the grid of God being our portion and reward.

Consider Abraham, who waited years for God to deliver upon a promise to give him a son. Remember David, the shepherd boy, psalmist, and giant slayer who became Israel's greatest king, but was also a fugitive for many years of his life. And think of Paul, who was shipwrecked, imprisoned, and beaten and left for dead several times. They all regarded God as their portion or reward – regardless of their circumstances.

When God – not money, success or any other person or thing - becomes our ultimate prize and reward, our lives will be radically altered. We won't have to worry about provisions, we will have hope for the future, we will find comfort in God's word, we will focus on our blessing and not our burdens, and generally be content with the life we have been granted.

Let us therefore strive to live by the motto:
"The lord is my portion".

DAY 22

January 22

Your hands made me and
fashioned me;
Give me understanding,
That I may learn your
commandments

Psalm 119:73

PSALM 119:73

As Christians we should all ask ourselves this question – When people look at you, do they see the characteristics of Christ? The Bible tells us that our purpose, as believers in Christ, is to be conformed into His image so that we can reflect His characteristics in all we do. "For whom He did foreknow, He also did predestine to be conformed to the image of His Son". (Romans 8:29)

Being conformed into Christ's image really is the goal of the Christian life. We need to learn how to walk in the Spirit, how to show forth His love, and how to live His life. We need to put into our actions what we already possess in our hearts. We are to love with Christ's love, share from His wisdom, walk in His power, and extend His peace, patience and joy.

"If I am not Christ-like at heart- if I am not becoming noticeably more like Him- then I have totally missed God's purpose for my life. It doesn't matter what I accomplish for His kingdom. If I miss this one purpose, I have lived, preached and yes, striven in vain."
-David Wilkerson

If God was small enough for us to understand, He would not be big enough for us to worship.
-Dietrich Bonhoeffer

DAY 23

January 23

But now, O Lord, You are our Father, we are the clay, and you our potter; and all of us are the work of your hand.

Isaiah 64:8

ALMOST THERE

ISAIAH 64:8

Clay is not easy to work with. Before it can be put upon the wheel it has to be properly prepared. It has to be supple enough to adapt to change, yet firm enough not to collapse under pressure. The Bible says that God is the potter and we are the clay. And, just like the clay, before God can begin remaking and changing us, certain preparations have to be made. It is only when we are open to God's will in our lives that He can begin to mould, transform, and sanctify us as we walk with Him.

However, in today's world, everybody is so busy with their own lives that spending time in fellowship with, and worshiping God, is sorely neglected. We think we are self-sufficient. We think we have everything we need in life, including all the comforts this world has to offer. It is only when something happens that brings us to a dead stop that we start to question and wonder how this could have happened. It takes those unexpected trials and tribulations to bring us back to our Saviour. They force us to slow down and re-evaluate our values and principles.

Sometimes God allows such trials and tribulations in our lives to humble us. When we are "self-sufficient" and proud, we are more concerned about our own selfish things than worshiping and honouring Him. But, when we realise our dependence on His love and grace, He can begin to mould us into His perfect image. When we come to the Potter, we need to surrender our all to Him, all our imperfections, and let Him be our Lord and Master. We need to let Him mould us and make us the vessel of honour He wants us to be.

DAY 24

January 24

> Though the mountains leave their place and the hills be shaken, my love shall never leave you nor my covenant be shaken...
>
> Isaiah 54:10

ISAIAH 54:10

The "everlasting covenant" gets mentioned 16 times in the Old Testament and once in the New Testament. It refers to a covenant between God and humanity. More precisely, it is a covenant between the Father and Christ – that Christ would take human form and shed his blood to save humanity from sin.

"For God so loved the world" - His everlasting love-"that He gave His only Son" - His everlasting covenant- "that whoever believes in Him"- the everlasting gospel- "should not perish but have eternal life" - everlasting redemption through the blood of the everlasting covenant. (John 3:16)

God's love and presence in our lives is more unshakeable than the greatest mountains he Himself created.
-Peter M. van Bemmelen

DAY 25

January 25

I am made glorious
in the sight of the Lord

Isaiah 49:5

ISAIAH 49:5

When I reached the heights on Mount Kilimanjaro and saw the world of clouds beneath me, I was awestruck. I have been amazed by the abundance of living creatures, vibrant colours, shapes and sizes that form the kaleidoscope of the undersea world.

Many other things, people, and places, have taken my breath away. Yet, in God's sight, we too are glorious and perfect - and we take His breath away.

How wonderful to know that our Father considers us glorious – we should strive to live a life worthy of such consideration and attempt to make him proud at every turn.

DAY 26

January 26

You alone are the Lord. You have made the heavens, the heaven of heavens with all their hosts, the earth and all that is on it, the seas and all that is in them, you give life to all of them, and the heavenly hosts bow down before you.

Nehemiah 9:6

ALMOST THERE

NEHEMIAH 9:6

In the book of Acts, we read about how the early believers devoted themselves to the apostles' teaching, to fellowship, to the breaking of the bread, to prayer, and to praising God (Acts 2:42-47). We see that as a result of their devotion, the Holy Spirit manifested the intimacy and awesomeness of God's presence to them as they praised and worshipped Him. God seemed so real to them, and they radiated peace, freedom and power.

As followers of Christ, we too should be able to experience this awesomeness of God. We too, should be able to be in His presence and feel His love and power. But, before we can experience these benefits of worship, we have to understand what worship is, why it is important, and what happens when we worship. By definition, worship is ascribing worth to someone or to something. But, true worship is also a matter of the heart – it must be felt. Every human being was designed to worship, and does worship something– food, sports, art, music, money, achievement, power, control or work. But God calls us to worship Him in spirit and in truth. And, in return, He promises to bestow on us His provision, grace, sovereignty, and power.

True worship is the heartfelt expression of love, adoration, admiration, fascination, wonder and celebration. It comes alive in your heart and soul when you praise God for who He is and give Him thanks for all He has done.

DAY 27

January 27

So God blessed the seventh day and made it holy, because on it he rested from all the work he had done in creation.

Genesis 2:3

GENESIS 2:3

Even God rested! It is comforting to know that God gives us permission to take time out from our busy schedule. He wants us to rest and spend time in quiet communion with him.

We get so caught up in the hectic pace of life that we keep pushing time we could spend with God, and with our family, to the side lines. By hanging onto the idea that "tomorrow is another day" these relationships are soon just a distant memory.

But God blessed the Sabbath and made it holy. He made it a day of religious observance and abstinence from work. He made it easy for us to prioritise the important things in our life. It is up to us to follow His example and to make time to nurture our relationship with Him, with our family, and with our friends.

DAY 28

January 28

Lo, I am about to create new
heavens and a new earth;
the things of the past shall
not be remembered
or come to mind.

Isaiah 65:17

ALMOST THERE

ISAIAH 65:17

Most believers are looking forward to an eternal life spent in the presence of God.

The beauty and mystery of our faith is that there is no doubt that before the new heavens come to the new earth, all the causes and results of our sins will be totally destroyed. Satan's control on this earth will be nullified.

As children of God, we are also assured that through Jesus, all our own sins are forgiven and totally forgotten. We too, have been created anew (born again), and things of the past shall not be remembered or come to mind.

DAY 29

January 29

The plan of the Lord
stands forever, the design
of his heart, through all
generations

Psalm 33:11

ALMOST THERE

PSALM 33:11

When it comes to faith related issues, there are many questions we can spend hours exploring: why do bad things happen to good people, why is there war, why is there sickness and pain? But, by far the most difficult Christian principle to grasp is the seemingly conflicting view that God has a plan for our lives, yet we have free will and can choose to do whatever we want to do with it.

How do we know that God really does have a plan for us? Jeremiah 29:11 grants us this insight: "For I know the plans I have for you", declares the Lord, "plans to prosper you and not to harm you, plans to give you hope and a future". But, is this plan one that will be carried out by God, and unfold before us while we sit back, do nothing and wait for good things to happen?

Even though God has laid out a plan for us and wants great things for us, we have to take the first steps to realizing the benefits of his plan. God might nudge us in the right direction, but ultimately we are free to choose our own course.
We have to live up to our side of the plan.

The Bible provides us with many clues as to how we can hold up our side of God's plan, but one of the clearest is found in Micah 6:8: "He has showed you, O man, what is good. And what does the Lord require of you -To act justly and to love mercy and to walk humbly with your God". The Ten Commandments also guide us - they basically instruct us to lead a morally pure life. We are asked to take care of our fellow man and to keep God foremost in our lives.

Man's free will is not inconsistent with God's plan for us. Even though our will may conflict with God's, our free will, and ability to choose, is a gift from God. It is up to us to use this gift wisely or not.

DAY 30

January 30

Let us bow down in
worship; let us kneel
before the Lord who
made us.

Psalm 95:6

PSALM 95:6

In Matthew 2:10-11, we read that the three wise men, when they found Christ, "rejoiced with exceeding great joy" and then "they fell down, and worshipped him".

Modern believers find the concept of "worship" difficult to embrace. By our very nature, we are self-centred and not God-centred. We become angry and lose faith when adversity disrupts our lives. We place more emphasis on what God can do for us, than on our duty towards God.

This Psalm helps the believer to reconsider the role of, and the practice of, worship in our relationship with God. It turns our attention away from our own needs and helps us to refocus on God and His greatness.

When our role in worship is addressed, we acknowledge that the cornerstone of our faith is reverence and obedience to God. Through worshipping our God, we cement our place in His heart and in His eternal home.

DAY 31

January 31

The child grew and became strong, filled with wisdom and the favour of God was upon him.

Luke 2:40

ALMOST THERE

LUKE 2:40

"Favour" is God's "I'm for you" attitude. It is the amazing, undeserved benefit of being His child – yet many of us simply do not understand His favour. Favour can be defined as "the friendly disposition from which kindly acts proceed to assist, to provide with special advantages, to receive preferential treatment". That is God's heart towards us. He wants to bless, help and promote us. He wants to treat us as "special".

There are numerous examples of favour in the Bible. David found favour with Saul (1Samuel 16:22), and with God (Psalm 30:7). Despite his failings, God refers to David as "a man after my own heart" (Acts 13:22). Mary found favour with God (Luke 1:30), and became the mother of Jesus. Jesus disciples had favour with both God and men (Acts 2:47), and the church grew. But, God never intended His favour to be found by just a handful of people. Every believer can find it and do things that could not be accomplished without it.

Jesus possessed many traits that should be part of every Christian's character. From His youth he was interested in spiritual things (Luke 2:49). He lived unselfishly, and served others (Matthew 20:28). He focused on accomplishing His Father's will every day of His life (John 6:38). He left us this perfect example so that we can follow in His footsteps.

When Luke boils down the first thirty years of Jesus' life, he writes, "Then He went down to Nazareth with them and was obedient to them. But his mother treasured all these things in her heart. And Jesus grew in wisdom and stature, and in favour with God and men" (Luke 2:51-52).The four areas we are told Jesus grew in– wisdom, stature, favour with God, favour with men – are all areas that we must also strive to grow in.

DAY 32-59

February

Just Because You Are My God

Oh, my God, I want to love you
Not that I might gain eternal
heaven nor escape eternal hell
But, Lord, to love you just
because you are my God.
Grant me to give to you and
not to count the cost,
To fight for you and not to mind the wounds,
To labour and to ask for no reward
except the knowledge that I serve my God.

- Saint Ignatius of Loyola

DAY 32

February 01

And observe what the Lord your God requires: Walk in his ways, and keep his decrees and commands, His laws and his requirements, as written in the Law of Moses, so that you may prosper in all you do and wherever you go

1 Kings 2:3

ALMOST THERE

1 KINGS 2:3

It was nearly time for David to die and his forty year reign as King was almost over. In order to prepare his son, Solomon, for the great responsibility that would soon be his, the King, as any loving parent would, set about giving him a few morsels of advice. The main things that David wanted Solomon to understand was the importance to obey God, to observe what he requires, to walk in his ways, and to follow his written instructions.

This advice is still pertinent to us as Christians today. But how do we go about adhering to it? How do we do what God requires; how do we walk in his ways? We can only do this if we know what his requirements are and what morals and principles denote his ways. We can begin by taking the time and effort to learn. We learn from studying the bible and from going to church and listening to God's word, as taught by his representatives on earth. We can spend time in fellowship with other believers and in prayer. But, ultimately, it is the Holy Spirit who lives within us who teaches, counsels, and instructs us in the way of the Lord. The Bible, the preaching, the fellowship with friends, are all tools that help us on our spiritual journey – but it is the Holy Spirit who guides us to correctly interpret and apply these principles.

Our reward, as pointed out by King David, if we follow this advice and commit our lives to God, is that we will prosper in all that we do. "I came that they may have life, and have it abundantly".
John 10:10

DAY 33

February 02

HAND OF GOD

The fear of the Lord is the
beginning of knowledge;
But fools despise wisdom
and instruction.

Proverbs 1:7

PROVERBS 1:7

The fear of the Lord is a healthy fear.
It compels us to surrender our life to him. When we surrender to the Lord and ask for forgiveness, he washes us and we become pure – "though your sins are like scarlet, they shall be white as snow"
- Isaiah 1:18

The fear of the Lord is about reverence toward God, respect for Him, love and appreciation, and holding Him, and His beloved Son, in high esteem. It can also be defined as "the continual awareness that our loving Father is watching and evaluating everything we think, say and do"
- Matthew 12:36

Nothing is hidden from his sight. In order to develop this fear we have to recognize God for whom he is. This means we cannot recreate Him in our own image- God is far greater than that. Part of our relationship with the Father has got to involve this fear of God. All true believers have this fear, and all nonbelievers do not fear him at all.

Proverbs 23: 17-18 teaches us that the fear of God is similar to "hope in the Lord"- because it holds the key to life. "Do not let your heart envy sinners, but be zealous for the fear of the Lord all the day; for surely there is a hereafter, and your hope will not be cut off".

DAY 34

February 03

There is no fear in love, but perfect love casts out fear. For fear has to do with punishment, and whoever fears has not been perfected in love

1 John 4:18

… ALMOST THERE

1 JOHN 4:18

When love beckons to you, follow him, though his ways are hard and steep. And when his wings enfold you yield to him, though the sword hidden among his pinions may wound you .And when he speaks to you believe in him, though his voice may shatter your dreams as the north wind lays waste the garden. For even as love crowns you so shall he crucify you. Even as he is for your growth so is he for your pruning. Even as he ascends to your height and caresses your tenderest branches that quiver in the sun, so shall he descend to your roots and shake them in their clinging to the earth.

Like sheaves of corn he gathers you unto himself. He threshes you to make you naked. He sifts you free from your husks. He grinds you to whiteness. He kneads you until you are pliant; and then he assigns you to his to his sacred fire that you may become sacred bread for God's sacred feast. All these things shall love do unto you that you may know the secrets of your heart and in that knowledge become a fragment of Life's heart.

But if in your fear you would seek only love's peace and love's pleasure, then it is better for you that you cover your nakedness and pass out of love's threshing-floor into the seasonless world where you shall laugh, but not all of your laughter, and weep, but not all of your tears. Love gives naught but itself and takes naught but from itself. Love possesses not nor would it be possessed; for love is sufficient unto love.

When you love you should not say "God is in my heart", but rather, "I am in the heart of God". And think not that you can direct the course of love, for love, if it finds you worthy, directs you course.
- Kahlil Gibran

DAY 35

February 04

The Lord is good;
His kindness endures
forever, and his faithfulness
to all generations

Psalm 100:5

PSALM 100:5

It is easy to proclaim God's goodness when life is running smoothly and we are happy and content with our circumstances.

It is not as easy to except that his "kindness endures forever", when a loved one is suffering and dying from cancer or some other illness. Where is His "faithfulness" when we face mounting debt and cannot see light at the end of the tunnel?

On our journey of faith, some days it will be easy to obey the Psalmists and sing praises and glory to God. However, on the mornings when life is hard and everything seems cloudy even though the sun is shining, we need to find strength in the words of Jesus - "I will be with you always".

We need to find the faith to know that "the Lord is good".

DAY 36

February 05

Every good and
perfect gift is
from above

James 1:17

JAMES 1:17

God's message at Christmas is – "With all my love….a little gift is on the way". His gift of love was the birth of Jesus. Jesus is the gift of God's love! God captures our hearts and minds with this little gift that is full of grace and truth.

Our lives are beautiful gifts from God, and how we live them is our prayer of gratitude for such a gift. In order to help us honour this precious gift, God has also given us the gift of faith, and, as children of God, we are expected to live by faith and not by sight.

When times get tough and our faith starts to waiver, we can draw strength from God's gift of hope. This hope is a future hope that looks forward to a time when there will be no more pain, no more suffering, no more tears or hunger, or sadness. It is the hope that rests in God's promise of eternal life.

But the greatest gift of all is the gift of love– a love that passes all understanding. God's love is perfect and is eternal – "for perfect love casts out all fear"
- 1 John 4:18

DAY 37

February 06

Where your treasure is, there your heart will be also.

Matthew 6:21

ALMOST THERE

MATTHEW 6:21

"Treasure" is not necessarily a specific collection of objects, but can be anything that one values in life. Jesus, during the Sermon on the Mount, stresses the point that treasure changes hearts. Instead of saying "Where your heart is, there your treasure will be also", Jesus puts it the other way round – "Where your treasure is, there will your heart be also". Money and wealth changes the heart more than the heart is capable of deciding on how to correctly handle these earthly possessions.

When we invest our deepest treasure in the attractions and things of this world, we find that we are no longer serving God but money (Matthew 6:24). We get caught up in the anxiety and uncertainty that loving money brings – what happens if the stock market crashes, is the effect of inflation eroding my bank balance, have I saved enough to secure my future?

If, however, we commit to the ways and means of God's kingdom, this commitment has to include the way we manage and share the wealth that we have. But how do we discern between appropriate and inappropriate attention to money and worldly things? Jesus tells us how – "Strive first for the kingdom God and his righteousness, and all these things will be given to you"
- Matthew 6:33

If we listen carefully to our hearts, we will realise that paying excessive attention to money and accumulating earthly goods, makes us greedy. If we let them displace God's role in our life, we become unfaithful. And if we acquire them at the expense of, and to the detriment of others, we become an oppressor who is not welcome in the Kingdom of God.

DAY 38

February 07

The Lord is near
to all who call
on him in truth

Psalm 145:18

ALMOST THERE

PSALM 145:18

Throughout the scriptures we are constantly told to "seek the Lord". As Christians, it is our duty to search for our Father on a daily basis. In seeking him we show that we have a desire to learn and know more of him, his love for us, and his will for our lives. It allows us to grow spiritually and build a personal relationship with him. It highlights our desperate need for God's wisdom, guidance and direction, as we go about our daily business.

God has promised - "and you will seek me and find me, when you search for me with your heart"
- Jeremiah 29:13

This promise is a constant encouragement when we are struggling, in pain, or battling with life's issues. When we feel like we are losing control, when we are tired of trying to find our own solutions, or simply need to escape the cares of this world, we can draw strength from yet another assurance – "give all your worries and cares to God, for he cares about you"
- 1 Peter 5:7

When we truly focus on the word of God, study the scriptures and keep on praying and knocking on God's door, the stronger we will become in our faith and we will experience a change of heart. God does not necessarily change our circumstances or the situation, but he changes our hearts and minds – he changes us.

God does not calm the storm, he calms the sailor!

ALMOST THERE

DEUTERONOMY 16:15

Our work is that activity which in many ways determines who we are. Often, in social interactions, the first thing we ask a new acquaintance is, "So, what do you do for a living?" We measure our worth through our work, the level of success and satisfaction we experience in that work, and, the amount of wealth we accumulate based on the success we achieve. Sometimes, we work primarily for the rewards it promises for a distant, unsure future.

However, as children of the Risen Lord, we have to rediscover that our primary call is to follow Jesus. This call encompasses the whole of our lives, including our everyday work. Our call should lead to a radically different lifestyle, seeking not to conform to the norm of the day, but striving to influence the world for the glory of God. For the Christian, life without work is meaningless; but work must never become the meaning of one's life. Our identity must be found in Christ, not in our work. It is the relationship and union we have with God that transforms our heart and gives us the desire to follow and serve Him - out of gratitude- while we go about our daily work.

God expects us to shape and influence the world and our work plays a major role in providing this positive impact. When we do our job with excellence and with accountability, in a distinctively Christian manner, we cannot help but have a profound effect on the world around us. It is then that we follow the Biblical Doctrine of work that "brings light into a dark world" (Matthew 5:16; John 1:5). When light is brought into a dark room it is transformed. The light of the Gospel has the power to radically change individuals and to transform the cultural norm of the day.

DAY 40

February 09

My presence will go with you, and I will give you rest

Exodus 33:14

ALMOST THERE

EXODUS 33:14

As Christians, God must be our number one priority. Interestingly, He puts our love for Him as the first and most important of the Ten Commandments. If we want to experience the rest that only God can provide, we have to allow Him to be our Shepherd and let Him guide us in all aspects of our life. God is a good shepherd. He is always looking out for our well-being, our happiness, our joy - hoping that we find passion and purpose, and everlasting peace. We spend our lives searching for these, in all the wrong people, places and things. We have to allow Him to lead us.

"Let go of your concerns! Then you will know that I am God. I rule the nations. I rule the earth". (Psalm 46:10) Every morning when you wake up you have a decision to make: Who is going to be in charge of your life – you or God? There are things we want to control. We want to make our own rules. But stress relief, and perfect peace, always starts with letting God be God. It is only when we fully believe and know that God is in the driving seat of our life, that we find serenity and lasting peace.

Millions of people pray the Serenity Prayer, which is based on the Lord's Prayer: "God grant me the serenity to accept the things I cannot change; courage to change the things I can; and wisdom to know the difference". But most people have never read the last eight lines of the prayer.

"Living one day at a time; enjoying one moment at a time; accepting hardships as the pathway to peace; taking, as He did, this sinful world as it is, not as I would have it; trusting that He will make all things right if I surrender to His Will; that I may be reasonably happy in this life and supremely happy with Him forever in the next. Amen".

DAY 41

February 10

Mercy, peace and love be yours in abundance

Jude 2

JUDE 2

The "American dream" is to pursue what is known as "the good life". This usually means owning your own home, having a couple of fancy cars in the garage, going on regular vacations and then, eventually, retiring in comfort and being free to do whatever we choose. This "dream" is kept alive by the media – the rich and famous, who supposedly have achieved and enjoy this good life, are constantly splashed across the pages of magazines, or being interviewed on TV. This reinforces the idea that the rich "have all the fun".

However, it is a sad reality that even those of us who are financially secure and seem to have attained "the good life" have missed the abundant life that Jesus promised to those who follow him. The materialistic "American dream" is a far cry from the abundant life that Jesus speaks about. The abundant life has nothing to do with collecting more stuff, but everything to do with being right with God, through faith in Jesus, and having the hope of spending eternity in His presence.

There are many avenues we can venture down but they won't lead us to eternal life. We can pursue pleasures – fancy cars or expensive holidays. We can try finding fulfilment in our work performance or achievements – even a sports star's thrill of victory lasts only a few minutes. We can chase money and possessions, or we can strive to reach a certain promotion or status. The truth is that life is not found in pleasure, performance, possessions, position or pursuits. It is found in the person of Jesus Christ – Jesus is the source of life.

"A thief comes only to steal and to kill and to destroy. I have come that they may have life and have it in abundance" - John 10:10

DAY 42

February 11

God does great things
Beyond our understanding

Job 37:5

JOB 37:5

"For my thoughts are not your thoughts, neither are your ways my ways, declares the Lord. For as the heavens are higher than the earth, so are my ways higher than your ways and my thoughts than your thoughts". (Isaiah 55:8-9)

It is wonderful to acknowledge and accept that God's thoughts, plans, methods, strategies, values and principles, are infinitely higher and greater than our own. What kind of God would he be if we could understand his mind, predict what he has planned for us or know how he will react and behave in any given circumstance. If we could understand the mind of God he would have to have the same small and limited view of the world as we do. It would then be acceptable to doubt him, or to question his judgements, because he would be equal to us. But God is infinitely big. His plane of thought is so vastly removed from ours that it is impossible for us to comprehend. With all his wisdom, knowledge and power, he planned all of eternity from start to finish.

It is often difficult to believe that God is in control. Where is he when a loved one suffers and dies from a debilitating illness, or financial strain robs us of our dignity? Why do innocent people die in a war they have nothing to do with, or when an Ebola epidemic grips their country? Our struggle to see what God sees shouldn't cause us to doubt Him, but to trust Him. He has a plan and is in control. If we understood the plan, how great could it be? It would be a human plan, at best. This leaves us with only one option-to trust Him. His plans are higher and better than anything we could possibly wrap our minds around. He sees the beginning and the end – all we have to do is have the faith that "in all things God works for the good of those who love him, who have been called according to his purpose" (Romans 8:28).

DAY 43

February 12

I will never forget you.

Isaiah 49:15

ISAIAH 49:15

Many of us can recall, quite vividly, the intense pain of losing a loved one. The desperate sense of loss that accompanies the grief is akin to losing a grip on reality and floundering around like a lost soul. Although the pain heals, we never forget them – they remain in our hearts.

I imagine that this must be what Jesus felt on the cross – all alone, abandoned by everyone. At that moment, while paying for our sins, he was forgotten, even by his Father.

Fortunately, God will never forget us. We have His word and Jesus consolidated that on the cross. The only challenge is that we never forget Him. It is easy to lose sight of God when the going is good – let us guard against that and stay loyal to Jesus who alienated himself for our salvation.

DAY 44

February 13

The earth is the Lord's, and all it contains
the world and those who dwell in it
For He has founded it upon the seas
and established it upon the rivers

Psalm 24:1-2

PSALM 24:1-2

As Christians, the most important thing is to acknowledge, in heart and in mind, that God owns everything.

In the Old Testament, King David understood this principle well and gave us a beautiful description of it: "Wealth and honour come from you; you are the ruler of all things. In your hands are strength and power to exalt and give to all. Now, our God, we give you thanks, and praise your glorious name. But who am I, and who are my people, that we should be able to give as generously as this? Everything comes from you, and we have given you only what comes from your hand. We are foreigners and strangers in your sight, as were all our ancestors. Our days on earth are like a shadow, without hope. Lord our God, all this abundance that we have provided for building you a temple for your Holy Name comes from your hand and all of it belongs to you."
(1 Chronicles 29:12-16)

David recognized and understood that God owns it all and that He gives to us out of His own abundance. We who are blessed should also remember where our resources truly come from. And, in so doing, we should strive to find ways to honour and glorify God with the money, possessions, and talents He has so richly and generously given to us.

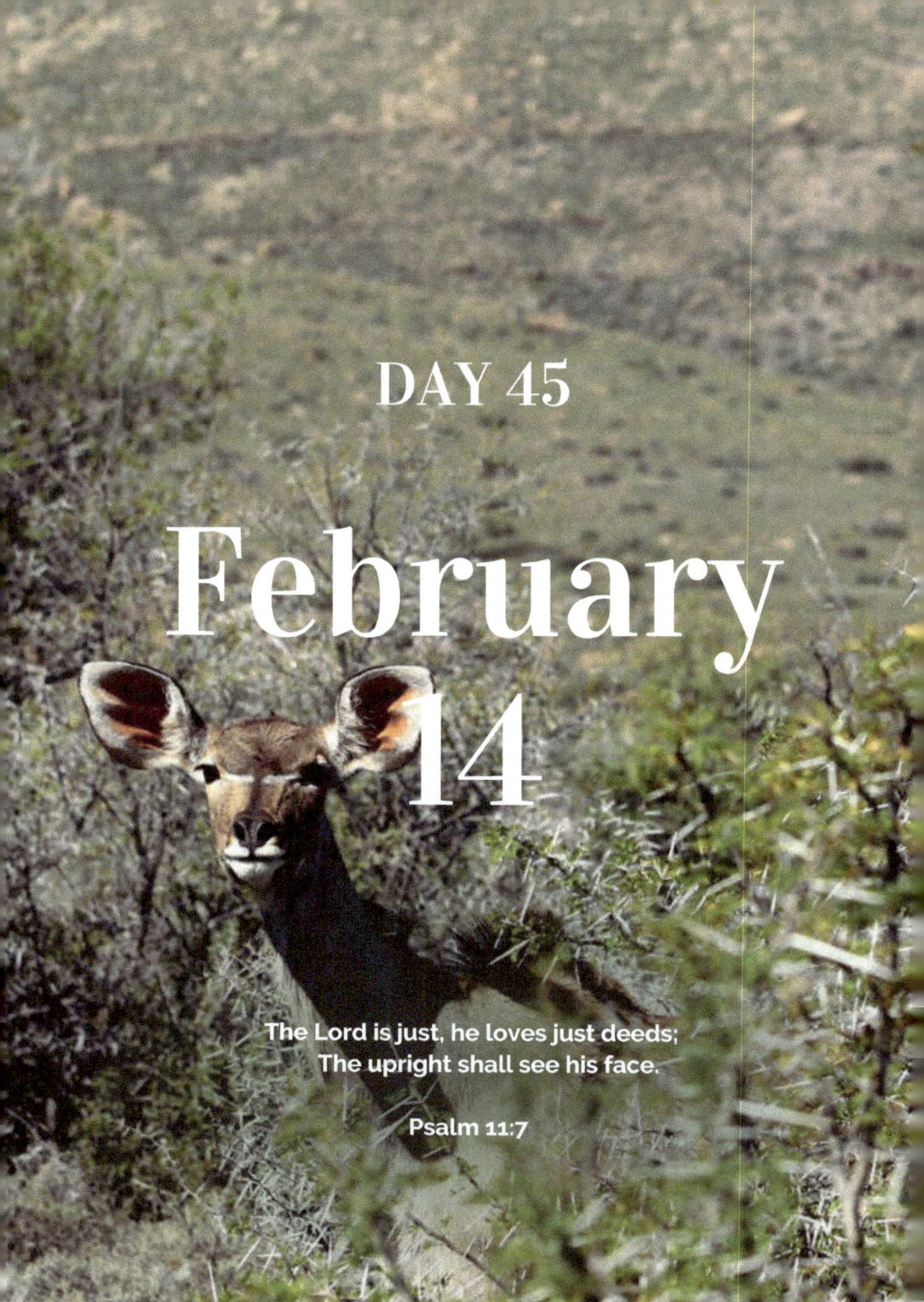

DAY 45

February 14

The Lord is just, he loves just deeds;
The upright shall see his face.

Psalm 11:7

ALMOST THERE

PSALM 11:7

Some of us have been privileged to see the expression on a mother's face when her newborn baby gets placed in her arms. No matter what the gender, size, or the health of the child is, pure joy, love and pride radiates from her as she gets acquainted with her precious new bundle.

As this child grows and gets exposed to the family's values and principles, he will learn to imitate them, and the foundation for his future spiritual life will depend on what his parents have taught him.

In the same way, in our relationship with God, we need to attempt to live according to His mind and heart. The scriptures tell us that the upright shall see God's face if we live according to His word. As we strive to grow in likeness to Him, God will draw us to himself and we will begin to see His face.

Then God, too, can gaze down on us with pride and joy radiating from his face.

DAY 46

February 15

Everyone who listens to these words of mine
And acts on them will be like a wise man
Who built his house on rock

Matthew 7:24

MATTHEW 7:24

From the moment we are born our parents start building the foundation for our future. They make sure that we are fed, that we are healthy, and that we are taught good values and principles. They even try to help us keep up with our peers in the sporting and social arenas. Sometimes, they make sacrifices to provide us with a decent education, so giving us a steppingstone onto the platform of adult life.

Jesus also loves us and wants to take care of us. He wants us to build a foundation that will take care of our soul. Only if we have a relationship with Jesus and study and listen to the Word of God, will our "house" be built on solid ground that can never be destroyed. We need to work on living a life that will help us get to the gates of heaven.

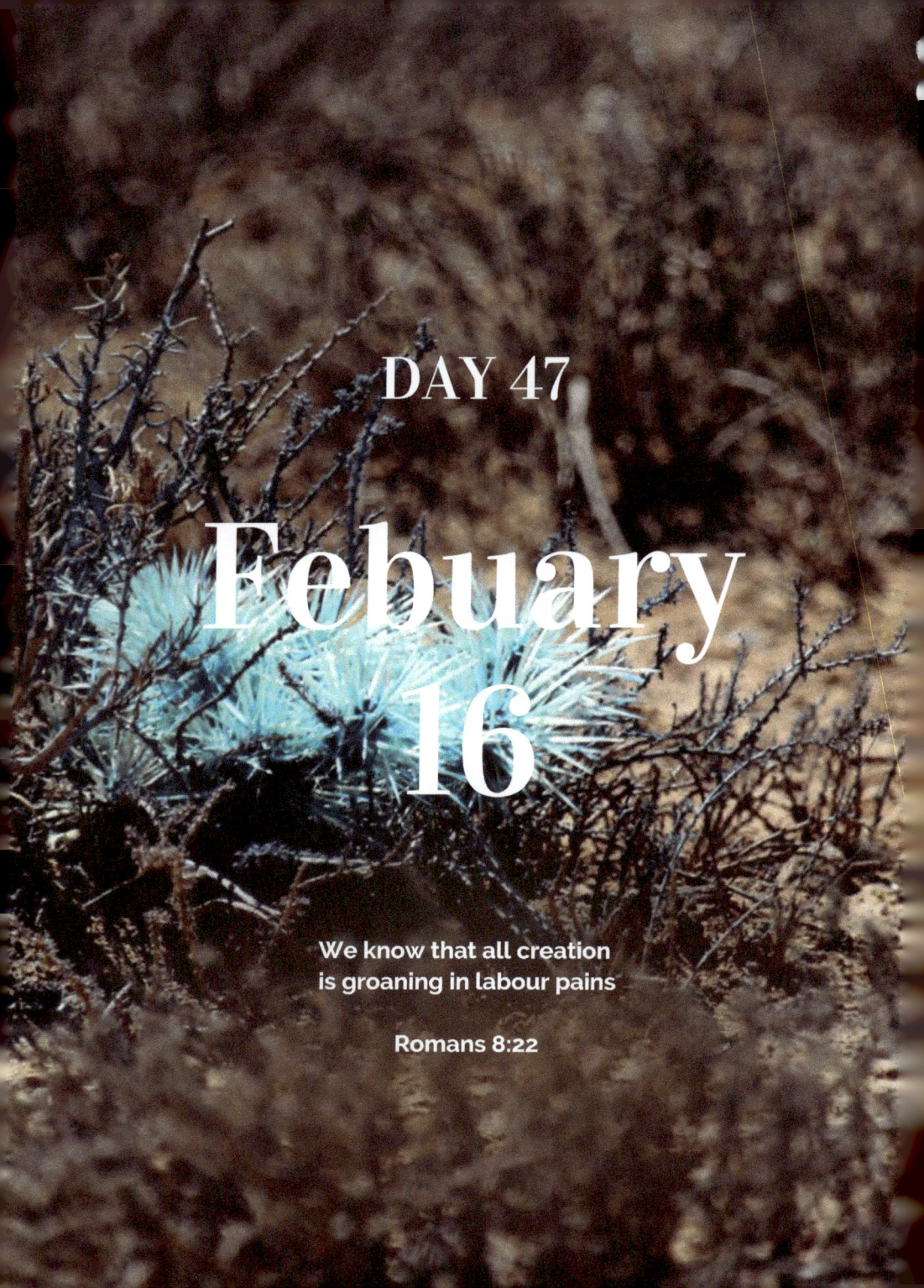

DAY 47

Febuary 16

We know that all creation
is groaning in labour pains

Romans 8:22

ROMANS 8:22

As Christians we all know that following Jesus is a "narrow gate" (Matthew 7:13-14). Truly following Jesus means "letting go". Jesus said, "the truth will set you free" (John 8:32). This freedom is only possible when we distance ourselves from the trappings of, and the consumerism of, this world. When we walk on the path that Jesus lays out for us, we have to let go of our false self, our cultural biases, and our fear of loss and death. Freedom to follow Jesus entails letting go of wanting more and better things, and of our desire to control and manipulate God and others.

By relinquishing our dependency on power and control, our need for personal safety and security, and our love of affection and our own self-esteem, we stop walking on the path of our own ego and begin to follow the "way of the cross".

DAY 48

February 17

Those who regularly give alms shall enjoy a full life; But those habitually guilty of sin are their own worst enemies

Tobit 12:9-10

ALMOST THERE

TOBIT 12:9-10

We are often our own worst enemies. By not believing in ourselves and in our abilities, we stifle our own success. By being too afraid to try in case we fail, we never reach our full potential. By refusing help and advice from others, we slow down our progress.

The same applies for our spiritual growth. By being attracted to the earthly rewards of money and power, we lose sight of the tenets of our Christian religion – faith, hope and love. When we nurture these tenets in our heart and allow them to guide us, charity follows. Jesus wants us to take care of the sick and the elderly. He wants us to provide for the poor. He wants us to forgive our enemies. Only through asking for His help, can we reach our full potential as children of God.

Sin is a kind of leprosy of the mind and heart – Jesus came to heal us.

DAY 49

February 18

Forgive and you will be forgiven.

Luke 6:37

LUKE 6:37

"Father, forgive them for they know not what they are doing". (Luke 23:34)

Jesus looked down from the cross to see the Roman soldiers casting lots for His clothing. The criminals on the crosses to either side of him were scorning Him. The religious leaders were mocking Him and the crowd was blaspheming Him. Even in His agony, Jesus' concern was the forgiveness of those who considered themselves His enemies.

And yet, I find it incredibly hard to forgive someone who has harmed me or done me an injustice. It almost feels like I am accepting and approving of what they have done. Forgetting is the most difficult part. By forgetting we have to let go of our feelings of superiority and allow the humility that forgiveness demands take over.

I pray for Jesus' intercession every time I need to forgive someone – I realise Jesus extended His forgiveness to me and wants me to extend this love to those who hurt or harm me in any way.

DAY 50

HAMBURGER PARADISE

February 19

The jar of flour did not go empty,
Nor the jug of oil run dry......

1 Kings 17:16

1 KINGS 17:16

How often do we tend to hoard our time, money or talents? When financial stress, or other hardships plaque us, we easily forget the words of Jesus – "Therefore you should not be concerned about tomorrow, for tomorrow will be concerned for itself. A day's trouble is sufficient for it". (Matthew 6:34)

The widow of Zarephath, despite the fact that her supplies were exhausted, heeded the promptings of the Spirit, and shared her meal with the prophet Elijah. By accepting the prophet's word that she would not lose by it, she secured food for her and her son for the next two years. Her faith saved her in a time of famine.

We too can believe in the providence of God. He promised to take care of and to provide for us. By having a trusting spirit we free ourselves from material concerns, allowing us to serve God and help his children on earth. Being kind and charitable is contagious and stimulates generosity in others.

DAY 51

February 20

Whoever seeks to preserve his
life will lose it, but whoever
loses it will save it.

Luke 17:33

LUKE 17:33

"I came that they might have life, and that they might have it more abundantly"
(John 10:10)

People are at their happiest when they live close to God. But our independence and desire to be our own boss often turns us away from God. And so, instead of living in harmony with him, we rely on our own strength and resourcefulness to get through life. This leads to disappointment, hardships, broken relationships and strife.

"If we choose to live close to God we allow His love to become our love, His strength to become our strength, His friendliness to become our friendliness". (Prof Jan van der Watt) In essence, we become the person God intended us to be.

We have the freedom to choose our own path. In choosing to serve God faithfully each day, we choose an abundant life on this earth and secure our place in the hereafter.

DAY 52

February 21

He guides the humble to justice,
He teaches the humble his way.

Psalm 25:9

PSALM 25:9

Humility is often considered a form of weakness. However, humility builds strength of character. A humble person is willing to learn. A humble person listens to, and serves others. Humility helps us to submit to noble values and to open our hearts instead of erecting walls. It joins and connects people, and frees us to build up our neighbour instead of ourselves.

Talent, education and leadership qualities are all important for success - but humility is necessary.

"Humility is not thinking less of yourself but thinking of yourself less". C.S. Lewis

DAY 53

February 22

"He must increase, but I must decrease.
He who comes from above is above all;
He who is of the earth is earthly
And speaks of the earth
He who comes from heaven is above all.

John 3:30-31

ALMOST THERE

JOHN 3:30-31

It is a sad reality that in today's world there are many people masquerading as ministers of the Gospel who actually just use it as platform for self-enrichment and self-aggrandisement. The news is full of these so-called pastors who abuse the trust and love of their congregation to fulfil their own needs.

Against that backdrop we have the magnanimity and humility of John the Baptist. Although it is a natural to be envious of the growing reputation of others, especially when it is likely to impact on your own, John was contented for the cause of Jesus to be advanced. He was totally unselfish and accepted that the goal of teaching and preaching is to lead people to follow Jesus.

The point of ministry is not to make the minister look good, but to help others in their walk with God.

DAY 54

February 23

All you who are thirsty,
Come to the water!
You who have no money,
Come, receive grain and eat;
Come, without paying and without cost,
Drink wine and milk!

Isaiah 55:1

ISAIAH 55:1

This invitation from God seems almost too good to be true. To be offered food and wine without paying and without cost is unheard of in this life. But is God's call to His banquet really without any cost at all?

God is offering water, milk and wine. All of these are beverages of a simple civilisation, but all are precious to a thirsty palate. Water revives, wine gladdens and inspires, milk nourishes. But the thirst is a spiritual thirst, and the hunger, our souls' desire to be in communion with God.

All we need and desire is to be found in Christ. Jesus then, is what each man desires. "He that comes to me shall never hunger, and he that believeth in me shall never thirst".
(John 6:35)

DAY 55
February 24

On that day there shall be open to the house of David and to the inhabitants of Jerusalem, a fountain to purify from sin and uncleanness

Zechariah 13:1

ZECHARIAH 13:1

Not one of us would dream of going out to a fancy restaurant after having run a marathon unless we have showered first. This physical picture has a spiritual analogy - "All have sinned and fall short of the glory of God" (Romans 3:23).

However, God has graciously provided a fountain for sinners to be cleansed so that they may become His holy people. Zechariah 13 makes 4 points:

- We all need God's fountain to cleanse us from sin and impurity. God's fountain stems from His grace, it is inexhaustible and it must be applied individually.
- Cleansing from sin should lead to separation from sin. In the words of St Paul "Therefore, having these promises, beloved, let us cleanse ourselves from all defilement of flesh and spirit, perfecting holiness in the fear of God" (2 Corinthians 7:1)
- God is the only one who can open a fountain for cleansing, and He has done so by killing His Shepherd.
- Those whom God cleanses from sin He purifies through the fires of affliction.

It is during times of trouble that we call on the Lord. When He answers us, we gain the assurance that we are His children and that He is our God.

DAY 56

February 25

You will grieve, but your
grief will become joy.

John 16:20

ALMOST THERE

JOHN 16:20

And the greatest grief you can ever experience, which is far greater than any loss that anybody ever talks about, is "the grief over love that you have never experienced" - Elizabeth Kubler-Ross

But God's love is unconditional– it does not matter who you are or what you have done– God loves you! God's love sent Jesus to Calvary to die for our sins. God doesn't love us for who we are; but rather because of who He is. Likewise, we need to love others because of whom we are, not because of who they are, what they do, or what they think.

FRINGE

DAY 57

February 26

"No one who believes in him will be put to shame"

Romans 10:11

ROMANS 10:11

We are all equal in the eyes of the Lord. Jew or gentile, rich or poor, black or white, male or female – God does not discriminate. "For whosoever shall call upon the name of the Lord shall be saved". (Romans 10:13)

Anyone who truly believes and calls on His name, through prayer, will be saved. Other than having faith and asking for His help, Jesus places no conditions on our acceptance into His holy presence.
All are welcome in his Fathers' house, and all of us are worthy of His unconditional love and acceptance.

As Christians, our challenge is to extend this unconditional love and acceptance, free from discrimination, to all we meet on our earthly journey.

"As I have loved you, have love one to another". (John 13:34)

DAY 58

February 27

Whoever has ears to hear ought to hear

Mark 4:9

MARK 4:9

"Whoever has ears ought to hear". Jesus had just addressed a large crowd on the beach and He had ended off the teaching with the words of todays' reading. He had been using parables, and even His own disciples didn't understand the meaning of them. They, however, were fortunate enough to get a special explanation afterwards, because, in the words of Jesus, "unto you (the disciples), is given the mystery of the kingdom of God". (Mark 4:11)

How do we, as the children of God today, get to understand the teachings of Christ? Have we been given the "mystery of the kingdom of God"? I believe we have. We can get our explanation through homilies, through bible readings and study, and through discussion with fellow believers. The more we open ourselves to the word of God, the more the mystery of our faith will be revealed to us.

DAY 59

February 28

Your ways, O Lord, make known to me;
Teach me your paths.

Psalm 25:4

PSALM 25:4

Living the life of a Christian isn't always simple or easy. We don't understand the mind of God, and His way of dealing with things doesn't always suite us or makes sense to us.

During the "Sermon on the Mount" Jesus teaches about "turning the other cheek". This could be interpreted in a number of ways. Most Christians, however, find this difficult to digest - because it seems to call for non-resistance and the facilitating of aggression against oneself. But, it could also simply mean that when "we turn the other cheek", we are not passively allowing someone to beat or rob us, but, if it happens, we are expected not to seek vengeance.

This is only one example where we battle to find the path that Jesus has laid out for us. We can only heed the words of the Psalmist and constantly pray for God's guidance and patience as we try to walk in His ways.

DAY 60-90

March

The Merton Prayer

My Lord God, I have no idea where I am going. I do not see the road ahead of me. I cannot know for certain where it will end.

Nor do I really know myself, and the fact that I think I am following your will does not mean that I am actually doing so.

But I believe that the desire to please you does in fact please you and I hope I have that desire in all that I am doing.

I hope that I will never do anything apart from that desire. and I know that if I do this you will lead me by the right road, though I may know nothing about it.

Therefore will I trust you always Though I may seem to be lost and in the shadow of death, I will not fear, for you are ever with me, and you will never leave me to face my perils alone.

- Thomas Merton

DAY 60

March 01

Whenever a person turns to the Lord the veil is removed.

2 Corinthians 3:16

2 CORINTHIANS 3:16

"And all of us have had that veil removed so that we can be mirrors that brightly reflect the Glory of the Lord. And as the Spirit of the Lord works within us, we become more and more like Him and reflect His Glory even more".
(2 Corinthians 3:18)

The "veil" is a covering and figuratively means an impediment – a hindrance or obstruction from doing something. In other words, it symbolises a cover over our minds and hearts that prevents us from understanding God's truth. We remain behind the veil when we allow the attractions of this earth to rule our decisions and we forego our Christian values and principles. However, when we acknowledge our sinfulness and accept the Lord as our saviour, He removes the veil. The Holy Spirit then opens our hearts and minds and, as we begin to understand the Greatness of God, our transformation into His image begins.

This transformation into His image is a process. The more time we spend in His presence, through fellowship and prayer, the more we reflect His Glory. The more time we spend in His presence, the more He removes the veil. In Matthew 5:14 Jesus says: "You are the light of the world". Our light must not be hidden or veiled – we are called to shine so that others can see and experience the love, beauty, and abundance, of His Splendour. Our radiance is His radiance shining through us – alone we can never be good enough. But, we are made in His image and, as we seek Him, He will remove the covering that hides our glow

DAY 61

March 02

Rely not on your strength
In following the desires
of your heart

Sirach 5:2

SIRACH 5:2

Most Christians are familiar with Psalm 37:4 – "Take delight in the Lord, and He will give you the desires of your heart". This verse is not suggesting that God will give us whatever we desire as long as we have enough faith. We all know what it is like to have desires. We experience pain, witness injustice, ache with loneliness or grief, and suffer all other sorts of trials and tribulations. It is only human and natural to pray for these onslaughts to pass, and for our situation to change for the better. However, even when all is going relatively well, our minds and hearts often imagine how wonderful it would be if we had just a tad more.

Most people desire good things – a job, a spouse, healing, children, friends, ministry etc. The question we face on a daily basis is not whether or not we have desires, but how to discern when they drift away from hopeful longings to become covetousness and entitled attitudes. It is important to note that the Psalmist tells us to "take delight in the Lord". It is only when we delight in Him that we begin to desire the same things He desires – mercy, forgiveness, obedience, love, wisdom, peace and kindness. God will grant these to us if we ask Him.

The other things like money, relationships and success, might be nice – and perhaps God may still give them to us. But they cannot be the desires of our heart. God wants something even greater for us than temporary happiness or fleeting success. He wants us to have a godly character, a loving heart, and deep desires that are in alignment with His own.

DAY 62

March 03

Those that sow in tears
Shall reap rejoicing

Psalm 126:5

PSALM 126:5

Sowing is hard work. For example, when growing your own vegetables, you have to make sure the rows are straight. You have to carefully measure the distance between each plant, and then dig the holes. Once the plant is in the hole, you have to water them. Even when the seeds or plants are safely in the ground the hard work continues – constant weeding, nurturing and protecting.

Our role on earth as followers of Christ is more about sowing than reaping. Whether we are working with people or with projects, we go through the same motions – we prepare the soil, plant and nurture. Sometimes, we have the joy of seeing the fruits of our labour. More often than not, we don't.

"As for the seed that fell on rich soil, they are the ones who, when they have heard the word, embrace it with a generous and good heart, and bear fruit through perseverance".
(Luke 8:15)

DAY 63

March 04

At nightfall, weeping enters in,
but with the dawn rejoicing

Psalm 30:5

PSALM 30:5

What is "the dark night"? What happens to our faith in the night seasons? We know that faith is simply being fully persuaded that God will do all that He has promised to do, in His timing, and in His Way. We also know that God continually pushes us to the limit in order to strengthen our faith and transform us into His image. When we willingly allow Him to purge our souls of sin and self, He can easily accomplish His will. However, when we block and prevent God from doing these things in our lives, either out of ignorance or disobedience, He sometimes takes matters into His own hands; i.e., the night seasons.

The dark night or the night season, is simply the transition we make from depending upon our own sight and our own selves, to a total dependence upon Christ and His faithfulness. This shift brings us into a new way of knowing God. During this time God moves us from simply "feeling good about Him", to a deeper awareness of Him and an intimacy never before known. Although we already belong to Christ and we already love Him, our union with Him will be incomplete as long as our mind, our judgement, our desires, our habits and our ideas, are still our own. God wants to rid us of our preoccupation with sight and feelings, and bring us into a new freedom and liberty of faith.

Unfortunately, this freeing process does not happen automatically. Most of us do not jump for joy when faced with the prospect of brokenness. Naturally, most of us run in the other direction. But God loves us so much that He doesn't let us get very far. The dark night is God's way of turning us around and forcing us to allow Him to do whatever is necessary in our lives to purge our souls and spirits so that we can have intimate fellowship with Him. God is not a "mean guy" up in heaven waiting to send us bad things – He is a loving Father who knows exactly what we need in order to accomplish His will in our lives. He knows that we will never be content, never enjoy real freedom and never be truly fulfilled, until we are "experientially" one with Him. The Dark Night of the Soul – Dr D. W. Ekstrand

DAY 64

March 05

I have set before you life and death,
The blessing and the curse
Choose life......

Deuteronomy 30:19

ALMOST THERE

DEUTERONOMY 30:19

These words are some of the last words that God gave Moses to write just before his death. They represent the most fundamental theme of the whole Bible: namely, the Lord seeks to enter into a covenantal relationship with His people. But precisely because a covenant of love must be chosen, rather than coerced, he also gives us the power to choose to reject his love. "This day I call heaven and earth as witnesses against you that I have set before you life and death, blessings and curses. Now choose life, so that you and your children may live..." That should be an easy choice – given the option of life and blessings, or death and curses, it seems natural that we would jump at the chance to choose life! But the command, "Choose life", is more than a decision to keep on breathing. God's command to choose life is further defined in Deuteronomy 30:16 – "For I command you today to love the Lord your God, to walk in God's ways, and to keep His commandments".

So, "choosing life", involves loving God – exclusively and wholeheartedly. "Love the Lord your God with all your heart and with all your soul and with all your strength". (Deuteronomy 6:5) "Choosing life" entails walking in God's ways. Like Adam and Eve, who had a choice to obey God or to do what they wanted – they chose to do it their way- we, by nature, want to do things our way. And, lastly, "choosing life" means keeping God's commandments. As humans, we tend to make excuses and find loopholes to continue doing things our way. But Jesus very clearly taught that "murder" includes anger and contempt; "adultery" includes lust and what is going on in our minds, our eyes and our hearts; "divorce" should be extremely rare; and "oaths" and "swearing" should not be necessary if we are trustworthy.

Therefore, to "choose life" we must have a change of heart. And that change can only come through faith in Jesus – "I am the Way, the Truth and the Life, no one comes to the Father except through me." (John 14:6)

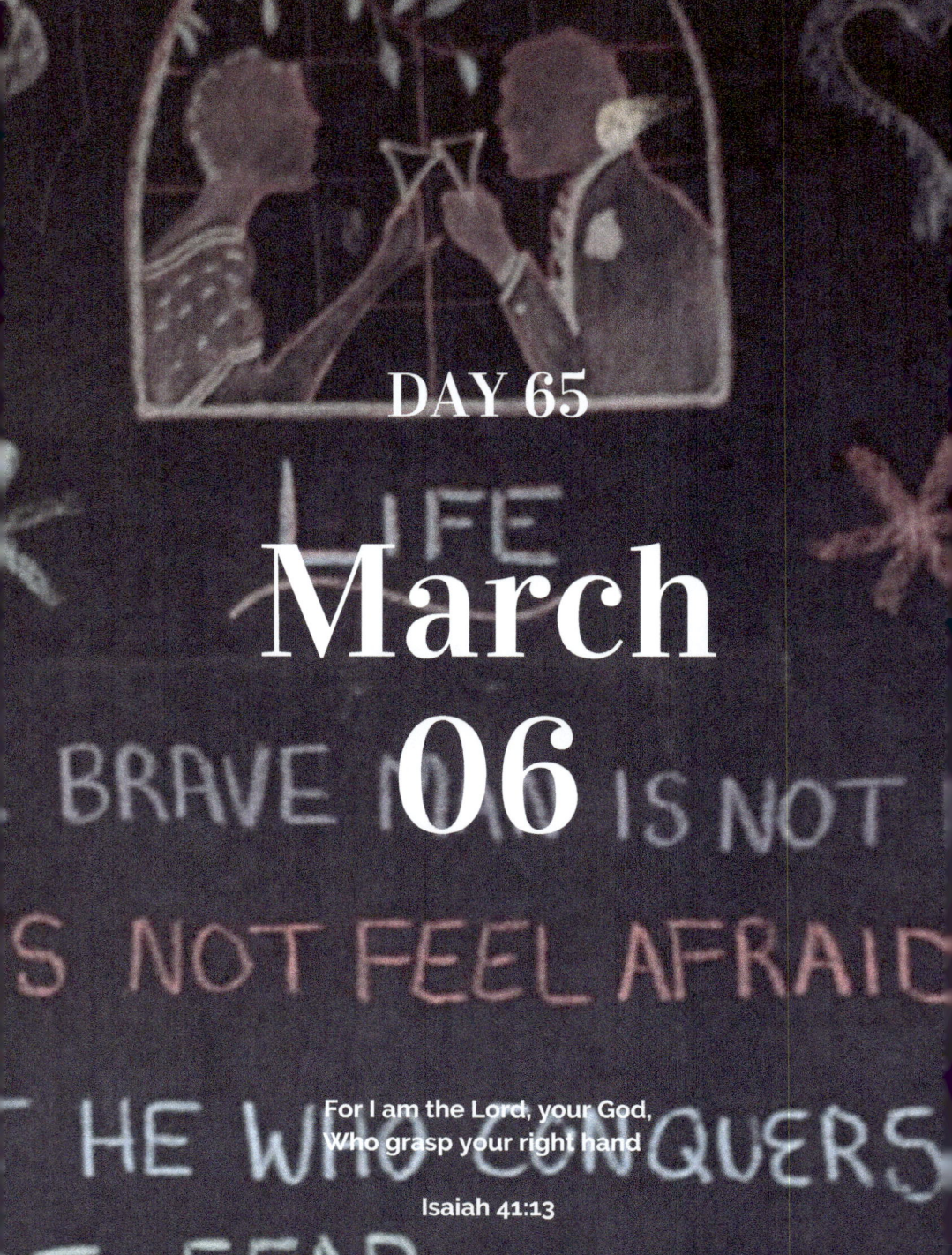

DAY 65

March 06

For I am the Lord, your God,
Who grasp your right hand

Isaiah 41:13

ISAIAH 41:13

Holding hands denotes affection, protection, and comfort. It is a connection between two people and a feeling of safety while in the company of a loved one.

Young children and their parents, romantic couples, adults and their elderly parents, are all examples of relationships that use hand-holding as a way of expressing togetherness. In each instance, however, the meaning of the physical contact is different. Children need affection and protection. Elderly people need balance and support. Romantic couples use it to display their love. One thing is certain, though, it always demonstrates a strong connection between the participants.

How privileged we are that the creator of the universe reaches out and wants to be in a relationship with us. Through accepting God's offer of life and love, we transform our destiny. Living in faith offers us safety, security, comfort and love, that only a life, holding hands with the creator, provides

DAY 66

March 07

The Lord lifts up all who are falling
And raises up all who are bowed down.

Psalm 145:14

ALMOST THERE

PSALM 145:14

How comforting these words of scripture are to all who are in need of God's forgiveness, His guidance and solace.

As humans, we all make mistakes and often fall prey to the attractions of this world. God loves us unconditionally anyway. When life's challenges and hardships leave us destitute and without hope, we can find strength in the certainty of His love.

The message throughout the gospel is that God's help and divine forgiveness are ours for the asking. By our faith we are healed. Through faith and trust in God, we are saved and gain eternal life.

Our failures, and life's challenges, are temporary. God's love and forgiveness are eternal. God will never forsake us, even in our darkest moments. That promise runs like a thread right through the bible and is a constant source of hope and encouragement.

DAY 67

March 08

Sing and rejoice, O daughter Zion!
See, I am coming to dwell among you
Says the Lord

Zechariah 2:10

ALMOST THERE

ZECHARIAH 2:10

These words of the Prophet, Zechariah, are words of encouragement and hope. In a world where reports of war, corruption, dishonesty, hunger, greed, and violence dominate the daily news, it is difficult to visualise a future of peace and prosperity.

Jesus came to live among us and, because he did, we stand a chance to have abundant life. "Abundant life" refers to life in its abounding fullness of joy and strength for mind, body and soul. "Abundant life" signifies a contrast to feelings of lack, emptiness and dissatisfaction - and such feelings may motivate a person to seek for the meaning of life, and to strive to change their ways.

In trusting in Jesus, we have every reason to want to sing and rejoice.

DAY 68

March 09

I believe that I shall see the bounty of the Lord in the land of the living

Psalm 27:13

ALMOST THERE

PSALM 27:13

The view that a person holds about the afterlife is bound to affect the value given to this current life. Christian beliefs about life after death are based on the resurrection of Jesus Christ. Jesus' sacrifice on the cross was a victory over sin and death. Therefore, after death, we will be taken into the presence of God and given eternal life with Him.

However, there are many things that we can rejoice in while we are still in this life. We should rejoice in the blessings that we do have. We should feel joy in being alive and give thanks for our loved ones.

God's bounty refers to His providence – to everything that He has given. We can see the bounty of the Lord in the beauty of His creation. We can see the bounty of the Lord in kindness shown to the elderly, the sick, or the poor. We can see the bounty of the Lord in the forgiveness and mercy shown to those who sin, or who have lost their way. God's bounty is not found in material wealth but in our knowledge of Him, in our faith, and in the goodness He has placed in our hearts.

DAY 69

March 10

The lamp of the body is the eye.
Therefore, when your eye is good,
your whole body also is full of light.
But when your eye is bad,
your body also is full of darkness.

Matthew 6:22-23

# MATTHEW 6:22-23

The above verses are part of the Sermon on the Mount. The Sermon on the Mount contains instructions on how to live a life that is both dedicated to, and pleasing to, God. Essentially it is a type of moral compass pointing the direction that God wants us to go. Therefore Jesus' description of the eye should not be seen as referring to the physical eye, but rather to the moral or ethical character of a person.

The "bad eye" is a "worldly eye". It is an eye that cannot see the beauty of grace or the brightness of generosity. It cannot see unexpected blessings to others as a precious treasure, and is blind to what is truly beautiful, bright, and God-like. Money and material reward clouds its vision. The "good eye", however, sees heavenly treasure as infinitely more precious than earthly possessions. So when our eye is good and not bad, we store our treasures in heaven. In order to do that, we simply have to live our lives with open hearts and open hands.

Open hearts means having a heart similar to God – one for the poor, the weak, the disenfranchised, and the marginalized. Open hands means living a life where our earthly goods are not used exclusively for our own enjoyment, but also to have an impact on those less fortunate than we are.

DAY 70

March 11

Because the foolishness of God
is wiser than men,
and the weakness of God
is stronger than men.

1 Corinthians 1:25

1 CORINTHIANS 1:25

"But the wisdom that comes from heaven is first of all pure;
then peace-loving, considerate, submissive, full of mercy
and good fruit, impartial and sincere".
(James 3:17)

Earthly wisdom appeals to our senses and emotions. In contrast, the wisdom that comes from God is a reflection of Him. Earthly wisdom says follow your heart, godly wisdom tells us in Jeremiah 17:9 that the heart is deceitful above all things. Earthly wisdom reiterates "seeing is believing", godly wisdom tells us that "blessed are those who have not seen and yet have believed" (John 20:29).

While earthly wisdom tells us to love our family and friends, godly wisdom, in Matthew 5:43-47, instructs us to love our enemies as well, and to bless them. While earthly wisdom says there are many ways to God, godly wisdom knows that there is only one way to God and that is through Jesus Christ – Acts 4:12. God wants to give His divine wisdom to all of His children. There are numerous modalities of learning and education available to us, but their value is limited unless built on the knowledge of the Lord himself. There are so many worldly distractions that confront us on our spiritual journey. We are constantly bombarded with viewpoints, ideals and principles that contradict the morals and ethics taught in God's word.

These belief systems are often appealing and sound impressive. But as believers we must remain diligent and steadfast in seeking godly wisdom. We have to guard against the wisdom of the world, and from blindly accepting advice from well-meaning family and friends. If it is our desire to be led solely by God, it is essential to spend time in prayer and in studying the scriptures – "If any of you lacks wisdom, you should ask God, who gives generously to all without finding fault, and it will be given to you".
(James 1:5)

DAY 71

March 12

When the whirlwind passes by, the wicked is no more. But the righteous has an everlasting foundation.

Proverbs 10:25

PROVERBS 10:25

Jesus often used hyperbole and contrast to teach important life lessons – "I will show you what it's like when someone comes to me, listens to my teaching, and then follows it. It is like a person building a house who digs deep and lays the foundation on solid rock. When the floodwaters rise and break against that house it stands firm because it is well built. But anyone who hears and doesn't obey is like a person who builds a house right on the ground, without a foundation. When the floods sweep down against that house, it will collapse into a heap of ruins". (Luke 6:47-49)

The word, "foundation", is defined as the ground on which other parts rest or are overlaid - like the base on which a house is built or the roots of a tree. Everyone's life has a foundation. We all put our trust and hope in something, and that becomes the foundation for our life. Some people build their lives around money, believing that it provides a better and more secure future. Others rely on possessions to bring happiness. Popularity is another way people try to find purpose and meaning – they think that if they have more friends they will never be on their own and life will be great.

All these things are not necessarily bad, but every one of them is temporary. When we face the storms of life – dealing with difficult relationships or a financial crisis, the death of a loved one, losing a job or handling rebellious teenagers – it is a strong spiritual foundation that will help us withstand them. We are called to build our lives on the rock – and that rock is Jesus. Life will still not be perfect – storms will still come. Jesus told his disciples, "Here on earth you will have many trials and sorrows. But take heart, because I have overcome the world" (John 16:33). Just as it takes time to lay a sturdy foundation for a house, it takes time to build the foundation of our faith. When we spend time with God in prayer, worship, praise, and reading the scriptures, he uses it as the foundation to solve our problems and transform our lives.

DAY 72

March 13

A faithful friend is a sturdy shelter;
He who finds one finds a treasure.

Sirach 6:14

SIRACH 6:14

The greatest example of friendship in the bible is that of David and Jonathan. In the story, Jonathan makes a covenant with David because he loves him just as he loves himself. With his pledge he was saying, "What's mine is yours". This friendship lasted throughout their lifetime and was based on trust and obedience to God.

A true best friend is hard to find, and the relationship needs to be nurtured and treasured. A best friend listens to you, prays with you, laughs with you, mourns with you, and shares your joy. A best friend shows up when you need her, and surprises you with her actions, based on love and concern, when you least expect it.

Victor Hugo describes it in Les Miserables -
" To love another person is to see the face of God".

"A faithful friend is something beyond price, there is no measuring his worth. A faithful friend is the elixir of life"
Ecclesiasticus 6:16

DAY 73

March 14

My soul waits for the Lord
More than sentinels wait for the dawn.

Psalm 130:6

PSALM 130:6

A sentinel is a guard, a lookout, a person keeping watch. It is most often associated with a soldier keeping watch at night, and it can safely be assumed that they long for and welcome daybreak.

But a sentinel represents anyone standing vigil over anything. Staying awake with a loved one who is terminally ill and in pain is one of the hardest tests of emotional endurance. During such times we pray for daybreak, and with the light of dawn the cross seems easier to bear. Somehow, everything seems better in the light of day.

Our soul too, is a sentinel, awaiting its own dawn. We all want our world and our life to have meaning and purpose. We try to find it through worldly possessions and worldly pleasures, but fail to recognise that it is really a deep hunger for God. The yearning for God draws each of us, and, just like the inevitability of dawn, we cannot avoid or ignore it.

DAY 74

March 15

The path of the virtuous is like the light of dawn,
Its brightness growing to the fullness of day;
The way of the wicked is as dark as night,
They cannot tell what it is they stumble over.

Proverbs 4:18

PROVERBS 4:18

We can see a contrast here between the righteous and the wicked, between light and darkness. When we have the light of Christ in us, it illuminates everything. We can see more clearly and understand more deeply - especially the things pertaining to the ways and purposes of God. Not so for the people of the world – those who walk by the dictates of the flesh, without the saving knowledge of Christ. They are still in darkness and have no idea, or understanding, of the ways of God. When we become Christians, our minds are no longer dull to our spiritual nature or the sinful nature. We begin to clearly see the contrast between light and darkness, and good and evil, that rule in the world.

This is an encouraging piece of scripture because it points to the reward in this life for being faithfully righteous. It takes time to develop an understanding of God and life, but that understanding brings a blessing and comfort to those that have it. Life may not get easier as we grow in the Lord, but our increased knowledge and understanding makes life make more sense, and makes it easier to bear hard times. This verse is not speaking of the full light of day being our next life – it is encouragement for this life – but the blessings of the next life might be considered an undertone in the verse.

DAY 75

March 16

For wisdom is more precious than pearls,
And nothing else is so worthy of desire.

Proverbs 8:11

PROVERBS 8:11

According to the Book of Proverbs, wisdom is more precious than pearls as well as rubies – "She is more precious than rubies: and all the things thou canst desire are not to be compared unto her". (Proverbs 3:15)

Wisdom surpasses anything we could dream about as being desirable, or necessary, for our success or happiness. Yet we spend great amounts of effort, and much time, pursuing things far inferior to wisdom and understanding. We chase education, physical fitness, career paths, estate building, a pretty wife or good-looking husband, and various other material investments that occupy our time. But these things, even added together and combined, are less valuable than wisdom.

It is an axiom of human nature that you love yourself. And, precisely because we care about our own peace, pleasure, prosperity and reputation, it is important to realise that these proverbs point us to the simplest and most dramatic change we can make in our lives in order to achieve our goals – learn wisdom and live your life by it. Wisdom is so important and precious because it brings long life, riches, and honour (Proverbs 3:16); it brings pleasantness and peace (Proverbs 3:17); and it brings life and happiness (Proverbs 3:18). Wisdom is the power of right judgement, the ability to please God and men in all situations. It is rooted in a deep and abiding fear of the Lord, a hatred of all sin and evil, a deep faith in God, and a profound understanding and knowledge of His precious word.

DAY 76

March 17

If you love listening you will learn,
If you lend an ear, wisdom will be yours.

Ecclesiasticus 6:34

ECCLESIASTICUS 6:34

"While ageing brings challenges to mind and body, it can also lead to an expansion in other realms. There is an abundance of emotional and social knowledge; qualities which scientists are beginning to define as wisdom…the wisdom of elders".

When King Solomon died, his son Rehoboam succeeded him as king of Israel. Early in his reign the people asked that he not repeat the harsh rulership of his father, and that he lighten the merciless labour and heavy taxes the former king had demanded of them. In return they promised to loyally serve him. The new king asked for some time to consult two groups of advisors – the elders who had served his father Solomon, and the young men who had grown up with him. The elders, who had much wisdom, encouraged him to hear the people and to grant their request. However, he rejected their advice and listened to his younger companions who advised him to tell the people – "My father laid on you a heavy yoke; I will make it even heavier. My father scourged you with whips; I will scourge you with scorpions". (1 Kings 12:14) This bad advice resulted in the rebellion of the ten northern tribes of Israel. They made Jereboam their king instead, leaving Rehoboam with only the tribe of Judah.

This piece of Bible history demonstrates the importance of paying attention and respect to what is called the "wisdom of the elders". The scriptures are filled with illustrations where good, sound, advice and counsel can be drawn from older men and women who have lived a long life and learned many valuable lessons. This doesn't mean that any older person is automatically a good source of godly advice. Only a life lived "in the way of righteousness", is a foundation of wisdom. We need to seek guidance from older people who have lived upright, godly lives for many decades. They must be mature believers who have "exercised themselves unto godliness" (1Timothy 4:7).

"To avoid the mistakes of youth, draw from the wisdom of age".

DAY 77

March 18

In a time of plenty remember times of famine,
Poverty and want in day of wealth.

Ecclesiasticus 18:25

ECCLESIASTICUS 18:25

Mother Teresa was a humanitarian. She was a tiny woman of just 4 feet 11 inches and less than 100 pounds. Yet, she spent many years lifting and carrying those who were dying or sick. Mother Teresa chose to "serve the poorest of the poor and to live among them and like them". She saw beauty in every human being. She, along with others of the Missionaries of Charity, strove to make the lives and deaths of those around them more peaceful and full of love. She fed, washed, and cared for anyone who needed the assistance.

In the words of Mother Teresa – "One day in a heap of rubbish, I found a woman who was half dead. Her body had been bitten by rats and by ants. I took her to a hospital, but they told me that they didn't want her because they couldn't do anything for her. I protested and said that I wouldn't leave unless they hospitalized her. They had a long meeting and finally granted my request. That woman was saved". Realizing the need for a home to care for those who were dying alone in the streets of Calcutta, Mother Teresa requested a place from city officials. She was a given a building next to the temple. She called the new home for the dying, "Nirmal Hriday", which means, "the pure heart". This became a place where homeless, dying individuals, were washed, fed, and allowed to die with dignity.

There is a Mother Teresa inside all of us. When we allow kindness, love and nurturing, all the Fruits of the Spirit, to control our thoughts and actions, we become true warriors in the Army of God. We then honour God's commandment to "love your neighbour as you love yourself", and begin to change the world one day at a time.

DAY 78

March 19

His anger lasts a moment,
His favour a lifetime

Psalm 30:5

PSALM 30:5

If we want to understand the meaning of "the wrath of God" mentioned in the Bible, we have to compare it to our human conception of anger and wrath. There are as many different kinds of anger as there are human kinds of love and desires. Generally, we can place them in two categories – positive or negative anger. If the love and desires giving rise to the anger are selfish and materialistic, it is a negative and destructive anger. However, if the love and desires that gives rise to the anger are spiritual and humanitarian, it is a positive and protective anger.

In either case, our anger is a force to protect what we love. However, if what we love is primarily ourselves, our own power, possessions, and pleasure, regardless of the wellbeing of others, the anger flaring up to protect what we value and love, becomes a destructive force destroying anything that stands in our way. On the other hand, when we love spiritual values such as justice, truth, kindness, and compassion, and we love other people, not for what they can give us, but for their intrinsic value as beautiful human beings, our anger is very different. It does not want destruction – only the protection of the people and the values we hold dear.

When we are driven by positive anger, the enemy is only our enemy as long as they are attacking what we love. As soon the threat is neutralized, they cease to be our enemy, and the anger subsides. This is the kind of anger Jesus displayed when he saw the merchants buying and selling and profiting at the temple. This also explains the "wrath of God" in the Old Testament. This anger flows from the love for our neighbours and love for the spiritual and divine values of justice, truth, kindness, and compassion.

DAY 79

March 20

More than all else,
Keep watch over your heart,
Since here are the wellsprings of life.

Proverbs 4:23

PROVERBS 4:23

In the Old Testament the word "heart" is often used to represent our thoughts and the emotions -the wellsprings of life, the things that motivate and mould us.

In Romans 12:2 we read, "Be not conformed to this world; but be transformed by the renewing of your mind". When we become children of God, we change the way we think. God changes our thought process. Before we can do anything we have to think about it. So our thoughts lead to attitudes. Our attitudes lead to actions, and our actions result in achievements. Therefore, all our achievements are the sum total of our thoughts.

"As a man thinketh in his heart, so is he" (Proverbs 23:7). When God is in the heart, then we think right, live right and do right. If God is absent, we think wrong, do wrong and live wrong.

DAY 80

March 21

He does not realise that the eyes of the Lord are ten thousand times brighter than the sun, observing every aspect of human behaviour, seeing into the most secret corners

Ecclesiasticus 23:28

ALMOST THERE

ECCLESIASTICUS 23:28

Man is strange. We have the sneaking notion that we can hide behind a barn somewhere, get hopelessly drunk, and nobody will know about it. We foolishly believe that we can hide our bad behaviour from other men, or that we can secretly, in dark places, do things unlawful to both God and our neighbours. But nothing is ever hidden from God. Not an activity, not a book we read, not a word we say, not a thought we think, not a place we go, morning, noon or night, is ever hidden from God.

Jeremiah 23:24 says, "Can any hide himself in secret places that I shall not see him?" Ezekiel 28:3 says, "There is no secret that they can hide from thee". So, despite all our efforts to have our sins hidden, despite all our efforts to hide from God, we never do anything in secret. The all-seeing eye, the all-hearing ear, the all-searching searchlight of God's omnipotence, shines constantly upon our lives. Not a broken home, not a broken heart, not a broken life, goes unnoticed. In the same vain, not a kind deed is ever done that the Father does not see – not even a cup of water given in His name. We cannot hide from God – both now or in the future.

"It is curious that physical courage should be so common in the world and moral courage so rare"
Mark Twain

DAY 81

March 22

Give thanks to the Lord, for he is good,
For his mercy endures forever.

Psalm 136:1

PSALM 136:1

In 1 Thessalonians 5:18 we are taught to "give thanks in all circumstances; for this is the will of God in Christ Jesus for you". Is it possible or, even realistic, to give thanks even when life seems to be one of discouragement, disappointment, disease, disaster and death? At the Last Supper, Jesus, after giving thanks, broke the bread, and then gave it to His disciples. Jesus's thanks was not based on the horror He was about to endure. He was thankful to His Father for the grace and glory that was about to follow because of His death and resurrection. This knowledge gave Him joy.

In the same way, God wants us to give thanks, not for our present circumstances, but for the future joy Jesus' suffering secured for us. Because we are an heir of the kingdom with Jesus, we can lay claim to all the future joy that is promised to us throughout God's holy word.

PSALM 146:6-7

During Jesus' ministry on earth he made it clear that he upholds the cause of the oppressed, the lonely, the orphans, the poor and the hungry. He regularly preached that He had come to "set the captives free", and to shelter the vulnerable from harm.

Jesus expects us as His followers to "keep faith", and to remain loyal to His moral principles. If we "break faith", we become like Judas who betrayed Jesus and lost His life as a result of it.

Jesus left us a legacy of love and respect for our neighbour. He asks us to help alleviate pain and suffering. He wants us to take care of the poor and lonely.

By "keeping the faith", we secure justice for all, and eternal life with our Heavenly Father.

DAY 83

March 24

The salvation of the just is from the Lord;
He is their refuge in time of distress.

Psalm 37:39

PSALM 37:39

I recall, all too vividly, the emotional agony we as a family endured at the time of my sisters' illness and death. During her, thankfully, brief encounter with the cancer that killed her, she suffered unbearable and intractable pain. The impotence and uselessness to somehow alleviate her pain was akin to being lost at sea. A total sense of desperation prevailed.

The Psalmist informs us that the Lord is our refuge in times of distress. I know that we prayed endlessly and constantly during this time. God did not prevent the pain or relieve our suffering. He did, however, play a role in making my sisters' transition from life to death a gentle one. We witnessed her calmness and acceptance as God held her hand. And in a strange way, that became our refuge and help. God does not abandon us in our time of need. God is the safest place of all.

DAY 84

March 25

The Son of Man did not come to be
served but to serve and to give his
life as a ransom for many

Matthew 20:28

MATTHEW 20:28

It is extremely difficult for man to accept that true greatness is expressed by a deep humility and a willingness to serve. Yet, it is our Lord's example - "The Son of Man did not come to be served but to serve and to give his life as a ransom for many". It's always been God's intention to make us like his son, Jesus (Romans 8:29). When we look at Jesus' life, there's no denying that he was a servant. His entire life was centred on serving God – by teaching, healing, and proclaiming the Kingdom. Then, on the night of his arrest, Jesus washed the disciples' feet, leaving them with a final teaching to serve one another: "I have set you an example that you should do as I have done for you". (John 13:15) That is the Heart of our God in one simple statement! We are to serve and sacrifice for others. We were bought and brought to freedom by the ransom price he paid. We are now called to follow his example and live his life in our world.

Throughout the gospel we see that Jesus served with passion. And so, we too, need to seize every opportunity to serve Him. We can begin by demonstrating kindness, and loving without boundaries. This could mean that we sometimes have to move out of our comfort zone and get our hands dirty. Genuine service cannot be separated from love. As such, we have to abandon any notion of social hierarchy – we must share equally in showing kindness, and should never be tempted to believe that certain acts of kindness, or service, are reserved for particular sections of society. But the most important lesson taken from Jesus is that our acts of love should be devoid of pride. When we consider that the act of feet-washing was usually reserved for the lowliest slave, we finally understand that Jesus wants us to serve others with humility. In order to do that it is essential to exercise modesty and manage any perceptions of our own importance.

DAY 85

March 26

The Lord sets captives free.

Psalm 146:7

ALMOST THERE

PSALM 146:7

"The Lord sets captives free". No matter what kind of yoke binds you, Jesus hears your cry for help. Whether tethered by physical, emotional, mental or spiritual bonds, Jesus promises to act on our behalf if we simply wait on Him. Jesus sets us free by the power of his Holy Spirit, and as we learn to live day by day in the power of that Spirit, we obtain freedom.

In real life, this could mean an addiction to sex, causing a pattern of falling into sexual sin. It could be being held captive by a critical and judgemental heart towards others, or a bitterness and inability to forgive as a result of an abusive childhood. The love for money and power lures and controls many of our fellow Christians, and often, they can become lost to the community.

"Turn your eyes upon Jesus,
Look full in His wonderful face;
And the things of the earth will grow strangely dim
In the light of His glory and grace"
-Alan Jackson

ECCLESIASTES 7:8

A world class sportsman, a chess master, a top musician, a successful business person or a renowned academic, all have one thing in common – patience. Patience is the cornerstone of any laudable achievement.

Patience is a fruit of the spirit of God and is of great use in the Christian life. It tends to make us humble, meek, and quiet before God. It helps us when we have to endure afflictions, when we ponder our lack of knowledge of the scriptures, or realise the poverty of our prayer life. It helps us as we walk towards sanctification.

Pride on the other hand leads to impatience. Impatience leads to an undisciplined spiritual life. Not making time on a daily basis to spend in the presence of God makes it extremely difficult to reach a deeper, and more intimate, relationship with our loving Father.

DAY 87

March 28

Give ear and come to me;
Hear me that your soul may live.

Isaiah 55:3

ISAIAH 55:3

Just as our physical body depends on good substantial food and water to survive, our spiritual life needs constant nourishing in order to flourish. If we want our soul to live, we must attend to Gods commands and embrace His promises. "Whoever comes to me will never go hungry, and whoever believes in me will never be thirsty". (John 6:35)

In John 6:63, Jesus tells us that God's word is full of life – of healing, health and happiness. It's full of everything we need at any given moment. God's word is where we find the answers to eternal life. "The words that I speak unto you they are spirit and they are life".

God's power is in His Word – we only need ears to listen and to heed to them.

DAY 88

March 29

For the Lord gives wisdom,
And from his mouth comes
Knowledge and understanding

Proverbs 2:6

PROVERBS 2:6

To have knowledge, is to have understanding or information about something. To have wisdom, is to have the ability to apply knowledge to everyday life. It is only in the reading and understanding of God's word that we obtain knowledge, and meditating upon that, brings wisdom.

In order to live a life in harmony with God, we have to have "the mind of Christ" (1 Corinthians 2:16). When we have the "mind of Christ" - the wisdom that trusting in Him and yielding to His Spirit brings- we begin to see people, circumstances and situations, like Jesus sees them. When we see things like Jesus sees them, we have "the wisdom that comes from above", and not "earthly wisdom". With Godly wisdom we receive Godly principles and Godly values, resulting in a life that reaps the fruits of the Spirit. Only then can we live a life in service of our neighbours and in fellowship with our creator.

DAY 89

March 30

If any of you lacks wisdom,
He should ask God,
Who gives generously to all
without finding fault
And it will be given to him.

James 1:5

ALMOST THERE

JAMES 1:5

As Christians, we are Christ's ambassadors on earth, and if we want to accurately represent him to the world around us, we have to pursue and prioritise wisdom. With wisdom, we move away from conduct towards character. As Christians it is important that we don't simply try to behave like a Christian, but rather that we strive to think like one, decide like one, and to plan like one. It is our thinking that determines our behaviour and controls our actions, and not the other way around.

When we begin to see godliness as more than just moral living, we will become greater witnesses of our faith and representatives of Jesus on earth.

God promises in His word that if we pray for wisdom, He will provide.

DAY 90

March 31

In him was life, and that life was the light of men. The light shines in the darkness, but the darkness has not understood it.

John 1:4-5

JOHN 1:4-5

Most people will do anything and everything possible in order to prolong their life on this earth. They will exercise, eat correctly, and sleep the appropriate number of hours each night. When sick, they visit doctors who run tests and investigations, and then prescribe medication or other treatments. If all this fails, they resort to alternative therapies. However, the fact remains, we are all going to die – our earthly life will come to an end.

The point John is trying to make when talking about life, light, and darkness, is that Jesus brought us physical life, but he wants to give us eternal life. Jesus is the embodiment of light and life, and he is the one who shows us the way to God and everlasting life. "For God so loved the world that he gave his one and only Son, that whoever believes in him shall not perish but have eternal life" (John 3:16). The coming of Jesus into the world was the dawning of a new day for sinful man.

Light is the perfect metaphor for Jesus, and it epitomises him as the personification of goodness, beauty and truth. Darkness is the direct opposite – spiritual confusion, distortion and ignorance. It is life without Christ, and especially represents that which has turned its back on him. When we live by the truth and follow "the way of the cross", we "come into the light", and darkness will have no reign over us.

"We can easily forgive a child who is afraid of the dark; the real tragedy of life is when men are afraid of the light." -Plato

DAY 91-121

April

Do It Anyway

Written on the wall in Mother Teresa's home for children in Calcutta:

People are often unreasonable, irrational, and self-centred. Forgive them anyway.
If you are kind, people may accuse you of selfish, ulterior motives. Be kind anyway.
If you are successful, you will win some unfaithful friends and some genuine enemies. Succeed anyway.
If you are honest and sincere people may deceive you. Be honest and sincere anyway.
What you spend years creating, others could destroy overnight. Create anyway.
If you find serenity and happiness, some may be jealous. Be happy anyway.
The good you do today, will often be forgotten. Do good anyway.
Give the best you have, and it will never be enough. Give your best anyway.
In the final analysis, it is between you and God. It was never between you and them anyway

Dr Kent Keith

ROMANS 8:18

Suffering must be the hardest, most confusing reality in a Christians' life. There's no denying that our world is far from perfect. When we watch the news, we often see so much pain, suffering and evil, that it breaks our heart. Suffering is inevitable and even followers of Christ are not exempt. Why? What is the standard, the moral code by which we are to live our lives, in order to bring about change?

According to the gospels, which are basically about the life and teachings of Jesus, the foundation of the Christian moral code is simply two principles: love God with everything you have, and love your neighbour the same way you love yourself. Everything that is right is in line with those two statements, and everything that is wrong runs contrary to those statements.

The first pillar means that the believer must put their worship of and relationship with God first and foremost. Their lives have to be centred around God. Right behaviour means orienting their lives around that centre, and wrong behaviour means orienting their lives around anything else - such as money, power, ambition etc. This devotion includes actions like worship, prayer and studying the bible. It also involves being active in the church and the community.

The second pillar of the Christian moral code, and the basis of all the remaining elements of that code, is to love others as we love ourselves, and to treat them the way we want to be treated. We must share what we have so that all children can be fed, all elderly can be warm and comforted, and all the sick be tended to with kindness.

In the end it all boils down to this – suffering sanctifies and purifies us. It draws us closer to God, because, when our earthly pleasures, possessions and relationships are taken away from us, we have nothing worldly to rely on. It is then that God reveals His glory.

DAY 92

April
02

The Lord is good to those
whose hope is in him
To the one who seeks him
It is good to wait quietly
For the salvation of the Lord

Lamentations 3:25-26

LAMENTATIONS 3:25-26

Jesus encourages us to "seek ye first the Kingdom of God, and His righteousness; and all these things will be added unto you" (Matthew 6:33). We find the Kingdom of God when we repent and believe in the gospel. Through repentance we change our way of thinking in order to turn away from sin, to abide by God's commandments, and to live by His principles and values.

Jesus promised that if we place Him first He will take care of all our earthly needs. It is when we spend time, quietly in the presence of God, that He helps us to develop, through our experiences in this life, His holy and righteous character. We need time, in prayer, to constantly strengthen our faith, to re-establish our values, and to replenish our souls.

ALMOST THERE

DEUTERONOMY 5:33

Obedience to God is essential to our Christian growth. It is most unlikely that we will become sufficiently sanctified in this life so that we always obey all of Gods' commandments. However, obedience to God is reiterated throughout the Gospel.

Jesus taught us how to "walk in the way God has commanded you". In John 14:15 we read, "If you love me, you will obey what I command". And in Matthew 22:37-39, "Love the Lord your God with all your heart and with all your soul and with all your mind". This is the first and greatest commandment. And the second is like it: "Love your neighbour as yourself."

Being obedient to God is more than simply participating in good works - being obedient to God means knowing Him, loving Him, and having a personal, intimate relationship with Him. Obedience to God is living according to His ways because we want to, and because we enjoy being filled with the love of God and the power of the Holy Spirit.

DAY 94

April 04

Though the mountains be shaken
and the hills be removed,
Yet my unfailing love for you
will not be shaken
Nor my covenant of peace
be removed.

Isaiah 54:10

ISAIAH 54:10

"The greatest disease in the West today is not TB or leprosy; it is being unwanted, unloved, and uncared for. We can cure physical diseases with medicine, but the only cure for loneliness, despair, and hopelessness is love. There are many in the world dying for a piece of bread, but there are more dying for a little love. The poverty of the West is a different kind of poverty – it is not only poverty of loneliness but also of spirituality. There's a hunger for love, as there is a hunger for God." -Mother Teresa

How often do we find that when we are stressed, hurting, or downhearted about certain life events our friends disappear? Or have you ever been offered unkind and painful advice like – "suck it up!", "get a grip!", "have faith", "it is God's will, so learn to accept it"? Another phrase that certainly doesn't help matters is, "forget about the past and move on". We are all human and none of us is exempt from pain and hardship. We all need compassion. We all want to know that someone truly cares about our feelings and that they are sorry that we are in pain.

What an example Jesus sets us about being compassionate! Jesus seemed to find those whom society had rejected – sinners, tax-collectors, prostitutes, lepers, and the unclean. He felt for them. He embraced them. He was compassionate towards them and, because of it, they were changed.

"Because of the Lord's great love we are not consumed, for his compassions never fail. They are new every morning; great is your faithfulness". (Lamentations 3:22-23)

God promises us unfailing love, compassion and faithfulness. We can count on Him and trust Him to be there for us, always. Even when we ignore Him because we are too busy with worldly things, he waits for us. God lives by His own word – "His compassions never fail, they are new every morning".

DAY 95

April 05

"How great is God-beyond our understanding!"

Job 36:26

ALMOST THERE

JOB 36:26

God thinks on a level far beyond our human comprehension. "For my thoughts are not your thoughts, nor are your ways my ways," says the Lord. "For as the heavens are higher than the earth, so are my ways higher than your ways, and my thoughts higher than your thoughts" (Isaiah 55:8-9).

Yet Jesus wants us to understand his thoughts and to begin to think like him. God gave us the desire to want to know, and learn, and understand. And although we are naturally limited by our tendency to focus on temporary pleasures instead of eternity, God has not left us stranded. He inspired the books of the bible to reveal his mind. The bible teaches us what is right and wrong, and points the way to peace, salvation and eternal life. Yet as incredible as the bible is, there are still many things that are challenging to understand. The apostle Paul points out that without God's spirit, we cannot truly comprehend things beyond the human realm. And, without repentance, we cannot receive the things of the Spirit of God. It is only when we ask for forgiveness, pray for the gift of the Holy Spirit, and place God at the centre of our lives, that we truly gain insight into his motivations and his thinking.

DAY 96

April 06

The Lord Yahweh will wipe away
The tears from every cheek

Isaiah 25:8

ALMOST THERE

ISAIAH 25:8

No one is a stranger to tears- crying is natural and a common human expression. Sometimes, the tears are tears of gratitude, happiness, or a sense of achievement. A mother attending her child's graduation ceremony often has to cope with a huge lump in her throat. Olympic athletes, standing on the podium listening to their national anthem, frequently have to fight back the tears. At other times, we shed tears because of mixed emotions – like the first day we dropped our little darling of at school and she waved goodbye from the classroom door? Or sometimes, when anger or frustration overwhelms, we resort to tears.

But, by far, the main reason for our tears is pain and suffering. Life is full of hardships – poverty, cruelty, illness, discrimination and war, are our constant companions. God, however, reminds us that our tears are not futile. He is intimately concerned with every aspect of our lives. He doesn't judge whether our sorrow is "valid". "You keep track of all my sorrows. You have collected all my tears in your bottle. You have recorded each one in your book." (Psalm 56:8) It doesn't matter how big or small, trivial or important, the sorrow might be - every tear we shed has meaning to Him.

The idea behind the keeping of "tears in a bottle" is remembrance. When we have a deep trust and faith in God, we know that he will remember our sorrow and tears, and He will not forget about us. God is a compassionate, tender-hearted Father to us, and he feels with us and weeps with us – (John 11:33-35). Ultimately, He will share His joy with us when "He will wipe away the tears from their eyes. There will be no more death, or mourning or crying or pain, for the old order of things has passed away". (Revelation 21:4)

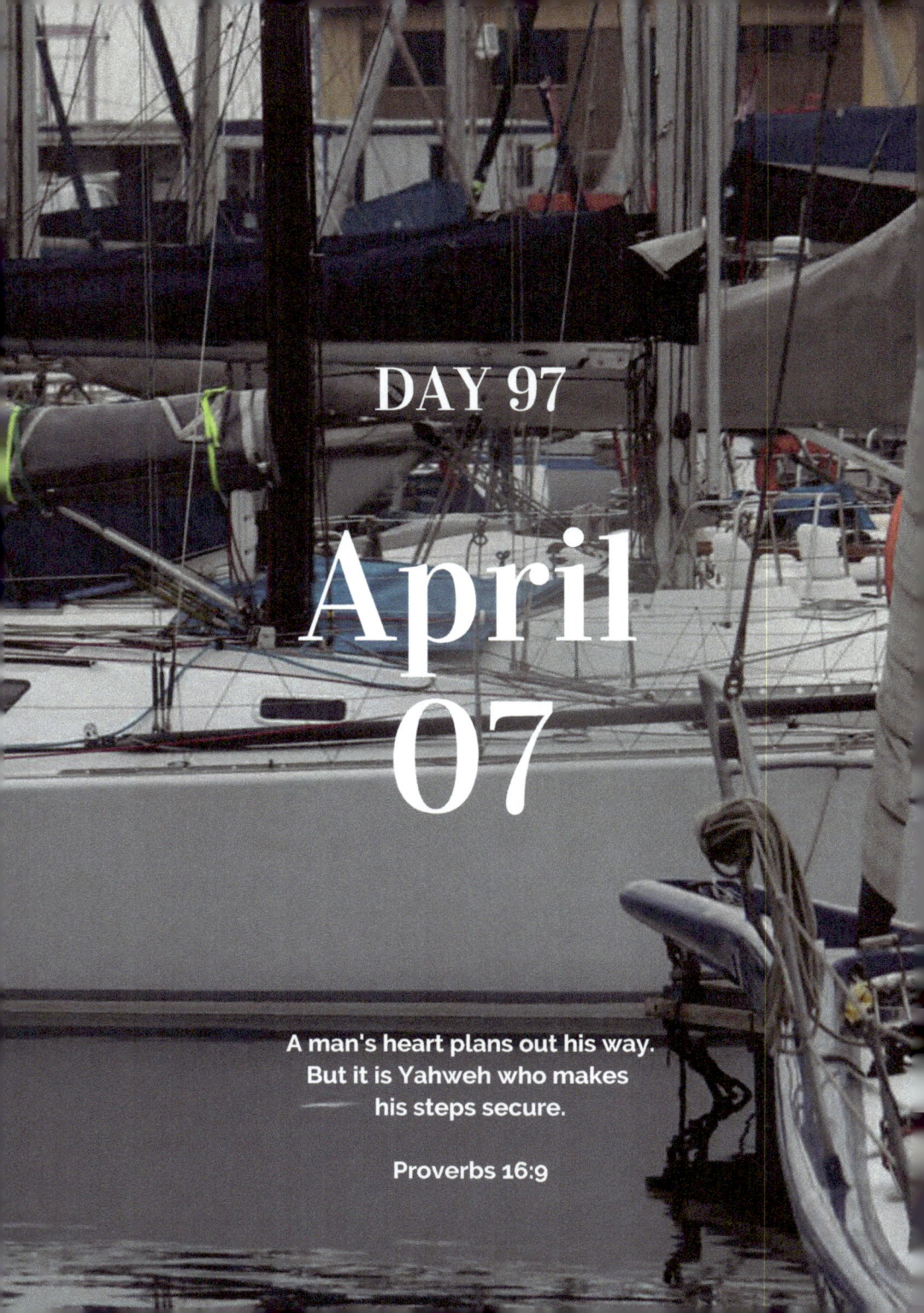

DAY 97

April 07

A man's heart plans out his way.
But it is Yahweh who makes
his steps secure.

Proverbs 16:9

PROVERBS 16:9

It is important to live life with purpose. Having a "purpose" gives us direction, helps us to make major decisions, keeps us moving, and helps to set us on a decisive path and journey for our life.

We have to make plans, and often these plans are formulated in our hearts – where do we want to be in ten years, and who would we like to have become by then? But once we have an idea of what we want to achieve, we need to start working towards it. That means taking a step forward – taking the first step or a leap of faith. Sure, there will be fear and trepidation. But we usually won't take the next step if we don't, at least, have some idea that our footing will be on solid ground, and that the planning we have done has already carried us some distance towards achieving our goal.

"Faith by itself, if not accompanied by action, is dead." (James 2:17) We have to get momentum - and this momentum gives God room to direct our steps. I once read some sound advice – "make plans and decisions, get some direction, but keep them fluid, don't set them in concrete. Keep your heart and life open for God to come and direct those plans and ultimately direct your heart. Move them around, if needed, to be in alignment with His word and purpose."

DAY 98

April 08

The fear of the Lord will gladden the heart,
Giving happiness and joy and long life
With him who fears the Lord it will be well
at the last and he will be blessed on the
day of his death.

Ecclesiasticus 1:12-16

ALMOST THERE

ECCLESIASTICUS 1:12-16

Fearing the Lord isn't an easy concept to understand. We fear the Lord because He alone holds the power over the destiny of our souls (Matthew 10:28). But fearing the Lord doesn't mean living in constant anxiety and dread of God! As believers, we know that Jesus paid the price for our sins and because of that, God doesn't condemn us. But, awareness of God's love and grace must never cause us to disregard His holiness, righteousness, and justice.

Christians are not supposed to be scared of God -we have no reason to be. We have His promise that nothing can separate us from His love (Romans 8:38-39). We have His promise that He will never leave us or forsake us (Hebrews 13:5).

Fearing God means having such reverence for Him that it has a great impact on the way we live our lives. The fear of God is respecting Him, submitting to His discipline, and worshipping Him in awe.

DAY 99

April 09

Do not be so sure of forgiveness
That you add sin to sin.

Ecclesiasticus 5:5

ECCLESIASTICUS 5:5

Friedrich Nietzsche, the 19th century philosopher, said, that when he looked at the ethic of Jesus expressed in the Beatitudes, he was listening to the most seductive lie that history had ever heard. When he came to the third beatitude, "Blessed are the meek, for they shall inherit the earth", Nietzsche rephrased it, "Assert yourself-it is the arrogant that take over the earth!"

"Pride is your greatest enemy- humility is your greatest friend" (John R W Stott). Pride and arrogance are conspicuous among the rich, the powerful, the successful, the famous, and celebrities of all sorts, including religious leaders. And it is alive and well in ordinary people, including each of us. In fact, what throughout history has been recognized as the deadliest of vices is now almost celebrated as a virtue in our culture. Humility, on the other hand, is seen as a weakness. But, for the good of our souls and our relationship with God, we need to gain a clear understanding of pride and humility, and of how to forsake the one and embrace the other. Pride can be summarized as an attitude of self-sufficiency, self-importance and self-exaltation in relation to God. Toward others, it is an attitude of contempt and indifference.

Humility is out of fashion in this world, and is unappealing to most of us. However, "We must view humility as one of the most essential things that characterises true Christianity" (Jonathan Edwards). Just as pride is the root of all sin, so "humility is the root, mother, nurse, foundation, and bond of all virtue". (John Chrysostom) The greatest example of humility in history is Jesus Christ. Throughout his life on earth he demonstrated profound humility, saying that he came "not to be served, but to serve". So, how do we gain the mind of Christ and humble ourselves? To put on the mind of Christ, we have to make a firm decision to ponder, understand, and adopt Jesus' way of thinking - his values and attitudes must become ours, and must take hold of our thinking, our desires and our conduct.

DAY 100

April 10

The word of Yahweh is integrity itself,
All he does is done faithfully.

Psalm 33:4

PSALM 33:4

Many people view integrity as an out-dated idea that is expendable, and not relevant in this age of moral relativism. But, just as honesty is essential for trust and trust is essential for sound relationships and good leadership, so integrity is essential to becoming trustworthy. Whenever we betray a trust, we compromise our integrity. Integrity is a prerequisite to credibility and is crucial in all aspects of our lives – professional, personal, social and spiritual.

Integrity is the basic element of a Christian's character. According to Webster it means "soundness of moral character". But, from a biblical viewpoint, what does being "morally sound" entail? It means knowing what is important to God, and consistently trying to live in the light of what He considers important. It involves more than simply living according to our values and principles – it necessitates buying into God's values and, with His help, to conform our conduct to those values.

Developing and maintaining integrity requires genuine humility, and not pretending to be someone we are not – what you see is what you get. It means embracing God's standards and learning to love what He loves and hate what He hates. But, mostly, it is accepting that we cannot live the Christian life on our own strength – without the Holy Spirit to lead, guide and mould us, inconsistencies will constantly weaken our moral foundation.

"People with integrity walk safely, but those who follow crooked paths will slip and fall." (Proverbs 10:9)

DAY 101

April 11

Make Yahweh your only joy
And he will give you what your heart desires.
Commit your fate to Yahweh,
Trust in him and he will act.

Psalm 37:4-5

PSALM 37:4-5

What does it mean to "delight yourself" in the Lord? Most people today take delight in wealth, material possessions, and other temporary things of this world. But, we will never be deeply satisfied or happy with the things this world has to offer. King Solomon learnt the same lesson in his pursuit of earthly treasure: "Everything is meaningless!"
(Ecclesiastes 2:11)

Taking delight in the Lord means that our hearts truly find peace and fulfilment in Him. This doesn't mean that if we diligently go to church every Sunday, God will give us our hearts desire! But, when we genuinely rejoice or delight in the eternal things of God, our desires will begin to parallel His, and the "things of the earth will grow strangely dim in the light of His glory and grace."
-Helen Lemmel

If we place our joy and hope in God first, He will meet all our needs. "See the birds of the sky, that they don't sow, neither do they reap, nor gather into barns. Your heavenly Father feeds them. Aren't you of much more value than they?"
(Matthew 6:26)

DAY 102

April 12

The people who sat in darkness
Have seen a great light, and upon
those who sat in the region and
shadow of death light has dawned.

Matthew 4:16

MATTHEW 4:16

"Even though I walk through the valley of the shadow of death, I will fear no evil, for you are with me; your rod and your staff, they comfort me" (Psalm 23:4)

Psalm 23 must rank as one of the greatest pieces of literature ever written. It flowed from the heart of King David during a dark, painful time in his life. He was experiencing a time of "doom and gloom"- hardship, peril, chaos and suffering, were invading his life. As a result, he felt as though death was close at hand. At some point, you and I will also make that long, slow, painful walk through the "valley of the shadow of death". We will not escape these things-hardship, peril, chaos and suffering- from invading our lives as well. We may have to confront illness, suffering, or death in our family. Our spouse may be unfaithful or ask for a divorce. Or we may have to pray for a child who has wandered away from the church and is caught up in the attractions of this world.

However, no matter what the circumstances, we need to remember the simple truth about this valley of death. In order for there to be a shadow, there must also be a light. That light is Jesus. He walks in the valley with us and we are never alone. And, not only is He the light, He is also the Shepherd who guides us. He comforts us with his presence, even in the "valley of the shadow of death".

ROMANS 13:12

"May each of us let our light shine as we strive to become like the perfect light – our Saviour, Jesus Christ."

In his Sermon on the Mount, especially the first part, the Beatitudes, Jesus gives us a revelation of his own character, which is perfect – and, in so doing he gave us a blueprint for our own lives. The Sermon can be seen as the foundation for a life that would be acceptable to God, our Heavenly Father. In fact, President Harold B. Lee (1899-1973), referred to the Beatitudes as "the constitution for a perfect life."

Jesus often described Himself as "the light of the world" (John 8:12), yet in this sermon He said, "Ye are the light of the world". With His help, we can become like Him! I don't think that we are supposed to be the light, or the source of light. The light – the light of truth, understanding, and knowledge – is already there, and that light will only shine in many dark places if we, as Christians, reflect it there. By reflecting light into the dark places of this world we change some things in, and for, many people. When we encounter people who are lost and struggling, it is our duty to reflect the Saviour's light to encourage and guide them. The Apostle Paul taught the Romans, "Let us therefore cast off the works of darkness, and let us put on the armour of light".
(Romans 13:12)

DAY 104

April 14

Thus says the Lord your redeemer,
The holy one of Israel: "I am the Lord your God,
Who teaches you to profit
Who leads you by the way you should go.
Oh, that you heeded my commandments!
Then your peace would have been like a river,
And your righteousness like the waves of the sea."

Isaiah 48:17-18

ALMOST THERE

ROMANS 13:12

"But be you doers of the word, and not hearers only, deceiving your own selves." (James 1:22)

When Jesus is asked which commandment is the greatest (Matthew 22:34-40, Mark 12:28-34), His answer is not found in the Ten Commandments. Jesus teaches that the greatest commandment is to love God, and the second is to love your neighbour. You will not find these, as such, in the Ten, but they are hidden in there. Jesus is showing us a different way to view the commandments – through love. However, this is not completely new – already in the Old Testament we are called upon to "love God with all our heart, soul, and strength". (Deuteronomy 6:5) So, we need to see the Ten Commandments not as laws, but as teaching us what it means to love – they all revolve around love. If we love God, we will trust Him and follow His teaching. If we love our neighbour, we will not steal, kill, or lie to them. If we love our spouse, we will not commit adultery. If we love our parents, we will honour them. Love provides us with a way to begin to know the mind of God. And so, in order to "heed His commandments" and be "doers of the word", love has to alter our life and direct us towards God's path. Jesus has paved the way – all we have to do is follow and believe.

"Greater love has no man than this that he lay down his life for his friends" (John 15:13)

DAY 105

April 15

I will bring the blind by a way they did not know;
I will lead them in paths they have not known.
I will make darkness light before them,
and crooked places straight.

Isaiah 42:16

ISAIAH 42:16

"Why do you look at the speck of sawdust in your brother's eye and pay no attention to the plank in your own eye" (Matthew 7:3)

We are all spiritually blind. The world was outraged when celebrated cyclist, Lance Armstrong, finally admitted that he had cheated to win. I, for one, fumed about the bad example he set for aspiring young athletes, and by his seeming lack of remorse.

Sadly, all of us are like Lance Armstrong. We are all human, and, being human, we fail. Christians get divorced, commit adultery, or become addicted to internet pornography or other worldly, sinful addictions. Christians commit fraud and end up in jail. Others battle with anger or take delight in harmful gossip. The truth is, that Christians, just like all people, are sinful beings and are prone to fail. The Apostle Paul touched on this in Romans 7:19 – "I have the desire to do what is good, but I cannot carry it out. For what I do is not the good I want to do; no, the evil I do not want to do – this I keep on doing".

According to 2 Corinthians 4, people are spiritually blind until God gives them eyes to see - that is, until we accept Jesus as our Lord and Saviour. God opens the eyes of the blind to see the truth, beauty and worth of Christ. When we accept that Jesus died on the cross for our salvation, we are given power over our sinful nature. Although sin does not die, it no longer has the hold over us that it once had. The Holy Spirit now gradually transforms us into righteous men and women.

"I am sending you to open their eyes". (Acts 26:18) As Christians, saving the spiritually blind becomes our responsibility. God entrusts us to spread His gospel – we can only do this successfully if we have hearts filled with love, and live a life in service to Him.

DAY 106

April 16

The sun shall no longer be your light by day, nor for brightness shall the moon give light to you; But the Lord will be to you an everlasting light, and your God your glory.

Isaiah 60:19

ALMOST THERE

ISAIAH 60:19

Let your light so shine before men, that they may see your good works and glorify your Father in heaven" (Matthew 5:16)

The German atheist philosopher, Nietzsche, once said that if he saw more redeemed people he might be more inclined to believe in their redeemer. Christians who do not have changed lives have a credibility gap. People need to see our light shine – we cannot tell them how great our Saviour is if our lives don't reflect that truth.

The Apostle John called Jesus "the life that is the light of men, the light that shines in the darkness" (John 1:5).The light in us is His light, the Holy Spirit, within us. The apostle Paul speaks of "the light of the gospel of the glory of Christ" (2 Corinthians 4:4). Our actions reflect the nature of Christ – His love, compassion and forgiveness. His light shines through our attitudes, words, and deeds. When we have and live Jesus' values, our testimony becomes convincing, and people are more inclined to believe in our Redeemer.

Our responsibility, as disciples, is to have lives so transformed by the Word, and the inward presence of Christ, that everyone can see His light reflected in our acts of kindness and love.

DAY 107

April 17

Do not rejoice over me, my enemy;
When I fall, I will arise;
When I sit in darkness,
The Lord will be a light to me.

Micah 7:8

MICAH 7:8

We all like our lives to run smoothly. When we encounter bumps along the road that mess with our perfectly structured plans, we cannot rest until we fix them. Our circumstances can easily rule our emotions if we let them. But, God does not want us to be at the mercy of our varied life events, or the hopeless perspective we sometimes have about them. The Bible directs us to look beyond these circumstances. This is a recurring message throughout. So, instead of getting swept up in the whirlwind of daily events, we should strive to become rooted in God's solid foundation. Psalm 62:1 gives us God's perspective – "My soul finds rest in God alone".

In order to be able to "rest in God", we have to acknowledge, and meditate, on His goodness. Focussing on God's love is the door to trusting him. When we finally grasp and accept that we are precious to Him, we will know that He will always take care of us.

God is good. He is good, when the puzzle pieces of our lives are falling into place. He is good, when our prayers are answered. He is good, when we are happy, surrounded by the ones we love. But, He is also good when our world is crumbling, when we are broken, or have lost our way. Life presents us with challenges - but that does not mean God has forgotten His promises. We will face moments of sin and failure - but that does not make the sacrifice of His Son any less real. John Ortberg said, "Peace doesn't come from finding a lake with no storms. It comes from having Jesus in the boat".

DAY 108

April 18

Awake, you who sleep,
arise from the dead,
and Christ will give you light.

Ephesians 5:14

EPHESIANS 5:14

"A wake-up call" is a common and well-known expression. For some of us, it brings back memories of a time before cell phones and travel alarms – remember the front desk of a motel calling the room in the morning so that we don't miss our taxi to the airport!

However, there is another, arguably greater, significance we may assign to the expression. When something happens to us, or we hear of, or witness something, that sets off some soul searching or internal awareness, we may refer to that as a "wake-up call". Someone who suffers a heart attack, or is involved in a serious car accident, may reflect on the event as a "wake-up call".

The problem is that we are only sobered momentarily. We are awakened and focused, but get over it very quickly. After a few days the impact of the event has diminished, and we simply resume our old habits and way of life.

The same thing can and, often does, happen in our spiritual life. When we have allowed Jesus to wake us out of our sinful nature, we can't afford to fall back into the slumber of our old life. Once we have had the "wake-up call", we have to guard against hitting the snooze button.

St Paul instructs us to "walk circumspectly, not as fools but as wise" (Ephesians 5:15). This means, paying attention to our conduct so that there is consistent wise living. Wise living is the healthy combination of good choices – about relationships, about money, about our use of time, and about our response to disappointments, pain and suffering. Everything we have is a gift from God, and if we squander it – if our habits amount to a wasting of time or using it primarily for selfish purposes- we have failed to respond to, and act on, God's "wake-up" call.

DAY 109

April 19

For my thoughts are not your thoughts,
Neither are your ways my ways,
Says the Lord

Isaiah 55:8

ISAIAH 55:8

It is human nature to compare ourselves to our peers and to strive to be better than they are. This often leads us to elevate ourselves above others by focussing on their flaws. The end result is self-delusion and self-righteousness that magnifies the lowliness of our spiritual state. When we believe that earthly pleasures, worldly possessions, status and power, define our happiness, we lose sight of true holiness. Yet, true holiness is the most dynamic, creative, and meaningful, way of life. It embodies a desire to have a relationship with God and to become more like Christ. If we want to be more like Christ, we need to pray for humility and meekness.

Humility and meekness go hand-in-glove. Humility's dominant thrust is its willingness to submit to God and to what is right and true. And the meek are kind, gentle, and sensitive to the needs of others. They are thoughtful and agreeable. They are not aggressive or argumentative. However, they are not weak. Jesus and Moses were both meek, but certainly not weak. They were firm and uncompromising regarding following truth, but they had no need to overwhelm and destroy those who were aligned against them.

DAY 110

April 20

See, I have set before
you an open door
That no one can shut.

Revelations 3:8

REVELATIONS 3:8

The open door being referred to in the book of Revelations most likely represents the door that opens into death and the life beyond. Jesus is the steward of the household of God, and, when we die, we will die through Christ. For those of us who have turned from sin and have confessed faith in Him, He has promised an open door which no one can shut.

When we face hardships and pain, when brokenness and turmoil become our daily companions, let us remember that Jesus encourages us to persevere. Let us not forget, in the midst of our turmoil, that we have been promised what all believers have been promised - that He has the key of David, and He has set before us an open door which no one can shut. This door leads to life everlasting. This door leads to freedom from the tensions, anxiety and pain of this life, and offers rest, love and peace, in the company of our loving God and Father.

DAY 111

April 21

I myself will send an angel before you
To guard you as you go and to bring
you to the place that I have prepared.
Give him reverence and listen to
all that he says.

Exodus 23:20

ALMOST THERE

EXODUS 23:20

"All we like sheep have gone astray: we have turned-every one-to his own way; and the Lord has laid on him the inequity of us all"
(Isaiah 53:6).

I find it interesting that God likens us to sheep – they are peculiar animals and are timid, defenceless, and not really known for their great intelligence. They don't know where to go, don't know what is best or good for them, and often wander of absentmindedly, getting into all sorts of dangerous situations. Although this comparison isn't very flattering, it is accurate and true. We also don't always know what is best for us. Left to our own wisdom and devices, we inevitably end up in trouble. We need a shepherd to guide us, and we need to understand exactly what he wants and expects us to do. God has a plan for our lives, and he wants to show us his will far more than we want to know it. It is only through following the divine Shepherd that this plan will be revealed to us. Failure to follow him is plain stupidity. The Apostle Paul told the Ephesians' the same thing – "So then do not be foolish, but understand what the will of the Lord is".
(Ephesians 5:17)

To do God's will, we must know God's will. The scriptures reveal it to us - David wrote: "I delight to do your will, O my God, and your law is within my heart." (Psalm 40:8) Timothy wrote: "All scripture is given by inspiration of God, and is profitable for doctrine, for reproof, for correction, for instruction in righteousness, that the man of God may be complete, thoroughly equipped for every good work." (2 Timothy 3:16-17). The will of God can be learned - David prayed: "Teach me to do your will, for you are my God". (Psalm 143:10) But, mostly, we must want to do God's will in order to recognise which doctrines come from him. Once we conform to His principles and values, we really begin to experience his will and the love that comes from following its instruction and direction. "And do not be conformed to this world, but be transformed by the renewing of your mind, that you may discern what is that good and acceptable and perfect will of God" (
Romans 12:2).

DAY 112

April 22

Open my eyes
that I may see
wonderful things
in your law.

Psalm 119:18

PSALM 119:18

As a medical doctor I am confronted, on a daily basis, with people who are anxious, unhappy, sad or depressed. Antidepressants have become one of the most commonly prescribed drugs in the modern era.

God encourages us to find strength and comfort in His Word. In our Christian life, bible reading is a primary source of power over sin and temptation. It is a source of intimacy with God and Jesus Christ, and, it is a source of fellowship with the Holy Spirit that makes us sensitive to His guidance.

The word of God deals either implicitly, or explicitly, with every question or issue that humans have about the most important things in life. When we are sad or depressed and life becomes too difficult to face - remember the Bible – it contains the answers to all our problems, difficulties and questions.

DAY 113

April 23

Create in me a clean heart, O God,
And renew a steadfast spirit within me.

Psalm 51:10

ALMOST THERE

PSALM 51:10

There are so many times I find myself praying for forgiveness – mainly because I realize that I keep falling short in my spiritual disciplines. It often feels like I am being insincere – asking forgiveness for the same sins over and over again. And, it's not big things that keep tripping me up – it is so difficult to regularly get up a few minutes earlier to do scripture readings, or to say my prayers before collapsing into bed at night. I love God. I love his ways and His Sabbath – yet I cannot prioritize my life around these much needed spiritual habits.

Psalm 51 emphasises that it is not only necessary to ask God to forgive us for placing other things before Him (sleep, entertainment, hobbies, etc.), but that we also need to pray for a steadfast spirit. Steadfast means "fixed in purpose, direction and resolution". This is exactly what God expects from us – to be fixed in our purpose, resolute in our spiritual pursuits, and to have a steadfast gaze on our final goal. This steadfast spirit will help us fight against our own desires and redirect us to what is most important- doing the will of God.

It is nice to know that we are not alone in our daily, and seemingly frivolous, struggles. Self-examination is hard, and it is encouraging that even King David, who God said was "a man after his own heart", had to pray for steadfastness of spirit.

DAY 114

April 24

Today, if you hear his voice,
do not harden your hearts.

Psalm 95:7-8

PSALM 95:7-8

During the course of our life there will be many people and situations which affect us deeply and intentionally, or unintentionally, cause us pain. The natural response to this is to build a wall of defence around our heart to prevent further and future pain.

"Hardening our hearts" however, can also lead to blocking God from taking control of our life and circumstances as we struggle to manage on our own. It is only when we open our hearts to a life with God in control, that He can bring new joys into our life. Through the power of the Holy Spirit He will give us gifts of wisdom, understanding, love, peace, joy, and whatever else our souls are in need of.

Once our hearts are open to God, they will be open to our neighbour as well. Only when we are no longer afraid to be of service to those needing a helping hand, or who seek companionship and love, will we have responded to the voice of God and heeded his call to continue His work on earth.

DAY 115

April 25

Since you are my rock and my fortress,
For the sake of your name
Lead and guide me.

Psalm 31:3

PSALM 31:3

"Therefore, whoever hears these sayings of mine, and does them, I will liken him to a wise man who built his house on the rock". (Matthew 7:24)

Foundations help protect our physical homes from disaster. But, what is our life built on? What's our foundation to protect us from spiritual disaster? In His teachings, Jesus points out that we can choose to live wisely or foolishly. He stressed that if we pay attention to what he said and follow Him, we will be like the wise builder. We will come through "the inevitable storms of life"- the trials and difficulties that are part of this life - because His teachings are rock-solid principles about how to live successfully. They provide a solid foundation for our lives, our families, our friendships, our associations, our work and our future.

There is only one sure foundation for living an abundant life - and that is Jesus Christ. That foundation includes His life, death, resurrection, and instruction for us. As a result, we should study what Jesus taught about life, and apply His teachings to how we live our lives. According to the Apostle Paul, the scriptures are a powerful foundation for living wisely and abundantly, allowing us to weather the inevitable storms of life and move forward – (the Bible) "is given by inspiration of God, and is profitable for doctrine, for reproof, for correction, for instruction in righteousness, that the man of God may be complete, thoroughly equipped for every good work". (2 Timothy 3:16)

DAY 116

April 26

Because small is the gate and narrow
The road that leads to life,
And only a few find it.

Matthew 7:14

MATTHEW 7:14

Following Jesus is difficult. In fact, without the grace of God, following Jesus would be impossible. Jesus demands total surrender and complete submission. He will not settle for second place in our lives. He calls us to be willing to give up anything, and everything, in following Him. Our most intimate family bonds, our careers, our material wealth and possessions- even our very own lives - must be subordinate to our love and allegiance to Jesus. (Matthew10:37-39)

If we want to follow Christ, we have to discipline our hearts, minds and bodies, to withstand the attractions of this world and to overcome the old sinful nature that naturally resides in us. Waging war against sin is hard because of its deceptive and alluring draw. (Ephesians 6:11-12) That is why following Jesus is a narrow path because it asks us to go against our natural, sinful nature and against the fallen and corrupted world system – we have to "swim against the stream".

As Christians, we know that following Jesus will grant us abundant life. The process of being conformed in the image of Christ is not always easy or comfortable, but, it is always a cause for rejoicing as it results in our maturity in Christ (James 1:2-4). God has promised those of us who follow Jesus that our sufferings are not worth comparing to the glory that will be revealed to us. In heaven we will be like Jesus and we will dwell with Him, forever, in a place devoid of pain and suffering. (Revelation 21:3-4)

DAY 117

April 27

But those who hope in the Lord will
renew their strength.
They will soar on wings like eagles;
They will run and not grow weary,
They will walk and not be faint.

Isaiah 40:31

ALMOST THERE

ISAIAH 40:31

Some days, even the strongest of personalities, or the best of leaders, get weary. Even those who know the truth, who walk closely with God, who believe in Him and in His power, can get tired. None of us are immune. Life is hard at times. And often it's not just one "big" thing, but lots of little battles, that drain us dry. Parenting, marriage, job, relationships, fears, worries, concerns about the future, experiencing loss, discouragement, illness, financial stress – all of it can leave us beaten and worn down.

But God has not left us to our own devices. He has given us His Holy Spirit, and our fellow believers, to help us when we feel, "I can't anymore…" We're all in this life thing together. God expects us to help, and to be there for, each other when the going gets rough. When we give an encouraging word, smile at someone, write a note, send a text, buy a friend a cup of coffee, pray for another soul and let them know that they are in our thoughts, we are doing our what our Saviour wants – we are helping those who have lost hope to "hold up their battle-weary arms".

God is with us and will never fail us. We can always lift up our hands, no matter how tired we might feel, to the throne of grace, our Lord Almighty. He will give us the strength to overcome any form of hardship, allowing us eventually to "soar on wings like eagles".

To be free is not merely to cast off one's chains, but to live in a way that respects and enhances the freedom of others.
- Nelson Mandela

DAY 118

April 28

No eye has seen,
No ear has heard,
No mind has conceived
What God has prepared
for those who Love him

1 Corinthians 2:9

1 CORINTHIANS 2:9

The word of God assures us that He has prepared the most wonderful things for those who love him. But a person's mind does not know about these things unless God's Spirit reveals them to us. Even the most intelligent people in the world, if they are non-believers, battle to understand the things every Christian already knows. God's plans, desires, and intentions are that we will share his glory, greatness, and honour in the future, but, He also promises to take care of us in this life.

It isn't necessary to have great knowledge or intelligence to know the mind of God – it is essential that we allow the Holy Spirit to teach us. God has prepared marvellous things for us in the afterlife, but, He also wants us to experience His love and presence while on this earth. Believing in the power of the living God opens doors to greater joy and fulfilment in our everyday existence, whilst promising rewards in heaven.

DAY 119

April 29

Therefore, if anyone is in Christ,
He is a new creation;
The old has gone,
The new has come.

2 Corinthians 5:17

2 CORINTHIANS 5:17

"For all have sinned and fall short of the glory of God". (Romans 3:23) Sinfulness is the general characteristic of all mankind; we are all guilty before God. We are sinners by nature, and by our own transgression. However, because of Jesus' death and resurrection, we are able "To be in Christ". To "be in Christ", means to be united to him by our faith and through our baptism. As believers, our sinful nature has died with Christ and we no longer live for ourselves – we "walk in the newness of life". (Romans 6:4) With this newness we let go of our old habits, our love of sin, our natural pride, our former opinions, and our reliance on earthly possessions, passions and positions of power. Love of self, self-righteousness and self-justification have "passed away".

We see the word differently. There are new feelings towards people – a new love towards family and friends, a new compassion towards those who do us harm, and a new desire to be of service to all mankind.

DAY 120

April 30

For everyone born of God
overcomes the world.
This is the victory that has
overcome the world,
even our faith.

1 John 5:4

1 JOHN 5:4

It is human nature to "be overcome by the world". We feel at home in this world, and earthly possessions and pleasures, status and power, are all things we strive for and are comfortable with.

And then, on the other hand, it is difficult to comprehend that believing in God helps us to "overcome the world". Pain, suffering, poverty and violence, reign supreme and it seems as if God has no control.

"I told you these things so that you can have peace in me. In this world you will have trouble. But be brave! I have defeated the world!" (John 16:33)

When Jesus accepted his Father's will to go to the cross, he conquered the power and attractions of this earth. He broke, and defeated, the power of sin and death. He brought life and immortality to light. He insured that death will not have the final say. So, in the midst of sorrows and trials, we can take heart and have peace. Not because life is easy, but, because the hard things are only fleeting and temporary. Our peace is not in the absence of trouble and strife, but in Jesus, and what he has done to secure our future.

DAY 121-151

May

St Paul's Prayer for Spiritual Growth

When I think of all this,
I fall to my knees and pray to the Father,
The Creator of everything in heaven and on earth
I pray that from his glorious, unlimited resources
He will empower you with inner strength through his Spirit.
Then Christ will make his home in your hearts as you trust in him.
Your roots will grow down into God's love and keep you strong.
And may you have the power to understand,
As all God's people should
How wide, how long, how high, and how deep his love is.
May you experience the love of Christ
Though it is too great to understand fully
Then you will be made complete with all the fullness
Of life and power that comes from God.
Now all glory to God,
Who is able, through his mighty power at work within us
To accomplish infinitely more than we might ask or think
Glory to him in the church and in Christ Jesus through all
generations forever and ever!

Amen.

– Ephesians 3:14-21

DAY 121

May 01

And Jesus said to them
"I am the bread of life. He who
comes to me shall never hunger,
and he who believes in me
shall never thirst"

John 6:35-36

JOHN 6:35-36

Hunger and thirst are natural expressions of the basic human desire and need for food and water. One of the first and clearest indicators that something is wrong physically is when we lose our appetite. It is the same spiritually - to hunger and thirst for God is at the very root of our being. It is the way God made us. When there is no hunger for the presence of God, it indicates that something is wrong spiritually.

Our spiritual appetite is dulled when we search for happiness and fulfilment in worldly things, and not in a relationship with our Creator. We may try to satisfy this hunger in a quest for power or money, in human relationships, or by indulging in physical pleasures. But, the saddest of all is when, as Christians, we allow our "busyness" in Church activities to rob us of time to "feast" with God. Time spent studying the scriptures, and in prayer and communion with God, often takes a back seat because we have allowed our hectic schedule to crowd out time with the Father.

"Blessed are those who hunger and thirst for righteousness, for they will be filled." (Matthew 5:6) Spiritual hunger is not always recognized for what it is. It may be an empty feeling, a sense of longing, even loneliness, in the presence of people. We then start looking for ways to make the feeling go away – to fill up the emptiness. Prayer and fasting are two of the most powerful tools God has given to help us in our search. "And, since the best teacher of prayer is the Holy Spirit, the best way to learn to pray is by praying. Whether and how much we pray is, finally, a matter of appetite, of hunger for God and all that He is and desires." Ben Patterson

DAY 122

May 02

For God so loved the world
That he gave his one and only Son,
That whoever believes in him shall not
perish but have eternal life.

John 3:16

JOHN 3:16

God wants us to know, believe, feel and see that He loves us. And, because love is an action, not just emotional feelings, God demonstrates His love in many ways – "Every good and perfect gift is from above, coming down from the Father of the heavenly lights, who does not change like shifting shadows. He chose to give us birth through the world of truth that we might be a kind of first fruits of all He created." (James 1:17-18)

God's love is perfect, and, it begins with faith. Upon receiving His gift of love we find unexplainable peace, joy, and confidence, even in the worst of situations. It is through His love that fear, worry and pain are removed. "There is no fear in love. But perfect love drives out fear that has to do with punishment. The one who fears is not made perfect in love." (1John 4:18) God's love can also be seen as a love of sacrifice – "For God so loved the world that He gave His only Son, that whoever believes in Him shall not perish but have eternal life. (John 3:16) And, because of Jesus' sacrifice, God's love benefits all – "Therefore, there is now no condemnation for those who are in Christ Jesus, because through Christ Jesus the law of the Spirit of life set me free from the law of sin and death." (Romans 8:1)

"No matter how many mistakes we make or how unworthy we deem ourselves to be, God loves us and wants us to have enough faith to receive it. The highest choice was to be willing never to use his powers and to be willing ever to give his life if he could help one fellow man to understand that death does not exist -that death is only a transition to a different form of living." Elizabeth Kubler-Ross

DAY 123

May 03

But he was pierced for our transgressions,
He was crushed for our iniquities;
The punishment that brought us peace was upon him,
And by his wounds we are healed

Isaiah 53:5

ISAIAH 53:5

If Jesus is the One who "heals the broken hearted and binds up their wounds" (Psalm 147:3), then why doesn't He simply do it? Here again, it is the principle at work that seems to govern the way the Kingdom of God operates: He operates by the law of love and so He waits for our willingness. God waits for us recognize our need, turn to Him, and ask for healing.

When the blind man cried out for mercy, Jesus asked him "What do you want me to do for you?"(Matthew 20:32) Surely it must have been obvious? But before Jesus heals him, He waits for his faith – respecting his freedom and looking for willingness. Why? These things engender love.

Jesus explained it this way, "For this people's heart has become calloused; they hardly hear with their ears, and they have closed their eyes. Otherwise they might see with their eyes, hear with their ears, understand with their hearts and turn, and I would heal them." (Matthew 13:15)

Our hearts become calloused when, instead of turning to the Lord for healing, we turn away and do sinful, protective and reactive things. Maybe it is motivated by the fear of being hurt. Perhaps it is our pride that doesn't allow us to admit that we are wounded and in need of healing. Sometimes we simply don't slow down long enough to listen. The reason doesn't matter. If we keep doing it long enough, our wounded heart will become so calloused that it becomes impossible for us to spiritually see God or to hear His words.

All it takes is to "understand with your hearts and turn," and look at what Jesus does – He heals us. He heals our wounded and calloused hearts.

DAY 124

May 04

I heard but I did not understand.
So I asked "My Lord, what will the
outcome of all this be?"

Daniel 12:8

DANIEL 12:8

The final chapter in the book of Daniel focuses on the end of time - the time just before and after Jesus Christ returns to earth. The Prophet warns of terrible times ahead, but, he also provides wonderful hope for those who put their faith in God.

The world as it is today is a living testimony of the Prophets predictions. Violence, corruption, betrayal, wars and destruction are the norm. Spiritual values and ethical standards have become the hallmark of the weak.

St Paul puts it all into perspective – "I consider that our present sufferings are not worth comparing with the glory that will be revealed in us." (Romans 8:18)

And so, when we too wonder "what the outcome of all this will be", let us remember that God is in control. He understands that we feel insecure, confused, and anxious at times. All He asks is that we turn our sights on him and rely on his grace.

"For by grace are you saved, through faith, and that not of yourselves" (Ephesians 2:8)

DAY 125

May 05

Do you show contempt for
the riches of his kindness
Tolerance and patience
Not realizing that God's
kindness leads you
Towards repentance

Romans 2:4

ROMANS 2:4

The Pharisees are the perfect example of those who showed contempt for the kindness, tolerance, and patience of the Living God. They believed that they were the "chosen ones of God", and, that they achieved that status through their own works and self-righteousness.

Paul, too, speaks of those that try to live by "what they do or don't do" - thereby relying on their own strength and goodness, instead of accepting the forgiveness and grace of Christ. True righteousness comes from faith. Faith in what Jesus has already done. The forgiveness of God is a gift- not something we can earn because of our own good deeds or achievements.

"For all have sinned and fall short of the glory of God." (Romans 3:23) When we eat from the tree of the knowledge of good and evil, we are operating from the system of this world .When we acknowledge the power and grace of God, we draw from the Tree of Life, which is Christ himself.

"God saves humanity not by punishing it but by restoring it" Richard Rohr

DAY 126

May 06

It is written
"Man does not live by bread alone,
But by every word that comes from
the mouth of God."

Matthew 4:4

ALMOST THERE

MATTHEW 4:4

The Word of God is essential in the life of anyone who claims to be a child of the Lord. The Bible, firstly, teaches us how to become a Christian, and then shows us how to follow Jesus on a daily basis.

We need to understand that the Word of God is our sustenance. It was equally important in the life of Jesus, because it sustained and helped Him, during times of temptation. The Word gives us strength to face the realities and difficulties of life. It gives us stability, security and an assurance of fulfilment. Jesus said that even if the heavens and earth pass away, His word will never pass away.

The Word stimulates us and inspires our faith. It provides clarity and comprehension during times of perplexity and confusion, and brings the message of hope. Therefore, when we diligently study the Word and fill our hearts with its lessons, we feed our faith and find revelation and peace.

The Word of God comforts and reassures us in times of sorrow and distress. It gives us rest and a sense of calmness in our hearts. It gives us hope and assurance of God's presence and guidance.

"I have hidden your word in my heart." (Psalm 119:11) People need more than bread to live; we have to feed on every word of God - because it helps us in our hour of need. It transforms us and furnishes us with the understanding and assurance of eternal life- where we will have "the right to eat from the tree of life, which is in the paradise of God." (Revelation 2:7)

DAY 127

May 07

When Jesus heard it, he said to them, "Those who are well have no need of a physician. But those who are sick I did not come to call the righteous But sinners to repentance"

Mark 2:17

MARK 2:17

In Mark 2, soon after calling Matthew to follow Him, Jesus ate a meal with "many publicans and sinners" in Matthew's house (verse 15). Matthew had been a tax collector (publican), and these were his friends and acquaintances now spending time with Jesus. The scribes and Pharisees complained, but Jesus' actions in spending time with sinners transcended His culture, and, should actually define Christian culture as we know it.

As Jesus' ministry grew, so did His popularity among the social outcasts of society. This was part of His mission: "I have not come to call the righteous, but sinners." Jesus went to where the need was, because "it is not the healthy who need a doctor, but the sick." By being at Matthew's dinner table Jesus broke many societal taboos, but, His presence there showed that He looked beyond culture into people's hearts. Whereas the Pharisees judged people by their profession or their past, Jesus only saw their need.

Jesus didn't let social status or cultural norms dictate His relationship with people. He saw individuals, not labels. He spoke the truth to sinners, and loved them. He offered them hope, based on their repentance and faith in Him (Mark1:15). Jesus, unlike the Pharisees, didn't require people to change before coming to Him. He sought them out and extended grace to them. Change would come to those who accepted Him, but, it would come from the inside. Like Jesus, cultural or societal norms should not dictate who we share the Word of God with, or who we are prepared to spend time with. We are God's healers on earth and we need to seek out those in need of healing.

"If we could only see that God is there in the cracks of our splintered human lives, we would already be healed"-Ilia Delio

DAY 128

May 08

He who conceals his sins does not prosper, But whoever confesses and renounces them finds mercy

Proverbs 28:13

ALMOST THERE

PROVERBS 28:13

In the words of Pope Francis: "True prayer is born of a heart which repents of its faults and failings, yet pleads for the grace to live the great commandment of love of God and neighbour."

Pope Francis was referring to the parable of the Tax Collector in which Jesus contrasts the arrogance and self-righteousness of the Pharisee's prayer, with the tax collector's humble recognition of his sinfulness and the need for the Lord's mercy.

"The Pharisee makes his way confidently to the temple, but he is unaware of having lost the way towards his heart. The Tax Collector comes to the temple humble, repentant and even afraid to raise his eyes to heaven. His was a beautiful prayer- Lord, have pity on me for I am a sinner."

"The parable shows us that being righteous or a sinner is not a question of social standing but of how we act towards God and others. Humbly recognizing his sin, the Tax Collector begs for God's mercy- and shows all of us the necessary condition to receive God's mercy. Arrogance compromises every good action while humility throws open the doors to His mercy."

JOHN 14:6

The above statement made by Jesus might seem politically incorrect, intolerant and unreasonable. However, the highway to heaven had been closed for centuries before Jesus came down to earth. God did not set up the road block – through our sinfulness, we erected the barriers that we could not move. God was the only one who could open the way.

Jesus is the way – through him, God comes to meet us, holding nothing back, and offering everything of who he is and what he has. Jesus is the truth. He is God's definitive and perfect word- expressing who God is, what He's like, who we are, and what we need to do to be saved from misery and futility. And Jesus is the life – He gives us not only commandments and noble ideals, but also the power to live them and to become new people.

The Power comes from the Holy Spirit, who Jesus pours out to those who accept Him.

"If we let him, he will use our lips to spread his truth, our lives to show the way, and our love to give to others. For the meaning of human life is to love, and the greatest gift we've received from Him is the power to give ourselves away."
- Dr M D'Ambrosio

DAY 130

May 10

For the message of the cross is foolishness
To those who are perishing, but to us
Who are being saved it is the power of God.
For it is written: "I will destroy the wisdom of the wise,
And bring to nothing the understanding of the prudent.
Where is the wise? Where is the disputer of this age?
Has not God made foolish the wisdom of this world?"

1 Corinthians 1:18-19

ALMOST THERE

1 CORINTHIANS 1:18-19

In this letter to the church in Corinth, St Paul focusses his attention on the Cross of Christ. The cross raised issues for both Jews and Greeks (Gentiles) alike - both populations were represented in the church. The Cross of Christ seemed like foolishness to the Jews who expected a powerful Messiah, and to the Greeks, who placed a high value on human wisdom. To the Jews, the cross appeared to be weakness, not strength. To the Greeks, the cross appeared to be foolishness, not wisdom.

Paul contrasts worldly wisdom with the wisdom of God, which finds its highest expression in the apparent foolishness of the cross. For those who pride themselves on their own wisdom, the cross appears to be stupid. Why would God send his Son to die on a cross? By the standards of human wisdom it makes no sense. But, sadly, human wisdom has no saving power. No matter how intelligent, people who rely solely on their own wisdom will perish. They are like people whose ship has sunk in the middle of the ocean. No matter how strong a swimmer they are, they will still need a lifeboat or, better yet, another ship to save them.

Those who are open to salvation acknowledge that they are powerless without God. They understand that they cannot defeat the sin that threatens to dominate them, and so, instead, they place their trust in the grace of God. That grace was manifested most fully at the Cross of Christ. There Jesus not only prayed that God would forgive those who crucified him, but he also opened the door to forgiveness for all who would come to believe in him.

And so, the cross, foolish to those stooped in worldly wisdom, is really the instrument of salvation for those who choose to accept it.

DAY 131

May 11

And Jesus, walking by the Sea of Galilee,
saw two brothers, Simon called Peter,
and Andrew his brother, casting a net into the sea
For they were fishermen. Then he said to them,
"Follow me, and I will make you fishers of men."

Matthew 4:18-20

MATTHEW 4:18-20

If you belong to God,
more is expected of you.
God does not want
money from you.
He desires the heart and
love of his children.
The currency of love is
not expressed in money
But in selfless devotion to
God and his people

- Prof Jan van der Watt

DAY 132

May 12

But what does it say?nThe Word is near you, in your mouth and in your heart. That if you confess with your mouth the Lord Jesus and believe in your heart that God has raised him from the dead, you will be saved. For with the heart one believes unto righteousness, and with the mouth confession is made unto salvation.

Romans 10:8-10

ROMANS 10:8-10

When we watch the Tennis Grand Slams or the Football World Cup, we may be admiring the impressive skill of the players and enjoying the thrill of competition. But, what are we actually witnessing? The winners-the champions-in any sport, are simply this-masters of the fundamentals. The game is the same no matter who is playing, whether it is an amateur or a professional. So how do professionals become champions? Practice, practice and more practice. Daily, for hours, they practice the fundamentals-the basics-of their sport. Mastering them determines their results. This pattern of focusing on the basics- the ABC's- is the hallmark of most successful coaches and athletes in any sport.

It is the same with our faith. If we want to be proficient in operating in great faith – to be a champion-we have to master the fundamentals. We have to master the ABC's of faith.

1. Believe the Word of God. The first, and most important, of the basics of faith, is to believe the Word of God. Faith begins where the will of God is known. But it isn't enough to simply know the Word of God – we have to believe the Word of God. We have to spend time in the Word, read the Word, and meditate on the Word, again and again and again.

2. Speak the Word of God. As Christians, there is power in the words we speak. Therefore, it is not good enough to simply renew our minds in His Word if we aren't going to put it to good use. Our words are often our biggest downfall. If we don't keep them in line with the Will of God, we allow sin to creep in. But if we guard our tongue and always speak the truth of His Word, we make room for the Holy Spirit to do God's work through us.

3. Act on the Word of God. James 2:14 says, "Faith by itself, if it does not have works, is dead." So, if we don't act on our faith, it isn't real Bible faith at all. Acting on the Word of God means altering our lifestyle to fit the Word, instead of altering it to fit our lifestyle. When we act on the Word, faith begins to grow, sin's power over us begins to wane, and circumstances begin to change. When our faith increases, our attitudes and our outlook begin to change – they become more in alignment with the Will of God.

DAY 133

May 13

For by grace you have been saved through faith, And that not of yourselves; it is the gift of God, Not of works, lest anyone should boast. For we are His workmanship, created in Christ Jesus for good works, which God prepared beforehand that we should walk in them.

Ephesians 2: 8-10

ALMOST THERE

EPHESIANS 2: 8-10

Years ago, C S Lewis was asked by a fellow theologian what he thinks makes Christianity different from any other religion. What makes Christianity unique? He replied – "that is the easiest question I have ever been asked – it is that Christianity shows the grace of God. It is God's grace. No other religion shows grace." Grace is an undeserved gift. That is simply what it means. It is God's love coming to us, free of charge, no strings attached.

John Newton knew the grace of God first hand…. Oh it was mercy indeed to save a wretch like me. John Newton wrote these words in his journal on 21 March 1796, at the age of 70. He never forgot that "great turning day" in 1748 when, as an obstreperous, rebellious young man, he was surprised to hear himself crying out during a violent storm at sea, "The Lord have mercy on us!" It was on that day he discovered, "How precious did that grace appear, the hour I first believed." The words of the hymn he wrote, Amazing Grace, were etched on his heart daily.

Amazing Grace! How sweet the sound,
that saved a wretch like me!
I once was lost but now am found; was blind, but now I see.
Twas grace that taught my heart to fear,
and grace my fears relieved;
How precious did that grace appear, the hour I first believed
Through many dangers, toils and snares, I have already come;
'Tis grace hath brought me safe thus far,
and grace will lead me home.
The Lord has promised good to me, His word my hope secures
He will my Shield and Portion be, as long as life endures.

DAY 134

May 14

Whatever happens to you, accept it,
And in the uncertainties of your humble state,
Be patient, since gold is tested in the fire,
And chosen men in the furnace of humiliation,
Trust him and he will uphold you.

Ecclesiaticus 2:4-6

ALMOST THERE

ECCLESIATICUS 2:4-6

As Christians, our faith often gets tested to breaking point. When we look at the world around us we are constantly confronted with earthquakes, tsunamis, famine, rape, war and pillaging, cancer, Alzheimer's, aids, genocide, and various other forms of atrocities. Yet, the Bible urges – "My child, if you aspire to serve the Lord, prepare yourself for an ordeal. Be sincere of heart, be steadfast, and do not be alarmed when disaster comes." Sirach 2:1

Do not be alarmed when disaster comes – you must be joking? It is not surprising that, for some, these tragedies trigger this kind of response: There's no way a loving God could allow this to happen. So either God isn't a loving God, or, he doesn't exist.

But faith does make a difference. During these times of disaster people from all walks of life spring into action and a multitude of hands respond to the call for help. It is then that the outpouring of compassion, love, concern, courage, prayer and spirit, becomes visible. Healing begins when all the disbelief, dismay, anger, grief and tears, that such anguish brings, can openly be shared among many.

Our faith is durable enough to be tested by fire because it is founded on the living Christ. "Trust him and he will uphold you, follow a straight path and hope in him." Sirach 2:6

Suffering and death, calamities and disasters: they happen with shocking regularity. Yet we know two things for certain: that God is love, and that faith in God offers no guarantees. Our faith embraces all of life, all of it, not just the pleasant parts, but also the tough, troubling and trying parts as well.

DAY 135

May 15

"But if you love those who love you,
what credit is that to you?
For even sinners do the same."

Luke 6:32

LUKE 6:32

It is easy to love those who love us. If someone is nice to us, we are more inclined to be nice back. However, God holds us to a higher standard – He calls us to love even those who hate and persecute us. How do we do that? How can we, in our human, sinful state, demonstrate the selfless love of Christ? The desires of our impure hearts are purely selfish – on our own, we seek only to further our well-being, and steer clear from anything that asks us to sacrifice and forsake any of our worldly pleasures.

The amount of love we have is limited and finite. We can only serve one master. Our restricted capacity for love only allows us to love one thing: ourselves or God. "No servant can serve two masters, for either he will hate the one and love the other, or he will be devoted to the one and despise the other. You cannot serve God and money." (Luke 16:13)

If we choose to love ourselves, we can only love the people and things that benefit us. There is no extra love for things that cause us pain or ask us for sacrifice. This untempered love for self only drives us further and further away from God, towards sin. However, if we give our love to God, we actually have hope of being content and of finding the ability to love others.

All our love should go to God. When we give Him all our love, we become a vessel for His love. This, in turn, gives us the power to love others unconditionally – the love I have for others is not a love from within me, but, it is God's love for me, flowing through me into the lives of others.

DAY 136

May 16

But Peter and the other apostles answered and said: "We ought to obey God rather than men."

Acts 5:29

ACTS 5:29

"Now behold, one came and said to Him, 'Good Teacher, what good thing shall I do that I may have eternal life?' So He said to him…If you want to enter into life keep the commandments."

"He said to Him, 'which ones? Jesus said, 'You shall not murder, you shall not commit adultery, you shall not steal, you shall not bear false witness, honour your father and your mother, and, you shall love your neighbour as yourself." (Matthew 19:16-19)

Obedience to God begins with accepting the Ten Commandments as the permanent standard and foundation for our values and behaviour. But our obedience has to encompass the full spirit of these commandments.

Jesus also said: "Do not think that I came to destroy the Law or the Prophets. I did not come to destroy but to fulfil. For assuredly, I say to you, till heaven and earth pass away, one jot or one title will by no means pass from the law till all is fulfilled." "Whoever therefore breaks one of the least of these commandments, and teaches men so, shall be called least in the kingdom of heaven; but whoever does and teaches them, he shall be called great in the kingdom of heaven."
(Matthew 5:17-19)

Sin is disregarding or refusing to do what God tells us to do. Jesus tells us that that He had no intention of annulling or abolishing God's commandments. Any man, therefore, who assumes otherwise, or teaches that, is in grave spiritual danger.

Saul said to Samuel "I have sinned, for I have transgressed the commandment of the Lord and your words, because I feared the people and obeyed their voice." (1 Samuel 15:24)

DAY 137

May 17

Let love be without hypocrisy, abhor what is evil. Cling to what is good. Be kindly affectionate to one another with brotherly love, In honour giving preference to one another; Not lagging in diligence, fervent in spirit, serving the Lord

Romans 12:9-11

ROMANS 12:9-11

One of the differences, and possibly the most important one, between Christians and the world, is our ability to love. This love comes solely from God, and stems from the fact that He first loved us. "Dear friends, let us love one another, for love comes from God. Everyone who loves has been born of God and knows God." (1 John 4:7)

It is not always so easy to show love and compassion to one another, but love is the hallmark of a disciple of Christ. Our love for each other, and for our neighbour, should speak louder than any words we can express. I do not believe that it is happenstance that love is the very first fruit of the Spirit listed in Galatians 5 – "But the fruit of the Spirit is love, joy, peace, patience, kindness, goodness, faithfulness, gentleness and self-control." (Galatians 5:22-23)
Love is the anchor for every other fruit, because, when we love, we allow God's love to flow through us.

When we love in the fashion God wants us to – without hypocrisy- we naturally begin to "hate and abhor what is evil and cling to what is good." As we strive to be unpolluted by worldly things, we are constantly reminded that God is good and perfect and that every good thing comes from Him. Through love, the other fruits of the Spirit become manifest in our lives. And, as we walk in fellowship with God and live according to the truth of His word, He changes our hearts to align with His heart. His characteristics become our characteristics, as evidenced by the fruit of the Spirit operating in our lives. "And now these three remain faith, hope and love. But the greatest of these is love."
(1 Corinthians 13:13)

DAY 138

May 18

Teaching us that,
Denying ungodliness and worldly lusts,
We should live soberly, righteous,
And godly in the present age

Titus 2:12

ALMOST THERE

TITUS 2:12

The Word of God tells us that God's grace, which brought us salvation, also wants us to deny "ungodliness and worldly lusts." Instead we should live "soberly and righteously and godly in this present world." According to Donald Guthrie in the Tyndale series of commentaries, this triad of adverbs expresses the Christian's ideal behaviour towards himself, his neighbour, and his God.

Our duty to ourselves is best expressed by Paul's command to live "soberly." W E Vine defines living soberly like this: "It suggests the exercise of that self-restraint that governs all passions and desires, enabling the believer to be conformed to the mind of Christ." Until we have mastered the ability to live within the limits of moderation and temperance, we are not ready to contemplate our duty towards others.

Our duty towards our neighbour is best understood by Paul's injunction to live "righteously." The word "righteous" pertains to honesty, justice, fairness, and integrity, in our dealings with others. Our supreme duty, though, is our duty to God. Paul urges us to live in a "godly" fashion. When we are devoted to God, our life is characterised by reverence and respect towards God. We believe, and acknowledge, His being and His perfection. The holy man loves God, fears God, and trusts God. The godly man depends on Him, prays to Him, praises Him, and meditates on His words and works.

"God is burning out of you everything that is unlike himself"
-Mother Teresa of Calcutta

DAY 139

May 19

Be sober, be vigilant;
Because your adversary, the devil,
Walks about like a roaring lion,
Seeking whom he may devour

1 Peter 5:8

ALMOST THERE

1 PETER 5:8

"But now that you have been set free from sin and have become slaves of God, the benefit you reap leads to holiness, and the result is eternal life." (Romans 6:22)

Can we really be free from sin? Isn't that impossible? In this context, "having been set free from sin", means that we are set free from the power of sin. Sin no longer reigns over us. (Romans 6:12) Obviously, we are very far from the purity and holiness of Jesus - but the Word of God makes it abundantly clear that we do not need to be enslaved to sin.

We become slaves to the one we obey – either sin, resulting in death, or righteousness, resulting in life and peace. We are the ones who decide whom we will serve. It is a matter of our own will. However, sin is a powerful force in our life –"but I see another law at work in me, waging war against the law of my mind and making me a prisoner of the law of sin at work within me." (Romans 7:23) We, just like Paul, serve the law of God with our minds, but at the same time, serve the law of sin with our flesh.

The only way to leave the sins of the flesh behind is to go the same way that Jesus went. The Bible tells us that He is our forerunner, and He opened the way for us to follow – "For to this you were called, because Christ also suffered for us, leaving us an example, that you should follow His steps: Who committed no sin, nor was deceit found in His mouth." (1Peter 2:21-22)

Following Jesus' steps means that we don't sin either. With the help of the Holy Spirit we are able to deny ourselves, and hate the things that lead to our destruction. By paying careful attention to our daily choices and decisions, and consciously striving to recognise anything that is not a fruit of the Spirit, we lose our taste for worldly lusts. As we begin to perfect the art of recognizing sin, we go from light to light, and from strength to strength – growing ever nearer to the purity and holiness of our Creator.

DAY 140

May 20

But one thing I do;
Forgetting what is behind
and straining toward what is ahead.

Phillipians 3:13

ALMOST THERE

1 PHILLIPIANS 3:13

A lot of things about our past are important to us. The past, and remembering it, has helped to mould and form us into the person we have become. Everything that has happened to us is a vital part of who and what we are.

Yet, there is much about our past which is best forgotten and left behind. We have littered the past with the mistakes of daily living. We have shed tears and caused others to shed tears. As much as we recall the joys and victories we have encountered along the way, we remember the failures which mark our journey through life.

To focus on the mistakes and failures of the past, brings a paralysis of anguish and remorse. Paul's statement in Philippians 3:13, demonstrates a better way of dealing with things: "forgetting what lies behind."

It is God who enables us to cover up the past, and to forget and erase those memories that cause anguish and remorse. God surrounds us with His love and assures us, "Your past is forgiven." God's redeeming grace helps us find the peace that enables us to forget and to begin anew.

This gift of forgetting makes the second direction of Paul's words, "straining forward to what lies ahead", possible. Once the past is absolved, we have a new future, with new possibilities, ahead of us.

DAY 141

May 21

Do not judge,
Or you too will be judged.

Matthew 7:1

MATTHEW 7:1

Two other verses in the Bible come to mind when I try to make sense of this one.

"How can you say to your brother, 'Brother, let me take out the speck that is in your eye,' when you yourself do not see the log that is in your own eye?" (Luke 6:42)

And "He that is without sin among you, let him first cast a stone at her." (John 8:7)

Only those who are faultless have the right to pass judgement on others. And so, because "all have sinned and fall short of the glory of God", no one has the right to pass judgement on their neighbour.

It is the tragedy of our Christian faith that many believers fall prey to the sin of hypocrisy. Hypocrisy is always motivated by self-love. We want to impress others, to make them think that we are something that we know in our hearts we are not.

The only way to avoid hypocrisy is to make sure that you are walking in reality with God every day. It is important to spend time in His word, and in prayer, on a regular basis. But, it is also essential to deal with the sin in your life- especially on the heart level- when His word confronts you with where you are wrong.

Only when we take an honest look at our lives and acknowledge our own sinfulness, are we worthy of being called disciples' of Christ.

1 JOHN 3:18

We are all familiar with the idiom "actions speak louder than words."

Actions are more revealing of one's true character because it is easy to say things or to make promises, but it takes effort to do things and to follow through.

Mother Teresa, an Albanian Catholic nun, who spent her life among the poor in Calcutta, was the very embodiment of "love in action." During her lifetime, her name became a metaphor for selflessness and goodness.

Not all of us have the fortitude to be a 'Mother Teresa'. "Not all of us can do great things. But we can do small things with great love." Being inspired to great things is good. However, Mother Teresa encourages us to take smaller steps to help kick start our spiritual journey. We may never be able to solve world hunger, but we can donate money to organisations that distribute food to the poor. We will never be able to stop all the injustices in the world. What we can do, is realise that a kind word, or a helping hand, can transform someone's day.

"By their fruit you will recognize them."
(Matthew 7:16)

DAY 143

May 23

Live by the spirit
and you will not gratify the desires
of the sinful nature

Galatians 5:16

GALATIANS 5:16

St Paul says in Romans 8:5 "Let those who live according to the flesh set their minds on the things of the flesh, but those who live according to the Spirit set their minds on the things of the Spirit." The 'flesh' is our natural tendency to be attracted toward sin and self – it is often referred to as our 'sin disposition' or our 'sin nature'.

As Christians we believe that Jesus died on the cross to free us from the gravitational pull of the flesh. Sin holds no power over those whose mind is set on the things of the Spirit. When our minds are set on the Spirit we conform to a different value system. It is not only about how we respond in the moment of temptation. It involves the reorienting of thoughts, desires, and motivations. We need to train our thoughts, behaviours, and actions to stay focussed on producing the fruits of the Spirit –love, joy, peace, patience, kindness, goodness, faithfulness, gentleness and self-control.

Turning from sin and learning to 'walk in the Spirit,' on a daily basis, is not easy or automatic. It involves a lot of little steps taken in submission to the Holy Spirit.

Helen Lemmel in her famous hymn urges us to "Turn your eyes upon Jesus, look full in His wonderful face, and the things of the earth will grow strangely dim, in the light of His glory and grace."

DAY 144

May 24

The path of life is to abide
By discipline, and he who ignores
correction goes astray

Proverbs 10:17

PROVERBS 10:17

Nobody likes criticism. It can hurt, especially when unsolicited, or delivered with unkind words and a harsh spirit. However, it is important to refrain from rejecting the reproof before considering whether or not it is valid.

God often uses an honest, direct person, to convey something we need to hear. His goal for us is to grow in spiritual maturity and holiness. But, we all have blind spots that prevent us from seeing, and accepting, areas in our lives that are in need of transformation. This is where criticism can be useful – it forces us to examine ourselves.

Instead of allowing criticism to lead us into anger and self-pity, we should let it do its work in our life. We can't allow hurt or anger to derail what God wants to do in us – namely, make us more Christ-like. However, not all critiques are necessarily valid. That is exactly why it is important to respond well and evaluate them adequately and correctly. Only once we have determined precisely what is under scrutiny – our beliefs, our character, our relationship with God – are we able to take the best course of action.

God is always available and willingly to help us discern the validity of the comment – all we have to do is ask.

DAY 145

May 25

Be quick to listen,
And deliberate in giving an answer.

Ecclesiaticus 5:11

ALMOST THERE

ECCLESIATICUS 5:11

"I really put my foot in my mouth." All of us relate to this idiom. We have all, at some point, offended someone by saying something we really wished we hadn't. The real problem though, is that we didn't think before speaking. "Rash words are like sword thrusts, but the tongue of the wise man brings healing."
(Proverbs 12:18)

Once harsh words are said, you can't take them back – you can only live them down. Hurtful words are more damaging than physical hurt, and leave scars on the soul and spirit. The words we speak have a direct impact on the lives of others. Harsh words, carelessly spoken, can destroy relationships. All it takes is one or two ill-placed words and you have gossiped, criticized, started a rumour, or offended someone. The guarding of our tongue takes effort – a conscious, daily, minute-by-minute effort- to think before we speak.

Galatians 5 reminds us that the Fruits of the Spirit are love, patience, kindness, and self-control. And, just as we can hurt others with our words, so we can speak kind, soothing, beneficial words, that can build, uplift, strengthen and heal those around us. "A word fitly spoken is like apples of gold in pictures of silver." (Proverbs 25:11) As Christians, these are the kind of words we should be speaking: "fitly spoken words."

DAY 146

May 26

Therefore, whatever you
want men to do to you,
Do also to them, For this is
the law and the prophets.

Matthew 7:12

MATTHEW 7:12

This famous quote made by Jesus Christ is often referred to as "The Golden Rule" (the principle of reciprocity – the practice of exchanging things with others for mutual benefit), which is a summation of Jesus' ethical teaching regarding our treatment of others.

This statement made by Jesus in Matthew 7, mirrors the same concept expressed in the Old Testament – "You shall not take vengeance, nor bear any grudge against the children of your people, but you shall love your neighbour as yourself: I am the Lord." (Leviticus 19:18) God's instruction is the same in the Old and the New Testaments.

Whether or not we apply the Golden Rule in our life, will have a direct impact on how God will deal with us. In the Gospel of Luke we are told how God expects us to be acting towards others if we expect to receive blessings and gifts from Him: "Judge not, and you shall not be judged. Condemn not, and you shall not be condemned. Forgive, and you will be forgiven. Give and it will be given to you: good measure, pressed down, shaken together, and running over will be put into your bosom. For with the same measure that you use, it will be measured back to you." (Luke 6:37-38) Once again, we see that the way we treat our neighbours sets the standard of how we will be treated by God – and this includes receiving His blessings and His gifts!

Many in our modern society espouse a general philosophy of looking out for the self – first taking what you want and need, and, only then, considering others. That is in direct conflict with the Golden Rule – "Therefore, whatever you want men to do to you, do also to them, for this is the Law and the Prophets." (Matthew 7:12)

DAY 147

May 27

The Father loves the Son, And has given all things into His hand "He who believes in the Son has everlasting life; And he who does not believe the Son shall not see life, But the wrath of God abides on him."

John 3:35-36

ALMOST THERE

JOHN 3:35-36

"I have set before you life and death, choose life…" (Deuteronomy 30:19)

"I made the choice for heaven and, having done so, I went in search of tools for living it."

"Will you engage this moment with kindness or with cruelty, with love or with fear, with generosity or scarcity, with a joyous heart or an embittered one? This is your choice and no one can make it for you.

If you choose kindness, love, generosity, and joy, then you will discover in that choice the Kingdom of God, heaven, nirvana, this-worldly salvation. If you choose cruelty, fear, scarcity, and bitterness, then you will discover in that choice the hellish states of which so many religions speak.

These are not ontological realities tucked away somewhere in space- these are existential realities playing out in your own mind. Heaven and hell are both inside of you. It is your choice that determines where you will reside."
- Rabbi Shapiro

DAY 148

May 28

Therefore be merciful, just as your Father also is merciful "Judge not, and you shall not be judged. Condemn not, and you shall not be condemned. Forgive, and you shall be forgiven."

Luke 6:36-38

LUKE 6:36-38

It is extremely easy for us to find fault with those around us – most of us readily judge our neighbour. However, a critical attitude hinders our walk with God, and distracts us from His purpose for our life. We judge because of our own selfish interests. We become critical when comparing ourselves to those who move in our circle. We try to find fault in them to prove that we are smarter, better looking, happier or wealthier. These are all selfish reasons, and simply serve to make us feel better about ourselves. We also get critical when others, often a family member or co-worker, fails to do what we ask, or does not do what we think is right. Our expectations lead to a judgemental attitude.

But Jesus told us not to judge "lest you be judged" (Matthew 7:1). When we judge, we invite judgement upon ourselves. The Bible teaches that "God will be as hard on you as you are on others. He will treat you exactly as you treat them" (Matthew 7:2). By judging others, we hide our own hypocrisy. When the religious leaders brought a woman to Jesus who had been caught in sexual sin, they wanted to kill her. Jesus responded, "If any of you have never sinned, then go ahead and throw the first stone at her" (John 8:7). Nobody threw one.

God alone reserves the right to judge each person. We are all sinners and fall short of the glory of God. That is why God sent Jesus into the world to pay for our sins. God offers all of us all His blessings – eternal life, forgiveness, peace, joy and hope. All we have to do is believe.

"Freely you have received, freely give" (Matthew 10:8). God has shown us grace and mercy- so we are expected to show grace and mercy to others. Therefore instead of judgement, if we profess to be His followers, we have to extend His love to those around us - our family, our friends and our colleagues.

DAY 149

May 29

If a son asks for bread from
any father among you,
Will he give him a stone?
Or if he asks for a fish
Will he give him a serpent,
instead of a fish

Luke 11:11

LUKE 11:11

"The Lord is my shepherd; I shall not want."(Psalm 23:1) This famous Psalm was written by King David, who once was a shepherd himself. Isn't it intriguing that David, who was also a warrior and a king, chose to look back on his time as a shepherd to paint a picture of how God cares for our needs? Maybe it is because a shepherd represents a closer and more intimate relationship. Whereas a King might do what is best for the majority, a shepherd knows each one of his sheep individually.

In the parable of the lost sheep, Jesus asks: "What man of you, having a hundred sheep, if he has lost one of them, does not leave the ninety-nine in the open country, and go after the one that is lost, until he finds it?" (Luke 15:4) A shepherd has a deep concern and care, not only for all his sheep as a whole but, also, for each and every single one. This is how God cares for us. He knows our comings and goings. He knows every hair on our heads. He knows when one of us is lost, and He has made provision to find us - through His Son, Jesus Christ. But, we can't see God as our Shepherd if we don't see and acknowledge ourselves as sheep. Sheep are prone to wander and are entirely reliant on the Shepherd, whether they realize it or not. Once we open our eyes to how much we need, and rely on God for everything, we will notice His provision in our lives. But if we continue to live the lie that we can do this on our own, we will wander and drift away from our true source - looking for satisfaction in artificial places.

When David says "I shall not want", he is acknowledging his total reliance on God. "I shall not want" because God, as a good shepherd, ensures that I have everything I need. "I shall not want", not because of what I have done or can do, but, because God loves me, and because I know God personally as my Shepherd. "I shall not want", because there are areas in my life that only God can fulfil, and He will fulfil them. And finally, "I shall not want", because I have made a decision not to desire anything outside of the scope of what God wants for me.

DAY 150

May
30

You are the light of the world.....
Let your light shine before men,
that they may see your good deeds
and praise your Father in heaven.

Matthew 5:14 & 16

ALMOST THERE

MATTHEW 5:14 & 16

When Jesus said, "Let your light shine before men," he went on to clarify why it is important for us to shine; "so that they may see your good deeds and praise your Father in heaven." Our goal should always be to bring glory to God, and not to gain recognition for ourselves. As God's children we are called to a higher standard. While others chase after physical pleasures and selfish gain, we are commanded to "cast off the works of darkness and put on the armour of light" (Romans 13:12).

So how do we put on the armour of light in order to shine for the glory of God? The Bible tells us to "not be conformed to this world" (Romans 12:2). Being considerate and kind to others, avoiding gossip, and guarding your tongue, are some examples of how we can treat our neighbour as we would ourselves.

But, in order to really shine, we need to let go of all arrogance, self-centeredness, and pride. It is only when we are truly God-centred that we can become beacons for Christ. It is in the letting go of self that we find and walk in the light.

DAY 151

May 31

Do your best to present yourself to God as one approved, A workman who does not need to be ashamed And who correctly handles the word of truth.

2 Timothy 2:15

2 TIMOTHY 2:15

Most of us need, and want, affirmation and acknowledgement from the people we care about, and from those who are important to our advancement in life. As scholars and students, we work hard to please our teachers and lectures. Our parents are our role models, and we strive to emulate them and make them proud. When we join the workforce our focus is on financial and job security, so we make every effort to provide a good service to our employer.

Just as we would desire to satisfy the expectations of our earthly boss, as disciples' of Christ, we should view our work for Him in the same way. God too, wants us to seek His approval, to emulate Him, and to make Him proud.

God has entrusted the ministry of His word to us, and we must perform it with diligence and pride. To be that diligent, approved workman, we have to "correctly handle the word of truth." Of necessity, correctly handling the Bible, the word of truth, involves much study, contemplation, and prayer. It involves an open mind, an open heart, and a faithful life, to the word of truth. But, mostly, it requires a spirit of dependence on the guidance of the Holy Spirit. Without the Holy Spirit we are simply workmen without the tools required for the job at hand.

DAY 152-181

June

Christ Be With Me

May the strength of God pilot me,
the power of God preserve me today.
May the wisdom of God instruct me,
the eye of God watch over me,
the ear of God hear me,
the word of God give me sweet talk,
the hand of God defend me,
the way of God guide me.
Christ be with me. Christ before me. Christ after me.
Christ in me. Christ under me. Christ over me.
Christ on my right hand. Christ on my left hand.
Christ on this side. Christ on that side. Christ at my back.
Christ in the head of everyone to whom I speak.
Christ in the mouth of every person who speaks to me.
Christ in the eye of every person who looks at me.
Christ in the ear of every person who hears me today.

St Patrick

DAY 152

June 01

I have come that they
may have life,
And that they may have
it more abundantly.

John 10:10

JOHN 10:10

God wants us to have a life of abundance. It is His desire for us to seek more out of life. However, from God's perspective, it never has to do with acquiring worldly possessions. Instead, it's all about what is eternal. We are supposed to desire more of God. "Oh God, you are my God; earnestly I seek you; my soul thirsts for you; my flesh faints for you, as in a dry and weary land where there is no water." (Psalm 63:1) But, instead of desiring more of God, we seek to fill our need with what the world has to offer – material possessions, fame, achievement, recognition, popularity, wealth and accomplishments. Then we read John 10:10, "I came that they may have life and have it abundantly", and we expect God to grant us all those worldly pursuits we crave.

Jesus came so that we can have life, because He is the embodiment of life. Because of His death and resurrection we have a way to be reconciled with God and spend eternity with Him. Yet, Jesus not only promises us eternal life, He assures us of an abundant life here on earth. This has nothing to do with worldly pursuits, and everything to do with obtaining those attributes that make us more like Him. He wants us to have the best possible life in a world that is sometimes intolerable – a world full of cruelty, injustice, sadness and pain. The only way to achieve this is if we take on His character. Only then will we be inwardly satisfied - because we know who we are through Him, we know who He is through God the Father, and we know where we will spend eternity.

DAY 153

June 02

You will seek me and find me when you seek me with all your heart.

Jeremiah 29:13

ALMOST THERE

JEREMIAH 29:13

True seekers of God seek Him with their whole heart. It doesn't matter if you already have a relationship with Jesus but want a deeper, more intimate one, or if you want to start a relationship with Him by trusting and accepting His saving grace on the cross – you still have to seek with your whole heart. Seeking requires a lot of focus and daily effort, but there is a promise of a reward – "For whoever would draw near to God must believe that He exists and that He rewards those who seek Him." (Hebrews 11:6)

So how do we seek God with our whole heart? Firstly, we have to believe that He exists. Although it would seem obvious that a seeker already believes in the existence of God, doubt is ever present. That is precisely why the psalmist stressed, "The heavens declare the glory of God and the sky above proclaims His handiwork." (Psalm 19:1) When doubt creeps in, all we have to do is go outside, look at the stars, and His glory will be revealed.

Next, we must commit to seek Him on a daily basis. This means reserving some time every day to focus on our spiritual growth. It entails using that time to study the Bible, and to pray. The Bible is full of examples of those who chose to seek God early – in the words of the psalmist, "Early will I seek Thee." (Psalm 63:1) If God is important to us, we will spend time with Him before doing anything else for the day. When we read the Bible, we see God himself – "In the beginning was the Word, and the Word was with God, and the Word was God." (John 1:1) But we need the help of the Holy Spirit to reveal God to us – without His guidance the Word of God is lifeless, and just a book of stories written a long time ago.

Be faithful in small things because it is in them that your strength lies. Mother Teresa of Calcutta

DAY 154

June 03

In the same way, faith by itself, if not accompanied by action, is dead.

James 2:17

JAMES 2:17

"Now suppose a brother or sister is without clothes and daily food. If one of you says to him, Go, I wish you well; keep warm and well fed, but does nothing about his physical needs, what good is it? In the same way, faith by itself, if not accompanied by action, is dead."

In this piece of scripture, St James explores the theme of faith and works. He points out that it is senseless to bless someone who is in need and to pray for them, if that is all we are going to do. Blessings and prayer may good for their spiritual needs, but is does not put food on the table, pay the bills, or keep them warm. "God-talk" in the absence of "God-acts", is a pointless exercise – it is all very well telling them that we will pray for them, but if we have the ability to help them here and now, to provide whatever it is they need, then why don't we do that as well?

When we become believers, we change inwardly – we become more Christ-like. Our faith is evident to others by our changed behaviour, by the way we speak and the things we do. We no longer over-indulge or use bad language. Racial and other prejudices, together with self-centeredness, belong to our past. We begin to think and behave as Jesus did.

As His disciples, we can't go around saying one thing and doing another. Our behaviour and lifestyle has to reflect our faith – we need to say, as well as, do. "God-talk" without "God-acts", is outrageous. We must practise what we preach, and demonstrate by our lives, and how we live them, that we are children of the Living God. Others find the love of God through our actions.

Feed your faith and doubt will starve to death.
-Andrew Murray

DAY 155

June 04

NON-SMOKING AREA

Do not merely listen to the word, and so deceive yourselves. Do what it says.

James 1:22

ALMOST THERE

JAMES 1:22

"Therefore whoever hears these sayings
of mine, and does them,
I will liken him to a wise man who built
his house on the rock:
"And the rain descended, the floods came,
and the winds blew and
Beat on that house; and it did not fall,
for it was founded on the rock.
"But everyone who hears these sayings
of mine, and does not do them,
Will be like a foolish man who built
his house on the sand:
"And the rain descended, the floods came,
and the winds blew and beat on that house;
And it fell. And great was its fall".
(Matthew 7: 24-27)

You choose where you will lay your foundation

If the world seems cold to you,
Kindle fires to warm it.
- Lucy Larcom

DAY 156

June 05

If you extend your soul to the hungry and satisfy the afflicted soul, then your light shall dawn in the darkness, and your darkness shall be as noonday.

Isaiah 58:10

ALMOST THERE

ISAIAH 58:10

Pope Francis, in "Evangelii Gaudium" (The joy of the Gospel), states this: "The joy of the Gospel fills the hearts and lives of all who encounter Jesus. Those who accept His offer of salvation are set free from sin, sorrow, inner emptiness and loneliness. With Christ joy is constantly born anew…I wish to encourage the Christian faithful to embark upon a new chapter of evangelization marked by this joy…"

As Christians, we are expected to pass along the life we have received from God – thereby spreading His love far and wide. We are told to "go and make disciples"-bear fruit." (John 15:8) This could seem daunting if it weren't for the grace of God. Jesus inspires and enables us to do far more than we could ever do on our own, things we might deem impossible.

Pope Francis also writes that we don't have to impose the Gospel on others – we can simply propose it in a loving and natural way. This we can do on a daily basis – as we encounter and interact with others we can open the door. All it takes is genuinely attempting to get to know them – and it can be as simple as inviting them to lunch. The presence of God in our life will do the rest.

DAY 157

June 06

I can do all things through Christ
Who strengthens me

Philippians 4:13

ALMOST THERE

PHILIPPIANS 4:13

This scriptural passage is often misquoted, especially by athletes. More than any other group of people, competitive athletes attempt to push boundaries way beyond the physical and mental limits of human ability. They are always chasing the elusive PR – just a little faster, a little higher, a little further. And so, with the best intentions, Christian athletes turn to the "Giver of all good things" (James 1:17), for extra strength, endurance, mental fortitude, or even, wisdom.

But, is this what the Apostle Paul intended? Is it meant to be seen as fuel for motivation, or as positive self-talk to improve performance? To get a clearer idea of Paul's intent, we have to include verses eleven and twelve - ...."I have learned that in whatever situation I am to be content. I know how to be brought low, and I know how to abound. In any and every circumstance, I have learned the secret of facing plenty and hunger, abundance and need. I can do all things through him who strengthens me." Paul's aim here is contentment, not achievement.

Contentment does not promote apathy or mediocrity, but allows joy, peace, and gratitude, in the best and worst of times. Contentment is achieved when we acknowledge the sufficiency of Christ in our lives – when we fully believe that God, as our Saviour, our Friend, our Provider and Lord, is enough for us. If we do all things for the glory of God, Christ enables us to be content with the outcome, win or lose.

On a long trip any traveller needs a map. Without it he or she is lost. The same is true of the journey of life. Without God's word, the light for one's feet and therefore one's journey, life becomes uncertain and without purpose. If you follow God's map on your journey, He promises to travel with you. God is your travel companion.

DAY 158

June 07

Your word is a lamp to my feet
And a light for my path

Psalm 119:105

PSALM 119:105

Anyone who has ever walked along a dark path, with a lamp as the sole source of light, knows that only the step they are about to take can be clearly seen. Everything else beyond that circle of yellowish-orange glow is darkened, and hard to make out. If you look behind you, you see only darkness. If you hold the lamp above your head, you cannot see the ground in front of you in any great detail- but you can see a little further around you to some extent. However, if you look right where you are about to place your next step, you can see remarkable detail.

That is exactly how it is with the Lord. He guides us step by step. He never lets us down. He protects us from any danger. He carries us through the hard times by taking us one step at a time. If we look too far ahead, we don't see things clearly. When we look behind, there is only darkness. If we raise the lamp in an attempt to see things further away, they become indistinct. But if we place it in the normal position, we clearly see the ground one step in front of us.

We only need to take the next step – and as we take that one step towards God, Jesus will be walking right beside us, also taking that step. But, we have to take the first step- then God does the rest.

DAY 159

June 08

By this will all men know that you are my disciples
If you have love for one another

John 13:35

JOHN 13:35

Martin Luther King, Jr. famously said that "Peace is not the absence of war but the presence of justice."

Our world changes when justice prevails. When we love each other, despite our differences, justice and peace become part of our reality. When we work for justice and equality, we begin to live in accordance with the love Jesus commanded us to show one another.

For Jesus, love did not mean a sweet sentimental feeling. It meant action. It meant actively loving – putting one's love into real world activities. We so often draw lines about who we will love and who we deem less deserving of our love. It happens in the hearts and minds of individuals, and sadly, also in the church. But the way Jesus loved was the precursor to Christianity. As He loved, that love spread within His inner circle, and it continued to spread - as long as the loving was done in His name.

This act of loving others is a distinguishing mark of a follower of Christ. Often, as Christians today, we do not embody this commandment, and this weakens the power of the Church of God.

Jesus makes it abundantly clear – if we want to be recognised as His followers, we have to love one another - "Let me give you a new commandment: Love one another. In the same way I loved you, you love one another. This is how everyone will recognize that you are my disciples – when they see the love you have for each other."
(John 13:34-35)

DAY 160

June 09

As the Father has loved me,
So have I loved you. Now remain in my love.

John 15:9

ALMOST THERE

JOHN 15:9

Even with an understanding of love, we often find it difficult to overcome barriers to love. These barriers arise from our past experiences – the hurts, wounds, rejections, and disappointments that left us unable to give, or receive, true love.

The key to overcoming these barriers can be summed up in one word – forgiveness. By asking forgiveness from those whom we have offended – beginning with God – and then forgiving those who have offended us, we move beyond the cycle of bitterness, and enter into the realm of God's true love.

Our own self-centred desires that give rise to pride, envy, jealousy and conceit, often separate us from God's true love. This barrier of self can only be overcome by turning away from sin and asking God to forgive our selfish desires and actions.

As we humble ourselves before the Lord and receive His forgiveness, we find the freedom to look beyond our own needs and the willingness to reach out to those around us.

DAY 161

June 10

"A new commandment I give unto you,
That you love one another;
As I have loved you, that you
also love one another."

John 13:34

JOHN 13:34

Genuine love – it's something all of us want, but many never find. All around us we see the endless pursuit of love. We look for it everywhere - in our homes and families, in friendships, dating relationships, marriage and religion.

But what is this elusive thing called love? It is most often described in terms of feelings. However, true love – what the New Testament writers called "agape love"- is not based on feelings at all. "Agape love" can change your life and set you free – and all it begins with a decision you must make.

"Agape love" is the decision to consider the needs of others ahead of our own needs - to live sacrificially; to give without demanding a return; to overlook an offense. Most of all, it is a decision to receive, and to respond to, God's love. All our efforts to love others will not bear fruit unless we are responding to His love – "We love because He first loved us." (1John 4:19)

DAY 162

June 11

Then Jesus spoke to them again, saying,
"I am the light of the world.
He who follows me shall not walk in darkness,
But have the light of life."

John 8:12

JOHN 8:12

Following Jesus is the condition of two promises found in John 8:12.

Firstly, His followers will never walk in darkness- which is a reference to the assurance of salvation we enjoy. As true followers of Christ, as followers of the Light, we will never follow the way of sin, never live in a state of continually sinning (1 John1:5-7). Instead, we repent of our sin in order to stay close to the Light of the world.

The second promise is that we will reflect the "Light of Life." Just as Jesus came as the Light of the world, He commands us to be "lights" too. (Matthew 5:14-16) Believers are commanded to reflect the Light of Christ so that all can see it in us and believe. The Light is evident to others by the good deeds we do in faith, and through the power of the Holy Spirit. We are expected to be credible witnesses in the world – witnesses who prove to be faithful, God-fearing, trustworthy, sincere, earnest and honest in all that we do.

DAY 163

June 12

"As long as I am in the world,
I am the light of the world."

John 9:5

JOHN 9:5

A famous poem by Cardinal John Henry Newman begins, "Lead, kindly Light, amid the encircling gloom. Lead thou me on."

Light is beautiful and mysterious – like God. It is also a perfect analogy for Jesus.

Light helps us see things – Jesus gives us the truth about God, about life, our origin, and our destiny. Light guides us as we travel – Jesus guides us safely through life to our heavenly home. Light promotes growth and life – Jesus brings us everlasting life. Light warms and comforts- Jesus welcomes us and calms us. Light prevents crime – Jesus is goodness itself. Light dispels darkness, which stands for evil – Jesus pierces the darkness of sin and death and conquers them. All the darkness in the world cannot put out one candle flame – Jesus cannot be overcome by evil.

"Night will be no more, nor will they need light from lamp or sun, for the Lord God shall give them light" (Revelation 22:5).

DAY 164

June 13

"I have come as a light into the world, that whoever believes in me should not abide in darkness"

John 12:46

JOHN 12:46

Physical light is necessary for life. The earth would change, rapidly, if there were no longer any sunlight. Plants, for example, never move away from the light – they are said to be phototrophic, drawn to the light.

In the same way, spiritual light is necessary for spiritual life. "When Jesus spoke again to the people, He said, 'I am the light of the World. Whoever follows me will never walk in darkness but have the light of life.'" (John 8:12). The allegory used by Jesus in this verse speaks of the light of His Truth, the light of His Word, the light of Eternal Life. Those who perceive the "True Light", will never walk in spiritual darkness.

In the same way as plants are drawn to the physical light, believers tend to lean towards spiritual things – towards fellowship, prayer, the Word of God. "Let your light shine before men, that they may see your good deeds and glorify your Father in heaven." (Matthew 5:16)

In declaring to be the Light of the World, Jesus was claiming that He is the exclusive source of spiritual life. No other source of spiritual truth is available to mankind. "I am the way and the truth and the life. No one comes to the Father except through me." (John 14:6)

DAY 165

June 14

I will make you the light of the nations so that my salvation may reach to the ends of the earth.

Isaiah 49:6

ISAIAH 49:6

In the Gospel of John, Jesus is called "the true light, which gives light to everyone" (John 1:9). Throughout the New Testament, the followers of Jesus are called to be lights in the darkness. As believers, we are expected to shine "so that my salvation may reach to the ends of the earth."

Being a light sounds great, but it is also a bit abstract. How, exactly, do we become this brilliant beacon to people all around us? One sure way is to guard our tongue. The Bible calls the tongue "a restless evil, full of deadly poison." (James 3:8) Words are powerful and can be used for good, as well as, for bad. "Let no corrupting talk come out of your mouths, but only such as is good for building up, as fits the occasion, that it may give grace to those who hear." (Ephesians 4:29) This verse should become our constant companion!

Another way is to pay careful attention to our form of entertainment. Where do we go for fun? What movies do we watch, and what kind of music do we listen to? It might be pertinent to ask if we would go to the same places, watch the same things, or listen to the same music, if Jesus were sitting right next to us. In the same vain, use social media wisely. People watch what we post, whether they interact with our posts or not. What we say, think, and do is a reflection of our true character – "Do not be conformed to this world." (Romans 12:2)

We can also reflect the light of Christ by being mindful of others- considering their needs and helping to meet them. We reflect His light when we encourage instead of criticize, by being patient, and giving others the benefit of the doubt.

When you encounter a difficult person, remember, that they were made and loved by God.

Above all, "Treat others the same way you want them to treat you." (Luke 6:31)

DAY 166

June 15

Love is as strong as death...
Many waters cannot quench love;
Rivers cannot wash it away.

Song of Solomon 8:7

SONG OF SOLOMON 8:7

Have you ever thought about the true definition of love? I have a strong notion that the majority of us will get it wrong. The Bible tells us that "God demonstrated His love for us in that while we were yet sinners Christ died for us." (Romans 5:8) Love transcends situations, it looks beyond faults and appeals to the levels of our character that are beyond the surface we see with the natural eye.

Love is the mother who continues to look for her lost child long after the authorities have told her all hope is gone. It is the father that yearns for reconciliation even though he keeps getting rejected. And, it is the child, struggling to turn from wickedness and temptations, continually fighting the demons that attempt to lead him down the path of loneliness and uncertainty.

When we have love for someone or something, there is nothing that can stop, or prevent it, from being manifested. Paul tells us about the depth and importance of love in the 13th chapter of his first letter to the Church in Corinth – "If I give all I possess to the poor and give over my body to hardship that I may boast, but do not have love, I gain nothing." (1 Corinthians 13:3) Here we are reminded that love has to be the foundation of our actions. We cannot allow what we do to be derived from things that are not of love, and, therefore, are meaningless ventures through this life.

One who is full of love is priceless – "Many waters cannot quench love; rivers cannot wash it away."(Song of Solomon 8:7) Love is the most important thing that we have to obtain. The Word says that God is love, and, so, in obtaining love, we obtain God – and that is exactly why it cannot be quenched.

DAY 167

June 16

Be happy young man while you are young, and let your heart give you joy In the days of your youth follow the ways of your heart and whatever your eyes see, but know that for all these things God will bring you to judgement.

Ecclesiastes 11:9

ECCLESIASTES 11:9

George Bernard Shaw said, "Youth is such a wonderful thing it is a shame to waste it on young people."

Youth is a time to plan, to try new things, to explore new opportunities, new adventures. It is the time to seize the moment and to follow your desires.

But – there is always a "but". Ultimately there must be an accounting – "For God will bring every deed into judgement, including every hidden thing, whether it is good or evil." (Ecclesiastes 12:14) Although there are great open doors of opportunity set before you that you will not have later on in life, you need to remember to enter them with the realization that you have to make wise choices. You must attempt to deny yourself the pleasures of sinful attractions; you must make choices in the light of what ultimately will be the evaluation of your life.

Youth in itself is empty. It is not the vitality that brings satisfaction, but having a relationship with the Living God.

Raise your children without fear and guilt and help to get rid of the Hitler in them, So you can create Mother Theresa. - Elizabeth Kubler Ross

May you live all the days of your life - Jonathan Swift

DAY 168
June 17

Light is shed upon the righteous
And joy on the upright in heart.

Psalm 97:11

PSALM 97:11

What is righteousness, and what does it mean to be righteous? Righteous is the perfect holiness of Christ. It is an essential attribute to the character of God. Literally, it means "One who is right." It can be seen as the polar opposite of sin.

God has many dysfunctional children – we struggle along on our spiritual journey, we hurt, we tend to do, and say, the wrong things. At times, we really try His patience and behave like the prodigal son in an emotional and intellectual sense. We drift away from God with our thoughts, feelings and actions – we get angry, impatient, and behave un-lovingly at times. And, as it says in Ephesians 4:30, there are times when we grieve the Holy Spirit.

In spite of all of this, God sees us as clothed in righteousness – "I will rejoice greatly in the Lord, my soul will exalt in my God. For he has clothed me with garments of salvation, He has wrapped me with a robe of righteousness." (Isaiah 61:10)

Although it is human, and natural, to believe that righteous living has more to do with behaviour modification than heart transformation, it actually is all about God's amazing grace. There is nothing we can do to inherit eternal life. We are told in Titus 3:5 that "He saved us, not on the basis of deeds which we have done in righteousness, but according to His mercy…"

DAY 169

June 18

Carefully determine what pleases the Lord.

Ephesians 5:10

EPHESIANS 5:10

"Freedom consists not in doing what we like,
But in having the right to do what we ought."
- Pope John Paul 2nd

How we live, day in and day out, affects our relationship with Almighty God. It is a stunning truth the Bible teaches plainly. God so cares about us as a Father, that He finds happiness in our obedience and sadness in our disobedience.

Pleasing God directly relates to our pursuit of holiness. When we say no to sin, and yes to righteousness, we are pleasing God, and he takes delight in us. Knowing that our obedience has the ability to bring happiness to the God of the Universe is incredible motivation. And knowing that our disobedience can bring sorrow and grief should keep us from treating sin lightly.

When C. S. Lewis thought about the promise of glory given to believers, he looked at how it relates to our pleasing God:

"The promise of glory is the promise, almost incredible and only possible by the work of Christ, that some of us, that any of us who really chooses….shall find approval, shall please God. To please God…. to be a real ingredient in the divine happiness… to be loved by God, not merely pitied, but delighted in as an artist delights in his work or as a father in a son – it seems impossible, a weight or a burden of glory which our thoughts can hardly sustain. But so it is. (The Weight of Glory)

Every decision that you make, every choice that you have in front of you to pursue sin, or to pursue righteousness, is a chance to bring happiness to God himself.

DAY 170

June 19

But the fruit of the Spirit is love, joy, peace, patience, kindness, goodness, faithfulness, gentleness, self-control.

Galatians 5:22

GALATIANS 5:22

Paul writes in his letter to the Galatians, "But the fruit of the Spirit is love, joy, peace, forbearance, kindness, goodness, faithfulness, gentleness and self-control. Against such things there is no law." According to Paul, these attributes sum up Christian life.

As we practice these virtues, the grace of the Holy Spirit becomes active in our lives, and our behaviour begins to align with that of Jesus. As these fruits transform us, we experience joy and recognize that happiness is rooted not in the things of this earth, but, in being believers of Christ. In a world full of chaos, violence and turmoil, we find peace that passes all understanding. We exemplify kindness and exhibit charity. When we care for those in need, we are doing God's will and allowing our behaviour to bear witness to the greatness of God.

As our faith deepens we learn to be more patient. Patience allows us to endure the hardships and difficulties we confront on a daily basis. Because of patience we are able to overcome temptations and sufferings because we know that God is ever-present. By being willing to place God first, we become more aware of His Goodness, and more conscious of our own sin.

As we grow in our spiritual life, the Holy Spirit refines our transformation by making us more generous and gentle with others. When the fruit of modesty takes root in us, our thoughts, words, and deeds, finally begin to mirror God's. Self-control helps to discipline our actions and emotions, thereby allowing us to overcome those attractions that separate us from the love of God.

The Holy Spirit and its fruits are a gift of God's love, given to those who place their faith in Jesus. But with this privilege comes great responsibility. Our lives must reflect God's goodness and love so that His message of salvation is spread to all the ends of the earth.

DAY 171

June 20

We know that we have passed from death to life Because we love our brothers

1 John 3:14

1 JOHN 3:14

"No one is born hating another person because of the colour of his skin, or his background or his religion. People learn to hate, and if they can learn to hate, they can be taught to love, for love comes more naturally to the human heart than its opposite."
- Nelson Mandela

Love, says John, is a mark that we are different from the world. 'We know that we have passed from death to life, because we love our brothers. Anyone who does not love remains in death."
(1 John 3:14)

There's an echo here of Jesus' words: "Whoever hears my word and believes him who sent me….has crossed over from death to life."
(John 5:24)

To "pass-over" or to "cross-over" figuratively means to "change from one state or condition to another state"- to "pass-on". Love from the heart is a true indication that something has changed deep within us. It is amazing that we Christians need to hear the message, the command, to love, so often – and still we don't get it. It is important that we don't let this message of love slip off our consciousness like water off a duck's back When we obey God's command to love, we choose to enter through the narrow gate, and begin our cross-over from death to life – we cement our place in eternity.

DAY 172

June 21

Even in darkness light dawns for the upright, For the gracious and compassionate and righteous man

Psalm 112:4

ALMOST THERE

PSALM 112:4

This is the message
which we have
heard from Him and
declare to you,
That God is light and in Him
is no darkness at all.
If we say that we have
fellowship with Him,
And walk in darkness, we lie
And do not practice the truth.
But if we walk in the light
as He is in the light,
We have fellowship with
one another,
And the blood of
Jesus Christ His Son
cleanses us
from all sin

- 1 John 1:5-7

DAY 173

June 22

Fragrant oil
gladdens the heart,
Friendship's sweetness
comforts the soul.

Proverbs 27:9

PROVERBS 27:9

In the New International Version of the Bible today's verse reads as follows: "Perfume and incense bring joy to the heart, and the pleasantness of a friend springs from their heartfelt advice. Do not forsake your friend or a friend of your family, and do not go to your relative's house when disaster strikes- better a neighbour nearby than a relative far away." (Proverbs 27:9-10)

What constitutes a "best friend"? Are they the ones that hang out with us at times and share a laugh or two? Are the best buddies the ones that always give positive feedback and avoid discussing the hard things, the real things, we need to be told?

According to Solomon, best friends are those who give us "heartfelt" advice. They are the friends that have the courage to take the "bull by the horns", and tell us what we need to hear – even if it hurts a little.

A true friend is one that trusts us, and that we trust in return. Solomon urges us to be available for our friend in need. And He advises that it be those same friends we turn to when we are in distress.

Christian friends must show wisdom, give wise counsel, tell the truth, be honest, be patient, be kind and forgiving. As "tall an order" as that may seem, we have the perfect example to follow – Jesus. He is our best friend and counsellor.

"One who has unreliable friends soon comes to ruin, but there is a friend who sticks closer than a brother." (Proverbs 18:24)

DAY 174

June 23

Blessed are you who hunger now, for you shall be filled. Blessed are you who weep now, for you shall laugh.

Luke 6:21

LUKE 6:21

If we want to be Children of God, we have to have a God-Centred worldview – our value system has to change. God has a different set of priorities and values to the worldly ones we have grown accustomed to. During the Sermon on the Mount, Jesus pronounced a blessing on those who are poor, hungry, weeping and hated. How radical is that? Our world view, and paradigm, would suggest that the rich, happy, and liked, are the ones who are blessed. Jesus is not saying that all poor people are blessed. He is, however, saying that His poor disciples are blessed. But their poverty is accompanied by grace - being poor in worldly possessions, but rich towards God. Jesus is declaring a blessing on His disciples because they have made certain sacrifices, from a worldly standard, in order to invest in eternity. They chose to forsake earthly treasures in lieu of heavenly ones – this is Christ-Centred Poverty.

Followers of Christ often need to make extreme choices in order to follow Him – this was especially true in the first century. To be His disciple often meant going hungry. Jesus encourages us to keep going and reminds us that the day is coming when God will forever satisfy us with riches untold, and that we will never be hungry again – this is Christ-Centred Hunger. When our daily life causes sadness, we need to remember that "though our outer nature is wasting away, our inner nature is being renewed day by day. For this slight momentary affliction is preparing for us an eternal weight of glory beyond all comparison, as we look not to the things that are seen but to the things that are unseen. For the things that are seen are transient, but the things that are unseen are eternal." (2 Corinthians 4:16-18)

Christ-Centred Sadness does not mean that everyone who weeps is blessed – it does mean, that if we place our trust in Jesus, He will dry our tears and comfort us until we find our rest.

DAY 175

June 24

"A good man out of the good treasure of his heart brings forth good; and an evil man out of the evil treasure of his heart brings forth evil." For out of the abundance of the heart, His mouth speaks.

Luke 6:45

LUKE 6:45

The Bible refers to the heart as the centre of a person's being – "The heart – it is the wellspring of life" (Proverbs 4:23). It is critically important.

When we have an emotionally painful experience, our heart aches! When we see the person we love, our heart flutters! It is the core of who we are – our personality, feelings, hopes, dreams and motivations. In His Sermon on the Mount (Luke 6:43), Jesus presents us with a simple fact: Trees bear fruit – that's what they do. And, just like trees can't help bearing fruit, our hearts can't help but bear fruit too. Jesus also states another simple fact – "each tree is known by its own fruit." In the same way, our heart affects our fruit – what we treasure in our heart, comes out of our mouth.

We produce good fruit when we care more about the Kingdom of God than the riches of the earth. Good fruit involves suffering "on account of the Son of Man" (Luke 6:22), loving our enemies, and taking sober account of our own sin before pointing out another's .And, having good fruit, helps us accept the pain, hardship, and tears, we suffer on this earth because we know that, one day, God will wipe away all tears and turn all sorrow into gladness.

DAY 176

June 25

For in it the righteousness
of God is revealed
From faith to faith;
As it is written "The just
shall live by faith."

Romans 1:17

ROMANS 1:17

"The just shall live by faith" – The Bible describes faith as "the conviction of the truth of God's Word that leads a person to obedience."

So, just how do the just live by faith? They believe and obey God's Word. Abel believed God's commands about sacrifice, and obeyed His instructions on how to properly sacrifice. Noah believed God's warning about a coming flood, and obeyed His instructions to build an ark. Moses believed God would deliver the Israelites, and obeyed the instructions to lead them out of Egypt.

But faith must not be confused with obedience – obedience alone, is not faith. Obeying God's instructions to love one another, to study the Bible, or to go to church, is not the same as faith. Lots of people go to church every Sunday, yet live their lives in accordance to worldly values. Many people are kind to others, but not because they believe in the existence of God. Faith accepts God's word, and the need of Jesus' death on the cross, for salvation. You can never be made righteous by obedience, but those who have truly been made right with God will live in obedience.

Faith is more than acceptance of a fact, or a personal opinion about something. Faith is, believing the truth of God's word, so fully, that you completely obey it.

Obedience to God's word is the fruit of true faith.

DAY 177

June 26

Love does no harm to a neighbour; Therefore love is the fulfilment of the law.

Romans 13:10

ROMANS 13:10

In the Gospels, Jesus says that the greatest two commandments are "to love the Lord with all our heart, soul, mind, and strength and, to love our neighbours as ourselves" – (Matthew 22:37-40) and (Mark 12:29-31). The Apostle Paul, also, on more than one occasion, said that the whole law is summed up by that one statement: "Love your neighbour as yourself" (Romans 13:9).

So how do we live out this command? Love is not simply a sentimental, fleeting feeling that we have. When Jesus says that we must love our neighbour as ourselves – and implying that everyone is our neighbour – we must consider how we love ourselves. We all love ourselves when it comes to fulfilling our needs. When we are hungry, we look for food. When we are tired, we look for a place to rest or to sleep. We love ourselves by looking for ways to meet all our needs.

Therefore, loving our spouse could mean sitting down, and patiently listening, when they have a need to talk about whatever is troubling them. Loving our children could mean helping to find the best way for them, whether or not they see it in the same light at the moment. Loving a colleague may mean having a desire for him to flourish, rather than trying to discredit him to make me look better. Loving a stranger could mean making sure that I am giving to the poor and marginalised in some way.

When we truly love our neighbours as we love ourselves, we will not commit adultery, we will not murder, we will not steal and we will not covet – love is an incredible thing – it is "the fulfilment of the law."

DAY 178

June 27

For you were once darkness,
But now you are light in the
Lord. Walk as children of light.

Ephesians 5:8

EPHESIANS 5:8

"To walk in the light" is a common metaphor in Christian culture, and is often taken to mean "acting correctly."

However, in the New Testament, "walking in the light" is directly linked to following Jesus, who said, "I am the light of the world. He who follows me shall not walk in darkness, but have the light of life." (John 8:12)

To "walk" means to live your life. One's lifestyle, or way of life, can be considered a "walk". The word can also denote progress. Walking is related to growth – it means moving forward, or taking steps towards maturity.

"Light", in the Bible, can be seen as a symbol for life, happiness, righteousness, or understanding. Light comes from God, the "Father of the heavenly lights" (James 1:17). And so, if we put it all together, "walking in the light", means growing in holiness, and maturing in our faith, as we follow Jesus.

As children of God, we are expected to live in the light God gives: "Now you are light in the Lord. Walk as children of the light." When we walk in the light, we cannot walk in darkness. Sin is left in the shadows as we let our light "shine before men." (Matthew 5:16)

DAY 179

June 28

And we know that all things
work together for good
To those who love God,
To those who are called
According to his purpose

Romans 8:28

ROMANS 8:28

Life is filled with disappointments, grief, difficulties, trial and strife. These things have touched all of us. It is the human experience. But in the midst of all the suffering, we cling to a promise found in Paul's letter to the Romans – "For we know that in all things God works for the good of those who love Him, who have been called according to His purpose." Christians find comfort, encouragement, and hope, in these words. We gain assurance that God is on our side. We find hope that situations and circumstances are heading in a positive direction. We turn to it when we are feeling down, and we offer it to others to lift them up.

But this is not a message of prosperity, or of security. It is not simply a message of wish-granting or prayer-request granting. Paul isn't promising safety, or uninhibited good times. We will endure hardships, sadness, pain, illness, and other afflictions of this world. The point being made is that we can count on God to use a bad situation for good. The pain and suffering might create opportunities for good in us and in the world. It might deepen our faith, or open our eyes. Maybe it inspires us with a new passion, or brings a new perspective. The "good" does not mean our happiness, physical comfort, or material abundance. It refers to our spiritual condition and sure hope of one day sharing in God's glory. God is working through the circumstances of our lives to make us like Jesus and to bring us to eternal glory.

DAY 180

June 29

"If you abide in me, and my words abide in you, you will ask what you desire, and it shall be done for you."

John 15:7

JOHN 15:7

Christianity is far more than having certain beliefs, or adopting correct behaviours. As children of the Living God, we enter into a union with Him that changes our status – we have a right standing with God. We have a righteousness that comes by faith, and that faith justifies us (Philippians 3:7-9). But, not only do we have a union with God, we also have communion with Him. We have access to a life-giving, soul-thrilling, joy-producing communion with God, through Christ (1 John 1:3). Jesus invites us to abide in Him. But how do we do that, and what does it mean? A few descriptions from some godly individuals might help us get the picture: John Piper says, "Hour-by hour abiding in Jesus means hour-by hour trusting Him to meet all your needs and to be all our treasure."

J.C Ryle explains, "To abide in Christ means to keep up a habit of constant close communion with Him – to be always leaning on Him, resting on Him, pouring out our hearts to Him, and using Him as our fountain of life and strength, as our chief companion and best friend. To have His words abiding in us is to keep His sayings and precepts continually before our memories and minds and to make them the guide of our actions and the rule of our daily conduct and behaviour".

In simple terms, I believe the essential meaning of our active abiding, is the act of receiving and trusting all that God is for us in Christ.

DAY 181

June 30

But you will receive power when the
Holy Spirit comes on you: And you will
be my witnesses in Jerusalem,
And in all Judea and Samoa,
And to the ends of the earth

Acts 1:8

ACTS 1:8

In his letter to the Corinthians, Paul addresses the issue of Christian witnessing: "And I, brethren, when I came to you, did not come with excellence of speech or wisdom declaring to you the testimony of God. For I determined not to know anything among you except Jesus Christ and Him crucified. I was with you in weakness, in fear, and in much trembling. And my speech and my preaching were not with persuasive words of human wisdom, but in demonstration of the Spirit and of power, that your faith should not be in the wisdom of men but in the power of God." (1 Corinthians 2:1-5)

So Paul is very clear that Christian witnessing is not about intellect or debating skills. It is merely sharing our sincere faith in Jesus – what He has personally done to change our individual lives. We are not expected to argue or debate in order to convince people in the saving power of the Cross. We are simply asked to share our experience. It can be compared to being in a courtroom – we are called to be a witness for the Gospel, not to be the lawyer, judge or jury – that is left up to God.

DAY 182-212

July

Shine Through Us

Dear Jesus, help us to spread your
fragrance everywhere we go.
Flood our souls with your spirit and life.
Penetrate and possess our whole being so utterly
that our lives may only be a radiance of yours.
Shine through us, and be so in us,
that every soul we come in contact with
may feel your presence in our soul.
Let them look up and see no
longer us but only Jesus!
Stay with us, and then we shall begin to shine
as you shine; so to shine as to be a light to others;
the light, O Jesus, will be all from you,
none of it will be ours; it will be you,
shining on others through us.
Let us thus praise you in the way you love best
by shining on those around us.
Let us preach you without preaching, not by words
but by our example, by the catching force,
the sympathetic influence of what we do,
the evident fullness of the love
our hearts bear to you. Amen.

Cardinal Newman

DAY 182

July 01

Pray without ceasing,
Give thanks in all circumstances;
For this is the will of God in Christ
Jesus for you

1 Thessalonians 5:17-18

ALMOST THERE

1 THESSALONIANS 5:17-18

How can I pray without ceasing? In his first letter to the Thessalonians, the Apostle Paul urges them to "rejoice evermore." "Pray without ceasing. In everything give thanks." The Greek word "without ceasing" means to pray continuously. How do we do that? We can't always be on our knees. With the daily demands on our busy lives, we are fortunate to kneel in prayer even a few minutes each day.

However, the context of the scriptural passage provides us with a clue – it focuses on heart attitude. "Rejoice always" is an attitude of joyfulness. Giving thanks in everything requires a mental attitude of thankfulness. The only way we can give thanks and rejoice, is through prayer. Therefore, effective prayer requires a proper heart attitude and a mental outlook of joy and thanksgiving. It expresses itself throughout the day with silent prayers of vital communication with the Lord.

An attitude of praying without ceasing means we have an ever-open heart to God's guidance. When we are always open to the teachings of the Holy Spirit – while driving, changing the baby, washing dishes, or mowing the lawn – we are ready to respond when He directs us to pray for someone or something. Praying without ceasing doesn't take away time alone in prayer with God. However, it is a joyful experience that unites us with our Saviour, and enables us to act when he lays a burden on our hearts. We can't always stop and kneel, but our heart attitude gives us the ability to be able to "pray without ceasing."

To pray is to let go and let God take over. Prayer is love in need appealing to love in power - R Moffat

DAY 183

July 02

Do not be anxious about anything,
But in everything,
By prayer and petition,
With thanksgiving,
Present your requests to God.

Philippians 4:6

ALMOST THERE

PHILIPPIANS 4:6

Most of us want to experience genuine intimacy in our relationship with God, yet this seems elusive, or difficult, to achieve. We either struggle with understanding what it means to draw near to God, or, we wrestle with the practicalities of practising an effective prayer life - which is the cornerstone of acknowledging God in our daily life.

We can only truly comprehend the value of prayer once we recognise that there are various types of prayer. There is the prayer of confession, the prayer of adoration, the prayer of thanksgiving, the prayer of supplication, the prayers of the heart, and the prayers for others. But, no matter what we are praying for, in order for it to be effective, the prayer needs to have certain qualities. It must depend on the Holy Spirit and on faith – "You can pray for anything, and if you have faith, you will receive it" (Matthew 21:22). We need to be still and wait patiently -"be still and know that I am God" (Psalm 46:10). When we grow quiet in the presence of God, and ask for His guidance, He will grant us the wisdom required to grow confident and comfortable in "presenting our request to God".

Prayer requires more of the heart than of the tongue
- Adam Clarke

DAY 184

July 03

Be joyful in hope,
patient in affliction,
faithful in prayer.

Romans 12:12

ROMANS 12:12

Joy, patience, and faithfulness, are all fruits of the Spirit. Also sometimes referred to as the "Triplet of Graces", they are the cornerstone of Jesus' character.

As Christians, we need to live a daily life of visible imitation of Jesus. That means we need to let these fruits of the Spirit flow through us- by living according to His word and constantly renewing our minds to the truth of His word.

"In his great mercy he has given us new birth into a living hope through the resurrection of Jesus Christ from the dead, and into an inheritance that can never perish, spoil or fade"
(1 Peter 1:3-4)

"The trying of your faith worketh patience. But let patience have her perfect work, that ye may be perfect and entire, wanting nothing"
(James 1:3-4)

"The prayer of a righteous man is powerful and effective"
(James 5:16)

DAY 185

July 04

Do not be impatient in prayer

Ecclesiasticus 7:10

ALMOST THERE

ECCLESIASTICUS 7:10

"Impatient" means "having or showing a tendency to be quickly irritated or provoked." Most of us have been irritated in heavy traffic, or when we have to wait for someone or something. Standing in line at the checkout in a grocery store, or waiting for food in a restaurant, are two examples that almost anyone can identify with – our lives are simply too rushed to have time to "wait".

"Be still before the Lord and wait patiently for him." (Psalm 37:7) All too often our prayers are not answered because we cannot seem to be able to wait on the Lord. Impatience wreaks havoc on our souls, and before we can help it, we take matters into our own hands and miss the opportunity to really experience God's power in our lives. But, waiting requires faith - faith that God really will answer our prayer. "But when he asks, he must believe and not doubt, because he who doubts is like a wave of the sea, blown and tossed by the wind." (James 1:6-7)

When you pray, rather let your heart
Be without words
Than your words without heart
- John Bunyan

DAY 186

July 05

Ask, and it will be given to you;
Seek, and you will find;
Knock and it will be opened to you.
For everyone who asks receives,
And he who seeks finds,
And to him who knocks it will be opened.

Matthew 7:7-8

MATTHEW 7:7-8

In Galatians 5:7, the apostle Paul laments: "You were running well. Who hindered you?" Many of us relate to these words during the course of our spiritual journey – we eagerly set off to do God's will, only to be blighted by a lack of perseverance. Jesus describes a similar tendency- in the parable of the sower- when he describes the one who "hears the word and immediately receives it with joy, yet he has no root in himself, but endures for a while" (Matthew 13:20).Perseverance, in the Bible, describes a quality in the believer and, is a fruit of the Holy Spirit at work in our life – "keep alert with all perseverance, making supplication for all the saints" (Ephesians 6:18). As Christians, we are often called upon to persevere in the face of opposition or trials, but, mainly in prayer.

During the Sermon on the Mount, Jesus is focussing on perseverance in prayer. He urges us to "ask, seek and knock." God wants us to bring our needs to him in prayer. Just as we would ask our earthly father for help, God wants us to trust him to provide and take care of us. We are expected to actively seek him so that we can draw closer to him – "You will seek me and find me, when you seek me with all your heart" (Jeremiah 29:13). Knocking is persistent asking and seeking, and denotes a seriousness in our searching for God's will.

So, when we pray, we need to be a supplicant, a seeker, and we need to be serious. True prayer demands all three.

DAY 187

July 06

Again I say to you that if two of you agree on earth concerning anything that they ask, it will be done for them by my Father in heaven. For where two or three are gathered together in my name, I am there in the midst of them.

Matthew 18:19-20

MATTHEW 18:19-20

In trying to understand what Jesus means in Matthew 18:20, we have to look at the context – the surrounding verses, the passage before and after, as well as the background of the book and the author. The heading for Matthew 18:15-20 is, "If your brother sins against you," or "Dealing with Sin in the Church." So, it becomes clear that this passage is about sin and discipline in the Christian community, specifically the church.

So, how do we know when, or how, to correct a brother or sister in Christ? Most people, including Christians, do not like being told that what they are doing is not acceptable to God. And, that is sad, because a rebuke can be good for the soul. "The wise of heart will receive correction" (Proverbs 10:8). Scripture, thankfully, gives us the answer – correct when the salvation of a brother or sister is in question.

Jesus taught us to correct one another because He understood the danger of unrepentant sin. In Matthew 18:15-18, He lays out the process for us. He does not reveal the nature of the sin, but He is quiet clear that repentance from sin is needed to remain in fellowship with God, and the community. Firstly, we should approach our brother or sister, who has strayed, alone. If that fails to bear fruit, we should ask for help from a few other believers, and then, finally, we should involve the whole church.

No one enjoys confrontation. As a result, going after, and seeking to restore a brother or sister that has fallen into sin, is one of the most neglected ministries in the body of Christ. If we are to be faithful to Jesus, we have to grow in our ability and willingness to perform this vital part of our discipleship.

DAY 188

July 07

"And whatever you ask in my name, that I will do, That the Father may be glorified in the Son If you ask anything in my name, I will do it."

John 14:13-14

JOHN 14:13-14

Once again, in order to understand Jesus' statement as is, we have to be clear about the time, the circumstance, and the audience. Jesus is talking to his closest disciples just prior to him being arrested and hanged for his teachings. He is preparing them to go out and continue his work when he is gone. He wasn't promising that he would give them anything they wanted – like fame or wealth. Rather, he was trying to communicate that he would be there to guide them, spiritually, regardless of how difficult the circumstances become.

Over and over again in scripture we come across the phrase "in my name." Demons were cast out in his name, healing occurred in his name, salvation comes in his name, we are to be baptised in his name.

But what does it mean to pray in Jesus' name? It means admitting the bankruptcy of our own name – we no longer act in our name, but in his. It means identifying with the person of Jesus Christ – He has given us his name, and when we use it, we acknowledge that we belong to him. We recognise that we are his representatives on earth, and have to uphold his morals and standards. Therefore, we pray with authority, only in accordance to his will, as revealed in this world. That is why prayers asking for things that are contrary to his word, can never be answered

DAY 189

July 08

He will respond to the prayer of the destitute; He will not despise their plea.

Psalm 102:17

ALMOST THERE

PSALM 102:17

As Christians, we draw strength from these words of King David. It is the cry of the troubled soul wrestling with despair and confusion that moves the loving heart of God. God assures us that prayer is our way of connecting with Him, in all life's circumstances, and, that "He hears us." (1 John 5:14)

"I have heard your prayer; I have seen your tears. Behold, I will heal you." (2 Kings 20:5) It is often difficult to see how God has heard and answered our prayer. In our human understanding of things, it might seem that He has paid no heed to our plight or request. But, if we wait faithfully on the Lord, He will respond to our prayer – and whatever He ordains for us will be good and according to His purpose.

When you Pray, God listens
When you Listen, God talks
When you Believe, God works.
- Unknown

DAY 190

July 09

So what shall I do?
I will pray with my spirit, but I
will also pray with my mind;
I will sing with my spirit,
But I will also sing with my mind.

1 Corinthians 14:15

ALMOST THERE

1 CORINTHIANS 14:15

According to Richard Rohr, St Paul's theology on the Holy Spirit is best summarized in Romans 8:16: "The Spirit joins with our spirit to bear common witness that we are children of God." Paul understands that Jesus left us his Indwelling Spirit as a permanent, strengthening gift. The Spirit gives us a source of true inner knowledge whereby we know spiritual things for ourselves.

However, certain gifts of the Spirit are often only for our own edification. St Paul wants us to engage our minds when we pray and worship, especially in public. As Christians, and apostles of Christ, we are expected to aid the spiritual growth and understanding of our fellow believers. Through praying and asking for the gift of prophecy, we will be better equipped to pray with our minds. "Praying with your mind" entails studying, and understanding, the scriptures in order to walk closer to God. When we pray with the mind, we guide and teach people in the Way of the Lord.

DAY 191

July 10

"And in that day you will ask me nothing. Most assuredly, I say to you, Whatever you ask the Father in My name He will give you."

John 16:23

JOHN 16:23

Are we to understand that God has given us carte blanche to ask anything of Him and He must oblige? We might like to think so, but 1 John 5:14 qualifies what He will grant: "Now this is the confidence that we have in Him that if we ask anything according to His will, He hears us." Real prayer is communion with God, and what is needed for communion, are common thoughts between His mind and ours. King David set us a great example: "As for me... I shall be fully satisfied when I awake to find myself beholding your form and having sweet communion with you." (Psalm 17:15) This is the heart of what prayer is all about. It is about seeking God's face, and enjoying "sweet communion with Him."

So often we are inclined to think that the only answer God can give our prayers is "yes". But "no", "wait" or "not now", is also an answer, (of love), from our Heavenly Father when we ask Him for things that are not really for our good, or for His glory. Bill Hybels writes - "If the request is wrong God says "No". If the timing is wrong God says "Slow". If you are wrong God says "Grow". But if the request is right and the timing is right and you are right, God says "Go".

In the Garden of Gethsemane, Jesus prayed – "let this cup pass from me."(Luke 22:42) This is the only request He made that was denied, and, it teaches us that there are some things we ask for – good as they may seem – that are simply not God's best for us. Jesus knew it was the Father's will that He should suffer on our behalf - He asked anyway. Some of our prayers may fall into this category. But, just as in Jesus' case, God sees the bigger picture – the ultimate outcome will be life out of death.

DAY 192

July 11

Wait for the Lord;
Be strong and take heart
And wait for the Lord.

Psalm 27:14

ALMOST THERE

PSALM 27:14

What does it mean to wait on the Lord? The command to wait on the Lord is found repeatedly throughout the old and new testament. As Christians, we are expected to wait on Him even if it seems as if He is reluctant to intervene or to answer our prayer – "I am worn out calling for help; my throat is parched. My eyes fail, looking for my God" (Psalm 69:3).

In the Bible, the word wait denotes hope and expectation, but, it necessitates complete dependence on God, and a willingness to accept the timing of His plan for us. Psalm 23:2-3, provides us with a lesson on waiting. It teaches us to be still and to rest in the Lord – "He makes me lie down in green pastures, He leads me beside quiet waters, He refreshes my soul."

Being still means that we have let go of our own agenda and no longer depend on our own strength and ingenuity. When we perfect the art of waiting, we gain confident assurance that, regardless of the difficulties and suffering we face in this life, God will never leave us stranded. This doesn't mean that we should spend our time doing nothing – we should continue doing the work he has given us to do. "As the eyes of slaves look to the hand of their master, as the eyes of a female slave look to the hand of her mistress, so our eyes look to the Lord our God, till he shows us his mercy" (Psalm 123:2).

DAY 193

July 12

Your love is better than life itself.

Psalm 63:3

ALMOST THERE

PSALM 63:3

Love suffers long and is kind;
Love does not envy;
Love does not parade itself;
is not puffed up;
Does not behave rudely,
does not seek its own;
Is not provoked, thinks no evil;
Does not rejoice in iniquity,
but rejoice in the truth;
Bears all things,
believes all things,
Hopes all things,
endures all things.

1 Corinthians 13:4-7

DAY 194

July 13

Now faith is being sure of what we hope for And certain of what we do not see.

Hebrews 11:1

HEBREWS 11:1

Faith is the foundation of our Christian life
– but how do we define it?

If we look at the passages in Scripture with reference to the phrase, "by faith", there is a noticeable common thread. All the people mentioned had one thing in common – they had simply taken God at His word, and obeyed His command. And they were remembered for their faith.

God told Noah to build an ark because He was going to cause a flood – Noah built the ark. God told the aged Sarah that she would conceive a son – "She considered Him faithful who had promised." (Hebrews 11:11) She took God at His word. The centurion told Jesus, "Just say the word and my servant will be healed." (Matthew 8:8)

Faith is simply taking God at His word:

"Heaven and earth will pass away, but my words shall not pass away. (Matthew 24:35)

"The word of the Lord abides forever." (1Peter 1:25)

Faith is to believe what you do not see;
The reward of faith is to see what you believe
- St Augustine of Hippo

DAY 195

July 14

Since you have asked for this
And not for long life or health for yourself,
Nor have you asked for the death of your enemies
But for discernment in administering justice,
I will do what you ask.

1 Kings 3:11-12

1 KINGS 3:11-12

In the Gospel of Matthew we get taught "to seek ye first the kingdom of God, and His righteousness; and all these things shall be added unto you." (Matthew 6:33) This means we should place more emphasis on our spiritual life than on things of the earth. The salvation that is inherent in the Kingdom of God is of greater value than all the riches and pleasures that the world can offer. When we make God's business a priority – seeking his salvation, living in obedience to Him, and sharing the good news of the Kingdom with others – then, Jesus promised, he will take care of all our daily business and needs.

In the same way, our prayer life should not focus exclusively on "self". Just as Solomon asked God for the ability to discern between right and wrong, we too, should pray for the wisdom to correctly interpret the Word of God. Only then can we guide our neighbours towards the salvation of God. It is hard to always ignore our own pain and hardship - Jesus wants us to lay our requests before Him. But, it is in the "losing of self", and acknowledging the sovereignty of God over our life, that we gain eternal life and the assurance that all our earthly wants will be taken care of.

Prayer is a wine that makes good the heart of a people
St Bernhard of Clairvaux

DAY 196

July 15

Rather think of yourself with sober judgement, in accordance with the measure of faith God has given you.

Romans 12:3

ROMANS 12:3

It is common human behaviour to measure ourselves against others. We do it all the time – do I make more money, do I live in a better home and more upmarket suburb, is my car more expensive, do I wear better clothes, am I physically more attractive? We constantly have the need to prove that we are more successful than our peers.

St Paul is well aware of this human failing and cautions us to apply "sober judgement." We are quick to make excuses for ourselves, but readily judge our neighbours harshly. Applying sober judgement involves staring at ourselves in the mirror of reality with brutal honesty. Are we measuring up to the role that God wants us to play in His Holy Church? We have been uniquely made by God to fill a specific purpose based on the gifts He has given us. We all form part of the body of Christ, and we all contribute towards its peace and unity. Our sins differ and our gifts differ, but, we all receive the same mercy and forgiveness through the blood of Christ.

And so, regular reality checks are necessary. Am I measuring up to my goals? Am I honest with myself about what I need to change, and what I need to seek forgiveness for? Am I willing to confront those that have harmed me and try to reconcile? Do I spend enough time in conversation with God?

As we let go of arrogance God builds His love in us and we become willing participants in building His Church on Earth.

DAY 197

July 16

For the one who is in you
is greater than the one
Who is in the world

1 John 4:4

1 JOHN 4:4

In this passage, "he that is in the world", means either the devil, or false teachers propagating false doctrines.

However, for us, as Christians today, it can also mean the attraction to, and accumulation of, worldly things. When money, fame, and power, rule our life, Jesus slips out of the back door. When life is good, God is forgotten. But Jesus cautions that worldly pleasures and wealth are only temporary.

Through our baptism, God lives within us. He will never forsake us. It is up to us to never forget Him. When things are going according to plan and life is good, let us thank and acknowledge Him for his role in it. When things are tough and our life is falling apart, let us call on Him and believe that "the one who is in you is greater than the one who is in the world."

Jesus taught us that we should be "in this world, but not part of this world." (John 17:15-16)

Let our light so shine that others may want to follow it.

HEBREWS 3:8

The American poet, Archibald MacLeish, wrote, "The great crime against life is not to feel."

God wants us to be sensitive to the promptings of the Holy Spirit within us. He wants us to be aware of, and sensitive to, the pain and needs of those around us. He wants us to notice the destitute, the elderly, and the abused. He wants us to comfort those who mourn. He wants us to follow Jesus' example of love, kindness, honesty and forgiveness.

But, we so easily get caught up in our own little world, forgetting that this is only our temporary home. Forgetting, that our treasures are stored in heaven and, that God our Father, frequently, in scripture, cautioned us to "harden not our hearts."

In the words of Mother Teresa - "Do good- Give the world the best you have" And, if we do, our Father will reward us with everlasting life, and a happiness that surpasses all understanding.

DAY 199

July 18

He said to them, "Go into the world and proclaim the gospel to every creature."

Mark 16:15

MARK 16:15

Jesus commanded his disciples to share the teachings of the gospel with everyone and every nation. As His representatives on earth today, we have been handed the mandate to guide and instruct our neighbours in the "way of the cross."

But not all of us are good teachers or preachers. Jesus accepts this, and, has given us all our own unique talents and strengths. In using these talents to serve the Lord, we honour this decree.

Doctors and nurses- showing compassion, easing pain, and helping people to maintain dignity in the face of suffering and impending death- reveal the light of Christ.

Business people- donating funds to feed the poor or help disaster management- reveal the light of Christ.

Ordinary people- taking time to visit the elderly, whether to provide some company, deliver meals, or help them bath and get dressed- reveal the light of Christ.

"Lord, make me an instrument of your peace. Where there is hatred, let me sow love; where there is injury, pardon; where there is doubt, faith; where there is despair, hope; where there is darkness, light; where there is sadness, joy." - St. Francis of Assisi

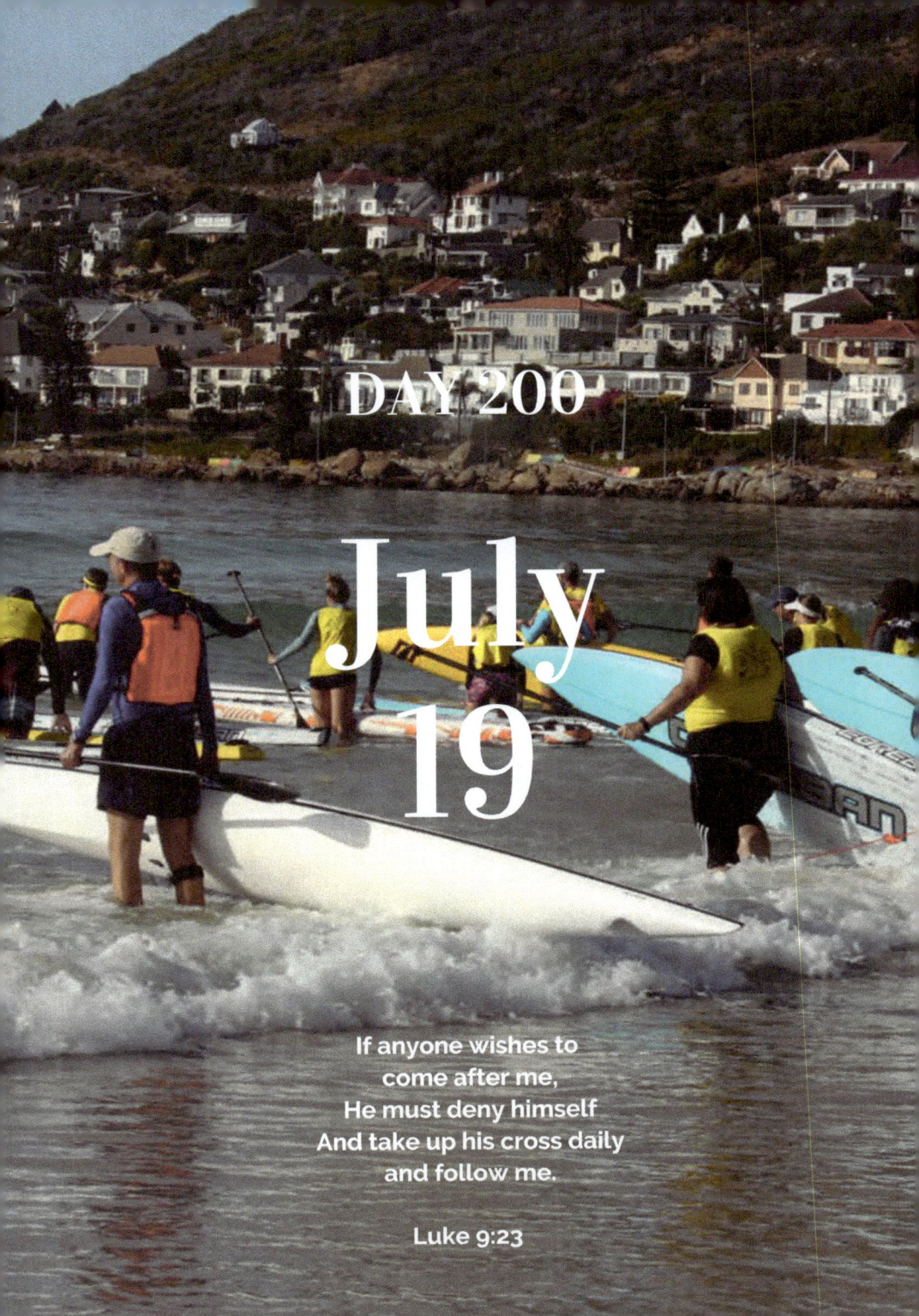

DAY 200

July 19

If anyone wishes to
come after me,
He must deny himself
And take up his cross daily
and follow me.

Luke 9:23

LUKE 9:23

Jesus tells us that if we believe in Him, we must become his disciples and follow Him. Every believer is called to yield to Jesus as Lord and dedicate himself to furthering His Kingdom, in accordance with the gifts He has entrusted to us. By placing these gifts in His hands, and allowing Him to use them as he sees fit, we discover that we make a difference.

By denying ourselves, we give up living for our own selfish interests, and embrace living for the sake of Christ and the gospel. Jesus reminds us, "If you want to save your life, you will lose it. But if you lose your life for the sake of Christ you will save it." (Matthew 16:25)

Following Jesus is a lifelong commitment and each day presents a new challenge. We make mistakes as we grow – but always in the knowledge that God is love, and quick to forgive and to forget.

"Getting rid of the 'self-life' is like peeling an onion: layer upon layer"   A T Pierson

DAY 201

July 20

What I say to you in the darkness,
Speak in the light;
What you hear whispered,
Proclaim on the housetops.

Matthew 10:27

MATTHEW 10:27

How do we listen to, and hear, the voice of God? As believers, it is something we need to do in order to live victorious Christian lives. However, it isn't easy to communicate with God, and, hearing His voice seems like an insurmountable challenge.

However, it is not impossible. According to Hebrews 4:12-"the word of God is alive and active. Sharper than a double-edged sword, it penetrates even to dividing soul and spirit, joints and marrow; it judges the thoughts and attitudes of the heart." So, it seems as if God has created us in such a way that we can hear Him. We can hear Him every day, if only we know how.

It is up to us to make time, and to create the space, to listen. God speaks in the whispers of Scripture, and reveals himself in the darkness of early morning and evening prayer. If we actively seek God, we will find Him in the stillness of the sacred, ordinary things that fill our lives. We will find, and hear Him, in the beauty of His creation, and in the depth of His kindness, mercy and love. We are created in the image of God. If we live our lives based on His principles, we will hear His voice and proclaim His word from the housetops.

DAY 202

July 21

Do not conform yourselves to this age
But be transformed by the
renewal of your mind...

Romans 12:2

ROMANS 12:2

Conforming to the values of our time comes naturally to us. Worldly pleasures, financial gain, and material possessions, are difficult to resist in a world that places more emphasis on the secular than on the spiritual.

Yet Paul exhorts us to godly living. He urges us to be transformed by the renewal of our minds. The mind is fundamental to a Christian way of life. It allows us to discern spiritual truth.

With repentance comes the notion of a change of mind. What we know in our minds to be true forms a conviction in our hearts of that truth, and, that conviction in our hearts, translates into action.

Transforming and renewing our mind is only possible if we fill them with God's word. Jesus taught us that when he prayed to the Father- "Sanctify them in the truth; your word is truth" (John 17:17)

DAY 203

July 22

If your brother sins against you,
Go and tell him his fault
Between you and him alone

Matthew 18:15

MATTHEW 18:15

One of the things that plague most Christians is the inability to handle confrontation, disagreement, and mutual accountability, when it comes to wrongdoings or sin. We simply don't know how to live together, fight together, or stay together.

Yet, Jesus urges us to confront our brother when he sins against us. No matter how much anxiety, fear, or anger the confrontation causes, it is the way Jesus wants us to deal with it. Jesus makes it even more difficult for us because he wants us to forgive those who do us harm 70 x 7 times – God's eternal forgiveness. In other words, He is commanding us to have forgiving hearts, and to continue forgiving, with as much grace, the thousandth time as the first.

God forgives us over and over, and unless we emulate his forgiving nature, we will not experience the fullness of His love and grace.

DAY 204

July 23

I will persevere in the way of integrity.

Psalm 101:2

PSALM 101:2

Integrity stems from the Latin word "integer", which means whole and complete. So integrity requires an inner sense of "wholeness" and consistency of character. When you are whole and consistent, there is only one you. You bring the same you wherever you are, regardless of the circumstance. In other words, you "walk your talk."

Our thoughts, attitudes, and actions, need to be congruent with what we believe. Today's Psalm reminds us that we have standards to follow, and, that in following them, the joy of the Lord should ensue.

It is important to live our life authentically and to reflect, often, on how we act, or do not act, in accordance with our core beliefs and values.

"Whoever is careless with the truth in small matters cannot be trusted with important matters" - Albert Einstein

DAY 205

July 24

Then Jesus said to the crowd,
"Take care to guard against all greed,
For though one may be rich.
One's life does not consist of
possessions."

Luke 12:15

LUKE 12:15

Today's reading is the key to understanding the "parable of the rich fool", found in Luke 12:13-21. Jesus uses this parable when a man asks him to arbitrate between him and his brother. He wants Jesus to help him procure an equal share of the family inheritance, even though he is not the firstborn.

The point of the parable is twofold. We are not to devote our lives to the gathering and accumulation of wealth, and, we will not be blessed by God if we hoard our wealth and keep it for ourselves.

What happens to all our wealth when we die? It gets left to others who didn't earn it, and might not appreciate it. If money is our master, God cannot be. We earn our blessings when we focus on enriching the lives of others, and in helping to build the Kingdom of God.

If we honour God with what He has given us, He will bless us with more. According to St Paul, if God has blessed you with material wealth "set not your heart on it", and, "be rich toward God." That is the message of the "Parable of the Rich Fool."

DAY 206

July 25

Rejoice in the Lord always.

Philippians 4:4

PHILIPPIANS 4:4

Joy is one of the hallmarks of our Christian faith, and St Paul exhorts us to "rejoice in the Lord always." Obviously we all want joy in life - but can we really rejoice always? Are we expected to deny pain and sorrow? Is it a sin to feel depressed or sad? How do we continue smiling when we face financial hardships, or possible retrenchment?

What we need to recognise is that St Paul is not simply asking us to have a cheerful disposition, but, that he is commanding us to have "joy in the Lord." In the gospel, John the Baptist preached the "good news", Zephaniah says "shout for joy", and, Isaiah tells us to be "confident and unafraid." It is because of our faith in the Living God and our belief in eternal life that we are able to "rejoice always" - despite all adversity and afflictions. The more we rejoice, the more we experience God's love, and notice His hand on the rudder of our life. Rejoicing opens our eyes to His power and grace.

DAY 207

July 26

Let the peace of Christ
control your hearts....

Colossians 3:15

ALMOST THERE

COLOSSIANS 3:15

Violence, war, and news of war, are persistent in human experience. Any history, including scriptural history, seems merely to alternate from war, to brief peace, and back to war. And, if current newspapers fail to report war somewhere, it is probably by oversight, or out of weariness. The drone of violence never relents. Yet the Saviour promised peace.

Clearly then, freedom from violence in this world is not promised. But with Christ's peace comes the deep, inner assurance that all things, even our greatest sufferings, will be for our good. Just as Jesus hushed the storm with the words, "Peace, be still", and brought forth "a great calm", so can he speak peace to the troubled mind and soothe the grieving heart.
- George S Tate

We do not live in peace with others because we are not at peace with ourselves; We do not have peace with ourselves because we do not have peace with God.
-Thomas Merton

DAY 208

July 27

If someone says, "I love God."
And hates his brother, he is a liar;
For he who does not love his brother
whom he has seen, How can he love
God whom he has not seen?

1 John 4:20

1 JOHN 4:20

"And now these three remain, faith, hope and love; but the greatest of these is love" (1 Corinthians 13:13)

Throughout the New Testament Jesus commands us to love. "Love your brother as you love yourself." Love defines who we are as Christians. Love allows us to feed the poor, look after the sick, forgive those who harm us, frees us from discrimination. Love is the cornerstone of our faith. It is in the act of loving our brothers, that we love God. Through injuring our brother, we injure God. We cannot fully submit to God if we don't accept that God is present in every person. Therefore, if we treat anyone without compassion, respect, or dignity, we are sinning in the eyes of God.

God is love and, as His children, we too, should be love.

DAY 209

July 28

Rising very early before dawn, he left
And went off to a deserted place,
Where he prayed

Mark 1:35

MARK 1:35

According to the scriptures, Jesus often sought solitude in order to pray. Quiet prayer gave Him the strength to continue His ministry, and to accomplish what He was sent to do. He was sent by God to save us from sin - by sacrificing himself on the cross. Even in His anguish, in the Garden of Gethsemane, Jesus went off by himself to pray.

Jesus placed so much emphasis on, and got so much comfort, from prayer. And yet, we are often too busy to take time out to spend in communion with God. If the Son of God needed prayer to stay focused and on track, how much more do we need it?

God wants us to have a personal relationship with him. Through prayer, we accept His invitation, and, through prayer, we grow closer to Him and learn to walk in His ways.

HEBREWS 12:2

In order to accomplish anything in life, we need to have a plan of action to help us achieve our desired goal. For example, if our goal is to run a marathon, we, firstly, need to find a coach to help formulate a training programme. We might consider joining a club- so that like-minded individuals can push us to stick to the programme, and offer advice on other aspects of training and nutrition. It would be prudent to enter races- to get used to the demands that racing and training places on our bodies. But, most importantly, it is through keeping our eyes fixed firmly on our goal, and believing in the plan of action laid out for us, that we are most likely to succeed.

The same applies to our religious life. Jesus is our leader, and He will guide us on our spiritual journey. He has given us our "plan of action", and, by following it, we will perfect our faith and find the path to eternal life. We have His teachings in the New Testament as our blueprint. We have the Church and our fellow Christians, to keep us focused and on track. We have Jesus' assurance that when we stumble and fall, He will be right there beside us. Through simply keeping our eyes "fixed on Jesus", we will achieve our ultimate goal - spending eternity with God our Father.

DAY 211

July 30

Come away by yourselves to a deserted place and rest a while.

Mark 6:31

MARK 6:31

Jesus knew the importance of going away to a deserted place for prayer and renewal. People hungered for His presence, His teachings, and His healing abilities. Because of this constant demand for His attention he had very little time for solitude and quiet contemplation- unless He removed himself from every day activities.

In the same way, we look forward to the holidays to rest and recover after a long, hard year. Work, family, and other commitments, keep us so occupied during the year that we have very little time for our own necessary solitude. The holidays provide us with part of the solution - to spend quality time with family and friends, and, to replenish our energy for the year ahead. But, our spiritual life also needs nurturing. Unless we deliberately take time out for prayer and contemplation, we run the risk of forgetting the importance of our inner life, and, our relationship with God.

"Somewhere we know that without a lonely place, our lives are in danger"
- Henri Nouwen

DAY 212

July 31

Whoever eats my flesh and drinks my blood
Remains in me and I in him

John 6:56

JOHN 6:56

Just as our physical body needs food to nourish it in order to survive, so, too, our soul needs Christ, received in faith, in order to obtain eternal life. Just as bread and meat cannot sustain us unless we eat it, we cannot enter the kingdom of God unless we believe in Jesus' death and resurrection.

Our relationship with Jesus can be likened to a marriage – where the two become "one flesh." It is the most intimate of relationships, and, it is one that allows the believer to walk, united with Jesus, in love. As Christians, we nourish our faith, and receive Jesus into our hearts, every time we partake in the Eucharist. And, by so doing, "He remains in me and I in Him."

I asked God for all things that I might have life. God said, "No, I will give you life that you may enjoy all things" - Francis Bacon

DAY 213-243

August

Disturb Us, Lord

Disturb us, Lord, when we are too well pleased with ourselves,
When our dreams have come true
Because we have dreamed too little,
When we arrive safely
Because we sailed too close to the shore.
Disturb us, Lord, when
With the abundance of things we possess
We have lost the thirst
For the waters of life;
Having fallen in love with life,
We have ceased to dream of eternity
And in our efforts to build a new earth,
We have allowed our vision
Of the new Heaven to dim
Disturb us, Lord, to dare more boldly,
To venture on wider seas
Where storms will show Your mastery;
Where losing sight of land,
We shall find the stars.
We ask you to push back
The horizons of our hopes;
And to push into the future
In strength, courage, hope, and love

- Sir Francis Drake

DAY 213

August 01

Serve the Lord with gladness; Come before him with joyful song.

Psalm 100:2

PSALM 100:2

This Psalm is a Psalm of praise. It is a celebration of the goodness and greatness of our God. It is a song of thanksgiving and joy.

"For the Lord is good;
his mercy is everlasting."
(Psalm 100:5)

As Christians, our daily lives should portray love, joy and happiness. Christ's light, shining in us, ought to draw others towards His mercy and grace. As His representatives on earth, we are likened to a beacon, guiding the way to joy and human fulfilment.

Serving the Lord with gladness takes effort and commitment to the will of God. The reward is eternal life and happiness in the presence of our Holy Father.

DAY 214

August 02

Moreover, God is able to make every grace abundant for you, So that in all things, always having all you need, you may have an abundance for every good work

2 Corinthians 9:8

ALMOST THERE

2 CORINTHIANS 9:8

"Do not be daunted by the enormity of the world's grief," -wrote Rabbi Tarfon- a couple of thousand years ago. "Do justly, now. Love mercy, now. Walk humbly, now. You are not obligated to complete the work, but neither are you free to abandon it."

St Paul, too, urges us to place God at the centre of our lives. If we do, God promises to provide us with the tools, knowledge and strength, required to do His work on earth. Allowing God to be at the centre also means trusting Him to take care of our everyday survival – He tells us we will have all we need. Knowing that our needs are taken care of, we are free to follow God's roadmap for our life. It is a route of loving others. A road filled with grace, forgiveness, patience and goodness. But mostly, a path that always pleases Him first –
a God-centred life

PSALM 128:1-2

"Blessed are you who fear the Lord" - in this context, the word fear, is a synonym for reverence.

Reverence means "a deep respect or admiration for someone." So, God is telling us that if we, out of respect, "walk in His ways", we will be blessed. If we love and revere God, the Fruits of the Spirit will emanate from our daily lives – love, joy, peace, forbearance, kindness, goodness, faithfulness, gentleness and self-control.

"Eat the fruit of your handiwork", suggests that the blessing entails success in what we do. But we know that "being good" doesn't always lead to success and happiness in this life. Sometimes, "the good", even die young. However, in the framework of eternity, good deeds get good results – nothing done out of love, goes unnoticed by God. Our labour is not in vain – our reward is waiting for us in heaven.

DAY 216

August 04

I have appointed you as
covenant of the people
and light of the nations.

Isaiah 42:6

ISAIAH 42:6

Christ is the light of the world. But, He was;
also the "servant of the Lord"- sent by God;
to be the mediator of the covenant, the;
meeting-point between God and man. It;
was because God could not save us;
without a mediator, or atonement for sin,;
that he sent Him into the world. He came;
as a peacemaker, and His crucifixion;
allowed us to be "at one, in
harmony with", the eternal God.

As God's "servants on earth" today, we, too,;
need to be a "light to the nations." Our lives;
need to reflect the love and peace of;
Christ. We need to be an example of;
Christ's humility, compassion, kindness and;
generosity. We need to be steadfast in our;
faith and not get caught up in the trappings;
of this world. God forgave all our sins. In;
return, we need to honour the covenant;
Jesus secured for us by continuing His;
work, building His church, and spreading;
His word. Our reward will be waiting
for us in heaven.

DAY 217

August 05

Therefore we are always **confident**
We live by faith, not by sight.

2 Corinthians 5:6-7

ALMOST THERE

2 CORINTHIANS 5:6-7

As Christians, we live by faith, in the belief of things that we cannot see. Our life on earth is a journey, and we walk it in confident expectation of things that are to come. We have a firm conviction of the reality and existence of heaven, and, of the fact that one day we will meet our Redeemer there. Through faith, we live and act as if Christ, the Holy Spirit, and Heaven are real- although they are unseen. And, because of our faith, we have the promise of life, and the knowledge that death holds no sway over us.

The people of this world live by sight and are influenced by things that can be seen. They strive for wealth, honour, worldly pleasures and praise. Unlike the Christian, they have no guarantee, or assurance, that they will achieve, or obtain, any of their hopes and desires. Their pilgrimage through live is uncertain, and often disappointing and frustrating.

Faith is the eye of the soul. Through it we look for Christ, for righteousness, peace, forgiveness, life and salvation.

DAY 218

August 06

So he said, "Come." and when Peter had come down out of the boat, he walked on the water to go to Jesus.

Matthew 14:29

MATTHEW 14:29

When Peter steps out of the boat and starts walking towards Jesus, he does it confidently and without a moments' hesitation. He walks on the water as if it is the most normal thing on earth. But, as soon as he feels the force of the wind, he starts to panic and begins to sink. In the instant that he takes his eyes off Jesus and relies on his own assessment and judgement, his fear creates doubt, and the miracle fades. In the same way, Jesus calls us to walk across certain waters towards him. The only prerequisite is absolute faith in His ability to protect us, and to keep our eyes firmly on Him. We need to ask ourselves if we can do it, and if we are willing to try.

Start by doing what is necessary;
then do what's possible;
and suddenly you are
doing the impossible.
- Francis of Assisi

DAY 219

August 07

Then he turned to his disciples and said privately, "Blessed are the eyes which see the things you see; for I tell you that many prophets and kings have desired to see what you see, and have not seen it, and to hear what you hear; and have not heard it."

Luke 10:23-24

ALMOST THERE

LUKE 10:23-24

The disciples had blessed eyes and blessed ears. They were common men, given an incredible blessing. They were able to see God's ultimate promise delivered, fulfilled, and embodied in Jesus. However, the joy of salvation does not belong exclusively to the disciples who saw, heard, and believed Jesus in His day. It is there for all of us who see Him as they did- by all who recognize Him to be God's Messiah and believe in His salvation.

"Because you have seen me, you have believed; Blessed are those who have not seen and yet have believed" (John 20:29)

DAY 220

August 08

But Peter arose and ran to the tomb; And stooping down, He saw the linen cloths lying by themselves; and he departed, marvelling to himself at what had happened.

Luke 24:12

ALMOST THERE

LUKE 24:12

Mary of Magdala, Joanna, and Mary, the mother of James, arrive at the tomb of Jesus, only to find the stone rolled away and the body of Jesus missing. When two angels appear and inform them that Jesus has risen from the dead, they rush off to share this with the apostles. Most of the disciples dismiss the story as pure nonsense and do not believe the women, or the angels, that had delivered the message. Peter, however, immediately runs to the tomb looking for Jesus, instantly believing that his Lord had risen just as He had told them He would while they were still in Galilee. His faith is immediate, and without hesitation.

For most of the followers of Jesus, His death shattered their dreams, hopes, and happiness. Jesus had to appear to them in person before they could believe again. However, throughout the Gospel wherever miracles are described, the word "immediately" is used. When the woman with haemorrhage touched the fringe of Jesus' clothes, "immediately" her bleeding stopped. We too, need to believe "immediately" in order to receive blessings. Like the Virgin Mary, there must be no delay in hearing the word of God. "Here am I, the servant of the Lord, let it be with me according to His word." (Luke 1:38)

Let us ask God to grant us the blessing of "instant belief", just like He granted it to Mary and Peter.

DAY 221

August 09

Charm is deceitful and beauty is passing,
But a woman who fears the Lord,
She shall be praised.

Proverbs 31:30

ALMOST THERE

PROVERBS 31:30

Mary, the Mother of Jesus, is a model disciple of Christ, who said "yes" to God's will throughout her life - from the time when Gabriel first appeared to her, all the way to the cross. The prayer to the Virgin Mary is based on the salutations of the angel Gabriel (Luke 1:28) and Elizabeth (Luke 1:42). It demonstrates her cooperation with the working of the Holy Spirit. It also emphasises the joy God found in her, and the great regard that He had for her.

"Hail Mary, full of grace, the Lord is with thee. Blessed art though among women and blessed is the fruit of thy womb, Jesus."

Have courage for the great sorrows of life and patience for the small ones. And when you have finished your daily task, go to sleep in peace.
- Victor Hugo

DAY 222

August 10

Whoever remains in love remains in God and God in him

1 John 4:16

ALMOST THERE

1 JOHN 4:16

When love beckons to you, follow him, though his ways are hard and steep. And when his wings enfold you yield to him, though the sword hidden among his pinions may wound you. And when he speaks to you believe in him, though his voice may shatter your dreams As the north wind lays waste the garden. For even as love crowns you so shall he crucify you. Even as he is for your growth so is he for your pruning. Even as he ascends to your height and caresses your tenderest branches that quiver in the sun, so shall he descend to your roots and shake them in their clinging to the earth. When you love you should not say, "God is in my heart," but rather, "I am in the heart of God." And think not that you can direct the course of love, for love, if it finds you worthy, directs your course.

- Kahlil Gibran

DAY 223

August 11

We love because he first loved us.

1 John 4:19

1 JOHN 4:19

All love starts with God. God is love, and, because He is love, He wants us to love. He showed that love when He created us. He created us in his likeness, and that likeness makes us vessels of love.

Life is all about love – about learning to love God, and learning to love other people. The love of God and our neighbour cannot be experienced differently. The way to one is through the other. We cannot say that we love God if we do not love our neighbour. We cannot enter the Kingdom of God if we do not love God, and if we do not love our neighbour as we love ourselves.

God showed His love again when he sent Jesus to earth to save us. "For God so loved the world that he gave his one and only Son, that whoever believes in him shall not perish but have eternal life." (John 3:16) Jesus taught us how to love, and then gave us the Holy Spirit to help us continue his legacy.

Through loving God and our neighbour we secure our place in the Kingdom of God.

DAY 224

August 12

And he said to them, "Cast the net on the right side of the boat, and you will find some." So they cast, and now they were not able to draw it in because of the multitude of fish.

John 21:6-7

JOHN 21:6-7

Once again Jesus shows himself to the disciples after his resurrection. This time, it is on the shore of Tiberias while they are out fishing. Here Jesus tells them where to cast their nets, allowing them to catch an abundance of fish. At once their eyes are opened, and they recognise him as the risen Lord.

Perhaps this story is about "spiritual abundance." If we recognise and acknowledge Jesus as the risen Lord, we will have life, and have it more abundantly. But what is "spiritual abundance"?

In the words of King David:
"The Lord is my shepherd, I shall not want. He makes me lie down in green pastures, He leads me beside quiet waters, He restores my soul. He guides me in paths of righteousness for his name's sake. Even though I walk through the valley of the shadow of death, I will fear no evil, for you are with me; your rod and your staff, they comfort me. You prepare a table before me in the presence of my enemies. You anoint my head with oil; my cup overflows. Surely goodness and mercy will follow me all the days of my life, and I will dwell in the house of the Lord forever." (Psalm 23)

DAY 225

August 13

I have set you as a light to the
Gentiles, that you should be for
salvation to the ends of the earth.

Acts 13:47

ACTS 13:47

It is comforting to know that God's love, compassion, forgiveness, and salvation is universal. He does not discriminate – rich or poor, black or white, Jew or Gentile, man or woman - we are all equal in His sight.

Most people today have very different values and principles. Racist tendencies, religious tensions, and gender inequalities abound. The poor, the elderly, or anyone deemed to "not fit in", are marginalised or victimised. As Christians, Jesus commands us to continue the work of His apostles. We are expected to look after anyone in need. We are called upon to provide comfort to those who mourn, to feed the hungry, look after the sick, and to love our neighbours as we love ourselves.

Like Jesus, our lives should be a beacon to those who have distanced themselves from God. His salvation is available to all who have ears to hear – we are His only voice here on earth.

DAY 226

August 14

For "who has known the mind of the
Lord that he may instruct Him?"
But we have the mind of Christ.

1 Corinthians 2:16

ALMOST THERE

1 CORINTHIANS 2:16

"Oh, the depth of the riches, both of the wisdom, and the knowledge of God! How unsearchable are His judgements and His ways past finding out!" "For who has known the mind of the Lord? Or who has become His counsellor? Or who has first given to Him, and it shall be repaid to him?" (Romans 11:33-35)

God thinks on a level far beyond human comprehension. "For my thoughts are not your thoughts, nor are your ways my ways," says the Lord. "For as the heavens are higher than the earth, so are my ways, higher than your ways, and my thoughts than your thoughts." (Isaiah 55:8-9) But God gave us the desire to want to know and learn and understand. We long to make sense of our world, and to comprehend the thoughts and plans of the Creator. Why do disasters strike? What is the purpose of my life, and what am I supposed to accomplish? Why do we face trials and hardship? Because our thinking, almost always, tends to focus on temporary pleasures and quick fixes, we are naturally limited, and face huge obstacles to actually begin to think like Him.

However, God has not left us to our own devices. He inspired the books of the Bible to reveal His mind. The Bible is full of practical wisdom, and tells us what God considers right or wrong. But, as incredible as the Bible is, there are still many things that are challenging to understand. According to Saint Paul, we cannot truly fathom things beyond a human realm without God's Spirit. And so, in order to have the mind of Christ, we need to pray ceaselessly for the gift of the Holy Spirit. Only when the Spirit of God is present in our daily lives will our thoughts and ways become more in harmony with those of our Heavenly Father.

DAY 227

August
15

For the word of God is living and powerful,
And sharper than any two-edged sword,
Piercing even to the division of soul and spirit,
and of joints and marrow, and is a discerner of
the thoughts and intents of the heart.

Hebrews 4:12-13

HEBREWS 4:12-13

The "Word of God" is Jesus, and He is living and powerful and a discerner of the thoughts and intents of our heart. That, in essence, means that no sin - not even a whispered curse or a fleeting evil thought, is hidden from the view of God. In fact, Jesus taught us that sin bottled on the inside, concealed from everyone else's view, carries the same culpability as sin that manifests itself in the worst form of ungodly behaviour. All sin is an assault against our holy God, whether committed in public, or in secret. Jesus is not suggesting that there is no difference, in degree, between sin that takes place in the mind and sin that is acted out. Not all sins are of equal enormity. For example, scripture tells us that the sin of Judas was greater than the sin of Pilate (John 19:11).

But, as Jesus pointed out in His Sermon on the Mount, anger arises from the same moral defect as murder, and, one who lusts suffers from the same character flaw as an adulterer.

Jesus cautions us against hypocrisy. Our secret life is the real test of our character; "As he thinks within himself, so he is" (Proverbs 23:7). So just as Jesus gazes into our hearts, we need to take a good look into His word - allowing it to disclose and correct the true thoughts and motives of our heart.

DAY 228

August 16

Once the hand is laid on the plough
No one who looks back is fit
For the kingdom of God

Luke 9:62

ALMOST THERE

LUKE 9:62

"Whoever wishes to come after me must deny himself, take up his cross, and follow me. For whoever wishes to save his life will lose it, but whoever loses his life for my sake will find it."
(Matthew 16:24-25)

As we journey through life it is impossible to avoid the reality of the cross. Whether mourning the death of a loved one, dealing with a debilitating, painful illness, caring for a parent drifting away in the clutches of dementia, watching a child lose the battle against addiction, facing the prospect of financial ruin, or, being betrayed by a lifelong friend - we all come face to face with our own cross.

However, when the cross is laid on our shoulders, it is a blessing, if, like Jesus, we have a Simon of Cyrene to help us carry it - to help lessen our burden. Sometimes we will be called upon to be a "Simon" for someone else - to help them during their time of suffering. When setting out on our journey each day, we don't need to search for, or create, crosses to bear. They will come our way. But when they do, we shouldn't run away from them either. They have meaning and value for us.

"In the cross is salvation, in the cross is life"

DAY 229

August 17

The word of God is living and effective...... able to discern reflections and thoughts of the heart

Hebrews 4:12

HEBREWS 4:12

The "Word of God" is Jesus, made flesh, who came to live among us. He is the living God, omnipotent and omniscient, and a critical discerner of the hearts of men. This knowledge extends to small, as well as, great affairs - to the hidden heart and mind of man, as well as to that which is open and manifest.

The "Word of God" we understand as the Gospel on the other hand, teaches us how to live a good life, and to stay true to the teachings of Christ. It is in studying and reflecting on the word, that we get a better understanding of the mind of God. This understanding, together with faith, gives us strength when we face adversity. This knowledge helps us remain firm when faced with temptation and sin. The "word" reminds us that all our thoughts and actions are visible to God – he is able to "discern the reflections and thoughts of our hearts." Lets' keep them pure and holy.

DAY 230

August 18

Immediately the father of the child
called out and said with tears,
"Lord, I believe; Help my unbelief!"

Mark 9:24

MARK 9:24

The Bible teaches us that "Everything is possible for one who believes." (Mark 9:23) The more we believe and trust God, the more limitless the possibilities become for our career, our family, our life. Having faith in God expands our horizons, and makes us more creative and innovative. Unbelief, however, limits and restricts possibilities, and our potential for success and happiness.

To live like Jesus, we have to live with faith, and therefore, with possibility. Scripture is very clear on the need for faith in order to enhance our life experiences. "The just shall live by faith" (Hebrews 10:38). "Without faith it is impossible to please God" (Hebrews 11:6). "Whatever is not of faith is sin" (Romans 14:23). "According to your faith it will be done unto you" (Matthew 9:29).

Let us too then, like the "father of the child" in todays' reading, call on Jesus to strengthen our faith- to help our unbelief.

DAY 231

August 19

You never know what will happen tomorrow;
You are no more than a mist that is here
For a little while and then disappears.
The most you should ever say is:
If it is the Lord's will, we shall be
alive to do this or that.

James 4:14-15

ALMOST THERE

JAMES 4:14-15

Most of us like to plan, and this planning often involves long, as well as, short term planning. Although planning is important, we need to stay God focussed – His timing and His will may not be exactly what we had in mind.

When someone we love dies and we start sorting through their belongings, we soon realise that life is but a vapour. We work so hard, and spend so much time, accumulating "stuff" that in the end means nothing. The only lasting thing we leave behind is our legacy. Our treasures and investments are best placed on eternal values and people. So, when we want direction in life, let us turn to our Creator. He knows what path we need to follow in order to live a fulfilling and gratifying life.

DAY 232

August 20

But let him ask in faith, with no doubting,
For he who doubts is like a wave of the sea
Driven and tossed by the wind.

James 1:6

JAMES 1:6

It would seem from the words of St James, that, someone who doubts is like someone without an anchor - which is slightly different to someone who has an anchor but is struggling to trust that it still works. God does not expect us to have "perfect faith." He is aware that we go through trials, and that these trials test our faith. It is in the midst of these difficulties that we become unsure, lose sight of God, and are tempted to not count on Him. What we should be doing, however, is to hand everything over to Him – not only our trials, but our doubts and misgivings as well. We need to say, like the man in Mark 9:24, "I believe; help my unbelief!"

God calms the storms of life, but mostly He calms the sailor

DAY 233

August 21

For it is God who commanded light to shine out of darkness, who has shone in our hearts to give the light of the knowledge of the glory of God in the face of Jesus Christ.

2 Corinthians 4:6

2 CORINTHIANS 4:6

"Light" in the Bible, is an emblem of knowledge, purity and truth. "Darkness", on the other hand, represents ignorance, error and sin.

The human mind is by nature ignorant of God, His laws, and, His expectations. This ignorance is amplified by the life we lead, by our education, by our indulgence in sin, and our striving for worldly possessions and pleasures. As Christians, we can have the knowledge of the glory of God if we allow the Holy Spirit to transform, or to illuminate, our minds. Then, we too, like the apostles, will have clear and consistent views. We will begin to see the beauty of our religion, see the beauty in the Bible, and, have a greater understanding of the doctrines governing our lives. When this happens, we will produce the fruits of the Spirit- love, joy, peace, forbearance, kindness, goodness, faithfulness, gentleness and self-control.

Allowing the light of Christ to be the source of our own light, will not necessarily have an immediate and direct effect on our intellect- but it will have an immediate and definite effect on our heart.

DAY 234

August 22

You have heard that it was said
"An eye for an eye, a tooth for a tooth"
"But I say to you, offer no resistance
to one who is evil"

Matthew 5:38-39

MATTHEW 5:38-39

Does anybody understand these words of Jesus? Does He really expect us to stay mute in the face of evil and injustice?

I, for one, find these words unsettling, and battle to comprehend why Jesus wants evil to triumph over goodness

Perhaps, all Jesus was attempting to say is that, as Christians, we need to behave and think differently to non-believers. We shouldn't have a "gut" response to circumstances, but, should rather consider the "Jesus way" before we react to any given situation.

DAY 235

August 23

Jesus said, "But I say to you,
Love your enemies and pray
For those who persecute you......"

Matthew 5:44

MATTHEW 5:44

Once again, Jesus challenges us with a statement that seems to be irrational. However, we know that His teachings are there to help us grow in our spiritual life, and to guide us to everlasting life. So, loving and praying for our enemies must somehow benefit us. It is in the act of forgiving someone who has done us harm, that we heal and purify our soul. It is in loving and praying for our enemies, that we draw ever closer to understanding the mind of God.

Love cures people, both the ones who give it and the ones who receive it
- Carl Menninger

DAY 236

August 24

But store up treasures in heaven,
Where neither moth nor decay destroy,
Nor thieves break in and steal.

Matthew 6:20

MATTHEW 6:20

This exhortation of Jesus must be one of the most encouraging and comforting ones in the New Testament. In this life it is a certainty that we will grow older, that we will experience sickness and pain, and that we will experience good times as well as bad. We could face financial ruin, or, a natural disaster could rob us of all our possessions.

But, Jesus assures us that if we remain faithful to His word and His teachings, we will store our treasures in heaven. Every effort we put into being good followers of Christ whilst we are on this earth- every random act of kindness, every bit of comfort offered to the sick, every cent donated to help the poor, will not go unnoticed or unrewarded. Jesus notices everything, and our hard earned treasures are safe with Him.

DAY 237

August 25

Why do you notice the splinter in your brother's eye, but do not perceive the wooden beam in your own eye?

Matthew 7:3

MATTHEW 7:3

It is a fairly common human characteristic to readily stand in judgement of others. It is easy, for example, to realise that our neighbour has racist tendencies. We are quick to express our disdain when a colleague is caught cheating on his wife. We vociferously voice our opinions concerning abortion and homosexuality.

And, all the while, Jesus is looking down on us and seeing us as we really are. We excuse and rationalise our own faults and mistakes, but refuse to be understanding when others fail.

Maybe, next time, instead of judging someone, we should be grateful that Jesus loves us all, despite our failings. In understanding and forgiveness we grow in holiness.

DAY 238

August 26

When Jesus heard it, he departed from there by boat to a deserted place by himself.

Matthew 14:13

MATTHEW 14:13

This passage has two strong messages for us. Jesus, having just heard about the beheading of John the Baptist, departs to a deserted place to be alone.

When we experience pain, like the pain the death of one that Jesus had known and loved, was likely to have caused, we too, need to withdraw to find solitude in the presence of our Saviour. In times of deep distress, turning to Jesus, who has experienced similar emotional distress, provides us with comfort and strength. Jesus knows and understands our pain. Jesus, however, was not granted the time to grieve. A multitude of people followed Him and ended up needing to be fed. Jesus performs the miracle of the loaves and fishes in order to take care of them. The lesson here is to never place our own requirements above those in need. Jesus always made time for the sick, the poor, and the lonely. In helping others we receive our own healing.

DAY 239

August 27

Jesus said to them,
"How many loaves do you have?"
And they said, "Seven and a few little
fish." And he took the seven loaves and
the fish and gave thanks, broke them
and gave them to his disciples;
And the disciples gave to the multitude.

Matthew 15:34-36

MATTHEW 15:34-36

"The miracle of the loaves and the fishes is not in the appearance of food by itself, it is in what people experience when God's table is open to all and each one becomes open to the idea that God loves them, heals them and changes them and is doing the same to everyone else. So the miracle is that a multitude of people felt healed by God, felt loved by God and walked away having sat at a common table after discussing an end to poverty, hunger and thirst, and to war and destruction. The true power of the miracle stems from the love of God that changes minds and changes the world."
Rev. Patrick Blaney

As Christians we are called to make the "power of love" the basis of our lives.

DAY 240

August 28

Then Jesus said to them, "A little while longer the light is with you. Walk while you have the light, lest the darkness overtake you; He who walks in darkness does not know where he is going.

John 12:35

JOHN 12:35

Light is beautiful and mysterious – it helps us to see things, it guides us as we travel, it promotes growth and life, it warms and comforts, and, it dispels darkness. Jesus said "I am the light of the world."(John 8:12) As this light He shows us the truth about God and life, He guides us on our journey to our heavenly home, He comforts and consoles us, and, in dispelling the darkness of sin and death, He leads us to everlasting life.

DAY 241

August 29

And now these three remain;
Faith, hope and love
But the greatest of these is love.

1 Corinthians 13:13

ALMOST THERE

1 CORINTHIANS 13:13

Mother Teresa understood the healing power of love:

"Let us always meet each other with a smile, for the smile is the beginning of love."

"We think sometimes that poverty is only being hungry, naked and homeless. The poverty of being unwanted, unloved and uncared for is the greatest poverty. We must start, in our own homes, to remedy this kind of poverty".

"I have found the paradox, that if you love until it hurts, there can be no more hurt, only more love."

"Spread love everywhere you go. Let no one ever come to you without leaving happier."

"Love begins by taking care of the closest ones – the ones at home."

"Each one of them is Jesus in disguise."

"The hunger for love is much more difficult to remove than the hunger for bread."

Mother Teresa showed us that following Jesus means being a peoples' person. It is impossible to love God if we don't have empathy, concern, or love, for our neighbour. Following Jesus means asking God to grant us the gifts of kindness, generosity, compassion, and concern. It is only then that we will be able to adhere to His command that we love our neighbour as we love ourselves.

DAY 242

August 30

Jesus said "I am the resurrection and the life, he who believes in me will live, even though he dies...."

John 11:25

JOHN 11:25

The Renaissance poet, John Donne, echoes these words of Jesus when he taunts "Death, thou shalt die."

As Christians we believe, and, at Easter celebrate, that the resurrection of Jesus means that God will no longer honour any covenant with death. Death has no hold over us, and we have no need to fear it. It is a "rite of passage" bringing us to our final home in the company of God our Father.

Through faith, fear is replaced with expectation and joy for the last phase of our journey. In living a life that God will be proud of, we store our treasures in heaven. In believing that Jesus died for our salvation, we pave the way to everlasting life and make our time on this earth a more worthwhile and happy experience.

DAY 243

August 31

Therefore God exalted him to the highest place and gave him the name that is above every name, that at the name of Jesus every knee should bow, in heaven and on earth and under the earth, and every tongue confess that Jesus Christ is Lord to the glory of God the Father

Philippians 2:9-11

PHILIPPIANS 2:9-11

Because Jesus was willing to humble Himself and be obedient to death on the cross, God highly exalted Him and bestowed on Him the name above every name. In order to undertake His earthly ministry, Jesus willingly laid aside the glory He shared with His Father and took on the form of a lowly servant. Man did not exalt Him – they cast insults and abuse at Him, and condemned Him to His death.

The lesson here, is, that we are to follow Jesus' example of laying aside His rights and taking on the form of a servant. It is in serving others that we find peace with God. "For everyone who exalts himself shall be humbled, and he who humbles himself shall be exalted" (Luke 14:11).

Jesus went to the cross out of love and obedience to His Father, and out of love for you and me. In the same way, our motivation to humble ourselves should be love for God and love for others. It is in loving God and others that, we too, will be lifted up to find eternal rest in the company of God our Father.

DAY 244-273

September

Do not look forward to what
may happen tomorrow;
The same everlasting Father who
cares for you today
Will take care of you tomorrow and every day
Either He will shield you from suffering,
Or He will give you unfailing strength to bear it.
Be at peace, then, put aside all
anxious thoughts and imaginations,
And say continually: "The Lord is
my strength and my shield;
My heart has trusted in Him and I am helped.
He is not only with me but in me and I in Him."

- Saint Francis de Sales

DAY 244

September 01

Anxiety in the heart of man causes depression, but a good word makes it glad.

Proverbs 12:2

PROVERBS 12:2

There is a very simple and easy way for Christians to touch, and enrich, the lives of others. A kind and thoughtful word is the cheapest and easiest gift we can give – and yet, it can do so much to uplift and gladden a heart burdened by sadness.

Unfortunately, most people, professing Christians included, are too selfish and preoccupied with their own lives to notice others. And, sadly, most of us lack the affection and concern for our neighbour, despite Jesus' teaching, to offer kind and helpful words when they are desperately warranted.

"The tongue has the power of life and death; godly saints use it for health and life." (Proverbs 12:18, 15:23, 16:24, 18:21, 27:9) "Only a pinch of salt-criticism or rebuke-should flavour a wise man's gracious words." (Colossians 4:6)

If you gladden a sad heart by a good word, you lay another brick for eternal life. Jesus, during His life, comforted and encouraged many - because God had given Him a wonderful gift of speech -"that I should know how to speak a word in season to him that is weary." (Isaiah 50:4) So, we need to remember that a kind thought, not expressed, is worthless. If you have a good thought about someone, tell them. The world would be a much better place if people complimented those who deserve it, and if people offered a kind word when it was needed.

DAY 245

September 02

Yet when I surveyed all that my hands had done and what I had toiled to achieve, everything was meaningless and chasing after the wind; Nothing was gained under the sun.

Ecclesiastes 2:11

ECCLESIASTES 2:11

It is so easy to get caught up in the ways of this world- so easy to "chase after the wind." We all find ourselves doing it at some point in our lives. Yet, it is important to realise that this is not our home – we are mere travellers passing through.

It doesn't help striving for worldly gain that brings no heavenly gain. Personal blessings are meaningless if they don't extend to those around us. Things that make us look good on this earth usually don't look good in the eyes of God. It doesn't matter how much money we have in the bank – what matters is how many people we serve with our finances, time, and energy. It doesn't matter if we are famous and known all over the world - it matters if we share Jesus with others, and live our life according to His principles. It doesn't matter what people write on our tombstone after we die – it matters what God will write in the Book of Life.

Our goal is not to "chase after the wind" – but to purposefully live out our days "chasing after God", and allowing Him to show us what it means to make a difference – both here on earth, and in our final home in Heaven.

DAY 246

September 03

In vain you rise early and stay up late,
Toiling for food to eat for He grants
sleep to those He loves.

Psalm 127:2

PSALM 127:2

Like so many things in the Bible, Kingdom thinking is paradoxical to our natural mind-sets. Sleeping could be productive, while rising early, and staying up late, could be in vain? However, this verse is not promoting laziness. The Bible makes clear its value for hard work and, warns of the consequences of being lazy – "Do not love sleep or you will grow poor; stay awake and you will have food to spare." (Proverbs 20:13)

Psalm 127 is directed to those who take the pressure of the future, of provision and protection, too heavily on their own shoulders. It is for planners and worriers, and those who push themselves too hard- putting provision before relationship, and calling it "responsibility".

This verse encourages us to step into a place of peace, knowing that God will always be a better manager of our lives than we are. He will work things out while we sleep – "He will not let your foot slip – he who watches over you will not slumber."(Psalm 121:3)

God is constantly watching over our needs. It doesn't mean that we will never have financial hiccoughs, or other hardships. It doesn't mean that we shouldn't work hard or have ambition. It does mean that we should work with God and stop trying to take His place – He is the master builder and the master watchman – let Him do the heavy lifting!

DAY 247

September 04

"And do not fear those who kill the body but cannot kill the soul but rather fear Him who is able to destroy both soul and body in hell"

Matthew 10:28

MATTHEW 10:28

God said, "And I have the keys of Hades and of Death." (Revelation 1:18) Possessing the "keys of death" means the risen Christ has control and authority over death. In John 10:17-18, Jesus says, "The reason my Father loves me is that I lay down my life – only to take it up again. No one takes it from me, but I lay it down of my own accord. I have the authority to lay it down and authority to take it up again. This command I received from my Father." When Jesus died, He died according to His own timing when He "gave up His spirit" (John 19:30).

Jesus, who had the authority over death, had the unique power to give up His spirit, and to rise from the dead. Moreover, He has the authority to release His followers from death, in order that we may be with Him forever.

Think of the concept of giving someone "the key to the city". Someone given "a key to the city" is considered welcome and honoured within that city. The Bible frequently speaks of keys as representing control over someone or something. In the same way, if you possess a master key to a building, you can open any of its doors and enter any room.

Eternal life through Jesus is the blessed assurance John describes in 1 John 5:6-13. Because He holds the keys to death, He has the power to release, from death, all of us who receive the gift of salvation He offers.

DAY 248

September 05

Therefore I say to you, do not worry about your life,what you will eat or what you will drink; nor about your bodies, what you will put on is not life more than food and the body more than clothing?

Matthew 6:25

MATTHEW 6:25

Anxiety, worry, fret, distress, agitation, tension and irritability – all these words describe a feeling of inner turmoil that results in an outward feeling of unease. This is a common feeling among us humans as we consider what the future holds for us, personally, and for the ones we love. These common emotions and feelings affect our outlook on life, our decision making, and, ultimately, the direction of our lives. Jesus does not want us to be anxious and full of concern. He wants us to live life differently. He doesn't want us to base decisions on fear of the future. Rather, He wants the direction of our lives to be established on eternal truths - not on the temporal things of this earth, and the hollow promises of man.

Dr Charles Mayo of the famous Mayo Clinic wrote, "Worry affects the circulation, the heart, the glands and the whole nervous system. I have never known a man to die of overwork, but I have known a lot who died of worry." In Matthew 6:27 Jesus echoes these words – "And which of you by being anxious can add a single cubit to his life's span." "Therefore do not be anxious for tomorrow; for tomorrow will care for itself, each day has enough trouble of its own." (Matthew 6:34) Worry is preoccupation, in the present, with the fear of what may take place in the future. There is no harm in having contingency plans – we must plan ahead. But, we must not be pre-occupied and fearful of the future – that is in the hands of God, and, we may not get there anyway. We need to live for God in the here and now, and not for ourselves, and in fear of what the future may bring.

DAY 249

September 06

"Do not fear, for you will not be ashamed; Neither be disgraced, for you will not be put to shame; For you will forget the shame of your youth, and will not remember the reproach of your widowhood anymore"

Isaiah 54:4

ISAIAH 54:4

"A man who had lived for many years the Christian life, told me how there was a place in Edinburgh which was associated with a sin. Every time in his early life he passed it, it brought back again the keen remorse and shame. It seemed to stain his life afresh whenever he saw the very place. But when he came to God and gave his heart and life to Christ, the first time he passed that place afterwards his soul was filled by a great transport of joy that all that was done, that it was no longer part of his life, that God had forgiven and forgotten and cast it behind His back. And he entered, for a moment at least in foretaste, into the perfect joy of soul, and he forgot the shame of his youth and remembered the reproach no more."

- Hugh Black, M. A.

DAY 250

September 07

And when I saw Him, I fell at His feet as dead. But He laid His right hand on me, saying to me, "do not be afraid; I am the First and the Last" "I am He who lives, and was dead, and behold, I am alive forevermore, amen. And I have the keys of Hades and of Death"

Revelation 1:17-18

REVELATION 1:17-18

"I fell at His feet as dead." This is the unrehearsed response of all who have been privileged to see the glory of God. Maybe, although years had passed, this brought to mind John's previous experience on the Mount of Transfiguration- where he had his first glimpse of the glory of Jesus? Daniel experienced a similar loss of strength at the imposing presence of his visitor at the river Tigris (Daniel 10:8). He was told not to be afraid, and was touched in a similar act of restoration.

The inevitable reaction of those who saw, even a glimmer, of God's glory, was to be afraid. And yet, how cavalier are we today in our attitude towards our Maker – we haven't the slightest notion, or appreciation, of His holiness. How badly we need to catch sight of His greatness so that we can develop a Scriptural fear of Him! A lack of fear of God is a characteristic of His enemies, and of unbelievers. But the fear that we, as His children, are to have is not the cowering response of someone fearing retribution. It is the healthy, reverent fear we would have towards a human father of perfect discipline and unconditional love – if one were to exist. And, along with the recognition of God's great power and might, comes the realisation that He is also our Protector. As Paul observed, "If God is for us, who can be against us." (Romans 8:31) "And I have the keys of Hades and of Death"

DAY 251

September 08

I tell you the truth, unless a grain of wheat falls to the ground and dies, it remains only a single seed. But if it dies, it produces many seeds.

John 12:24

JOHN 12:24

"But he who received seed on the good ground is he who hears the word and understands it, who indeed bears fruit and produces: some a hundredfold, some sixty, some thirty."(Matthew 13:23) The concept of bearing fruit is often used in Scripture. In the Gospels, Jesus told the story of a sower who went out to sow seed. The seed fell on various types of ground. Some was rocky and hard. Other was receptive, but the weeds chocked out the seed. But there was a portion of ground that was neither rocky nor weedy, and the seed took root. This was Jesus' analogy of the different people who hear the Gospel – those who truly believe are those whose life brings forth much fruit.

But, what is bearing fruit, or producing many seeds? Essentially it entails becoming like Jesus. Spiritual fruit will manifest itself in our lives as a change in character, outlook, and behaviour. It will become visible as we begin to pursue spiritual values in lieu of worldly riches and possessions. And, as we spend more and more time with Jesus in prayer and fellowship, we will get to know Him better. His thoughts will become our thoughts. His purpose will become our purpose. We will become like Jesus.

"But the fruit of the Spirit is love, joy, peace, longsuffering, kindness, goodness, faithfulness, gentleness, self-control." (Galatians 5:22-23) This is what others need to see in our lives. God is not asking that we be perfect. He is asking that these fruits be the primary characteristics of a life lived in accordance to His word, and in service to Him.

DAY 252

September 09

**The mystery of Christ...
Has now been revealed**

Ephesians 3:3-5

EPHESIANS 3:3-5

No matter how hard I try to understand, God's plan remains a mystery. Think about how He reigns over his creation, how He makes himself known in our hearts, how He shares His love and joy with us. All of these things are deeply mysterious and confounding.

And, He doesn't become less mysterious the more He reveals himself. It is a common experience among Christians that the more we begin to know about Him, the less we feel we understand Him.

Yet, in Jesus, we have someone we can relate to. Jesus felt pain and hunger. He experienced anger, and was subject to betrayal by people he trusted and loved. And, in His darkest hour, He felt isolated, rejected, and alone.

The mystery of Christ is that we are never alone – we will never be rejected, or left to suffer in isolation. Jesus is ever present to share our agony, dry our tears, and provide comfort. Although all of our faith remains a deep mystery, it is in fact very simple – all we have to do is accept the reality of the Cross, and to celebrate God's love for us with thankfulness – and also with awe.

DAY 253

September 10

Let your life be free from love of money
But be content with what you have,
For He said, "I will never forsake you..."

Hebrews 13:5

HEBREWS 13:5

St Augustine says we are made to love.
But made to love does not mean
we know how to love.

St Paul dispels any myths we might have.
To love is not comfortable or easy. It is not a
surge of feeling, but rather, a great thirst. In
order to find rest, we are called into a
struggle. He tells us to open our lives to
strangers, to treat outsiders as angels in
our midst, and, to show prisoners care
as if we were locked up together.

St Paul's description of love really destroys
the illusions we have of it. In this world it is
easier to love money, possessions, power
and fame - at least we benefit from that.
But, the Bible is very clear that we have
to avoid falling under the spell of
money and earthly things.

Loving God and our neighbour unlocks God's
promise to us – "I will never forsake you…"

DAY 254

September 11

Daughter, your faith has saved you.
Go in peace and be cured of your affliction.

Mark 5:34

MARK 5:34

"Your faith has saved you." These are the words Jesus uttered to a woman living as a nameless outcast in her community. Her days of bleeding had stretched into years; she was considered impure, and could not stand among the righteous. She felt unworthy to be heard and could not simply ask Jesus for help. And so, hidden in the crowd, she reached out and touched His coat – a silent plea for help.

"Your faith has saved you." We often forget where our strength and greatness comes from. It is not magic or luck – our failures don't vanish into the wind and we re-emerge victorious and successful. Like the bleeding woman, our greatness lies in reaching out to those who love us, in, and despite, our brokenness.

In fear, the beauty and wonder of our being slips from view. However, faith transforms fear. Through faith, our frailty is transformed into greatness, and we are freed to take up our rightful place in the presence of our loving Father.

DAY 255

September 12

We have given up everything
And followed you

Mark 10:28

MARK 10:28

Mother Teresa's life should be living proof that there is always hope – even when we get confronted with "faithless" days. It is well documented that she struggled with doubt and melancholy for many years. Despite a wholehearted commitment to serve Jesus in the most difficult situations possible, she wrote in her journal that she felt like she went for long periods without hearing from God, and, that she even sometimes wondered about His existence. Yet she never gave up her faith – despite her depression, God's perceived silence, and her doubt that he noticed that she followed His command to care for His most destitute children.

Mother Teresa deserves our respect and awe for how she lived her life. She may have doubted God, but, ultimately, she never stopped believing in Him. She lived a life none of us would ever choose- through years of doubt and years of darkness, years of questions, without answers, about His love and plan for her.

But, the Bible promises us hope. Mother Teresa held on to the hope that the silence was birthed on her side of the relationship, not His. Hope that one day she will hear His voice again, hope that He would show His face, love, and mercy to the people she served every day, and, one day, again to her. We can't live without hope. But hope doesn't really start with us; it starts with God. He is the one who promises to always love us, never leave us, be strong when we are weak, give direction when we are lost, and provide wisdom when we ask for it. Our hope has to be in Him, the author of hope.

"The paradox is that for her to be light, she was to be in darkness." Rev. Brian Kolodiejchuk – the editor who read through 6000 of Teresa's letters for the 2007 book, "Mother Teresa, come be my light".

PSALM 79:8

What bring us low? The list is endless – physical danger or illness, mental or moral dilemmas, fear of failure or loss. But usually, our distress stems from lack in the physical, visible world around us.

However, we don't often consider our spiritual unhappiness. Spiritual impoverishment manifests in so many ways – doubting that God can transform evil into good, lacking the desire to spend time with Him in prayer and silent contemplation, refusing to examine our lives honestly, and then attempting to root out the habits of sin that stem from pride, arrogance, vanity, greed and sloth.

Thankfully, God does not turn away from, or disdain, our weakness. He encourages us to be aware of, and face, them. He wants to lift us up – He wants us to turn to Him and acknowledge that He is the only supplier of all our strength. Then, His "compassion will quickly come to us."

DAY 257

September 14

Sing to the Lord a new song,
For He has done wonderous deeds;
His right hand has won victory
for Him, His holy arm.

Psalm 98:1

PSALM 98:1

I BELIEVE IN YOUR VICTORY, Lord...[yet] I fight for it on the battlefield as though it still had to be won by your might and my effort. That is the paradox of my life: to have tension at times but certitude always. You have proclaimed your victory in the face of the whole world, and I believe your word and spread your proclamation with total confidence in the face of all doubts and all attacks...

Your victory is here because you are here; you have walked the earth and spoken the human language; you have experienced human plight and proclaimed and effected human redemption; you have tasted death and restored life. I know all that, and now I want to make it all real in my own life and as a witness for others. Make me taste your victory in my soul, that I may proclaim it with my lips.
- FR Carlos G. Valles, S.J. (Psalms for Contemplation)

DAY 258

September 15

Let us confidently approach the throne of grace to receive mercy and to find grace for timely help.

Hebrews 4:16

HEBREWS 4:16

Have you ever wished there was someone you could talk to? Someone who would understand the challenges you face on a daily basis? And, perhaps, as you considered everyone in your life – your friends, your family, even your priest – you realised that there is no one who fills the gap? Many of them could be compassionate and wise – give a hug, or an encouraging word. But, there is no-one with whom you could have a real heart-to-heart, intimate chat, or even shed a tear or two?

But, how does anyone really understand what we are going through – the hurt, the pain, our innermost thoughts and feelings? After all, it is our life, so how can an outsider really understand? Jesus can, and does! "For we do not have a High Priest who cannot sympathise with our weakness, but was in all points tempted as we are, yet without sin. Let us therefore come boldly to the throne of grace that we may obtain mercy and find grace to help in time of need." (Hebrews 4:15-16)

Jesus extends an invitation for us to draw near. As believers, He has told us that we can approach boldly, and with confidence. And, if we are brave enough to come before the Throne of God, we will find a compassionate and caring Father. Why? Because He understands what we are going through – He has Himself endured everything we will ever face – He has first-hand knowledge and experience of pain, suffering, persecution, and temptation. There is nothing He is unable to relate to - and He extends all His compassion and love to us.

DAY 259

September 16

For God has not given us a spirit
of fear, but of power and of love
and of a sound mind

2 Timothy 1:7

2 TIMOTHY 1:7

All of us would love to go through life brimming with self-confidence – never having to confront doubt or fear. But, that simply never happens. Just as Timothy did, we recognise that our world can be an intimidating place. We aren't always the strong, self-disciplined person we want to be. Nor do we always have mature, experienced people we can rely on or turn to for mentorship.

The "sound mind" Paul is referring to, is a disciplined mind that does not allow emotions to take over and control us when we experience difficulties. It is natural to become discouraged during periods of tribulation. But, God's Spirit is one of power and love. It gives us strength to persevere when there seems to be little hope. It gives us the ability to avoid the damaging emotions of anger and resentment, which so often surface when we face these hard times.

Paul's advice to Timothy as he faced the future without his mentor and trusted friend, was, that he needs to trust God's Spirit of love and power. We need to follow and trust that same advice. God is our Mentor and Father, and He will sustain us in any situation.

DAY 260

September 17

But even if you should suffer for righteousness' sake, you are blessed. "And do not be afraid of their threats, nor be troubled."

1 Peter 3:14

1 PETER 3:14

In the Gospel of Matthew we also read about being persecuted for righteousness – "Blessed are those who are persecuted for the sake of righteousness…" (Matthew 5:10) Righteousness means acting in accordance with God's law or His will. It means that, in our hearts, we are making an effort to conform our own will to that of our Heavenly Father. And, in so doing, attempting to make our daily actions and choices work towards bringing about God's Kingdom on Earth.

As Christians we will be challenged, just as Jesus was challenged. All people, not only believers, carry the stain of original sin, and suffer from human failings. Life is all about perspectives, especially in our dealings with others. What we consider "right" or "correct", might not be what our brother or sister thinks is right or correct. Their priorities are not ours, and ours are not theirs.

We may suffer because of the understandings of others, for their perspectives. The important thing is that we do not inflict suffering on those whose understanding is different from our own. Jesus showed us how do to that. He taught - we should teach. He showed love and compassion - we should show love and compassion. He bore the sufferings of others - we should carry that burden.

We should not be afraid of suffering for righteousness. When we do, and do so in the loving example of Jesus, we receive grace and blessing from God.

DAY 261

September 18

For you did not receive the Spirit of bondage again to fear, but you received the Spirit of Adoption by whom we cry out, "Abba, Father"

Romans 8:15

ROMANS 8:15

This verse contrasts two spirits – an impersonal "spirit of bondage", and the Holy Spirit, called the "Spirit of Adoption". These two spirits reflect two different mind-sets that we can have in our approach to God. We can approach Him as slaves in bondage, or we can approach Him as adopted children.

There is a big difference between the way sons serve their fathers, and the way slaves serve their masters. Slaves perform duties; sons perform acts of love. Slaves dutifully obey; sons gladly obey. Slaves are motivated by fear of punishment; sons are motivated by love of relationship. Slaves ask, "What is required?" Sons ask, "What else can I do for you?" The "Spirit of Adoption" changes us from fearful slaves, to joyful sons and daughters. It allows us to "come boldly before the throne of grace" (Hebrews 4:16) - as a beloved child runs to his father in times of trouble.

God sent the Holy Spirit into our heart to testify to the fact that He loves us. It has nothing to do with who we are, or what we have done. It has everything to do with who He is, and what He has done. He loved us, gave His son to die for us, forgave us, and gave us righteousness –He made us worthy to be a part of His family.

DAY 262

September 19

"Be strong and of good courage,
Do not fear nor be afraid of them;
For the Lord your God, He is the one
who goes with you. He will not
leave you nor forsake you."

Deuteronomy 31:6

DEUTERONOMY 31:6

Most of us are well acquainted with weakness and fear. We know what it is like to feel weak, to have the desire to run away in the face of fear. But, fear and weakness aren't our inheritance. Throughout the Bible we read that there is nothing we should fear more than God. And this fear isn't a dreadful anxiousness – it is a reverent, awe-like fear that is motivated by wanting to please Him. We know that He is our strong tower. He protects us and fights for us. "Have I not commanded you? Be strong and courageous. Do not be afraid; do not be discouraged, for the Lord your God will be with you wherever you go."
(Joshua 1:9)

God often calls us to do things we don't believe we can accomplish. That's because without Him, we can't. He calls us to do things, like, have impossible strength and courage because, at the end of the day, we realize that those were things we were never going to be able to achieve on our own. He calls us to step out in faith, and trust that He is going to be there to put a firm foundation under our feet. We start, but He is the one who completes the mighty, powerful work, in our life

DAY 263

September 20

But now், thus says the Lord, who created you, O Jacob, and He who formed you, O Israel: "Fear not, for I have redeemed you; I have called you by your name; You are mine."

Isaiah 43:1

ISAIAH 43:1

"Fear not, for I have redeemed you; I have called you by name, you are mine. When you pass through the waters, I will be with you; and through the rivers, they shall not overwhelm you; when you walk through fire you shall not be burned, and the flame shall not consume you." (Isaiah 43:1-3)

The first part of this verse reminds us what God has done for us in the past – He has redeemed us, and called us to Him. However, the latter part contains a promise for the future. The promise is not one of smooth sailing waters and deliverance from trials, but rather His faithful presence in the midst of madness. We were never promised an easy life. But, we were promised His constant presence.

In his commentary on Isaiah, Ray Ortlund said, "Whatever life throws at you, including the tough love of God himself, He will go with you into it." Going through waters, rivers, fire, or flame? Be rest assured – we are not alone.

DAY 264

September 21

Say to those who are fearful-hearted,
"Be strong, do not fear! Behold your God will
come with vengeance, with the recompense
of God; He will come and save you."

Isaiah 35:4

ISAIAH 35:4

Fear can be caused by almost anything. It can be triggered through people, hardship, loss, the past, or the uncertainty of the future. Fear is that feeling of anxiety and dread concerning the outcome of something – the sense that your needs and desires will not be met. But, what is it that causes this, often unrealistic, feeling of fear and dread? Sometimes, it is because we look at the situation we find ourselves in and feel exposed and alone, without any control or help. We feel lost, and don't know what to do or where to turn.

A part of God's greatness is that He is omnipresent, meaning, He is everywhere at the same time. In John 14:23 Jesus says, "If anyone loves me, he will keep my word, and my Father will love him, and we will come to him and make our home with him." He makes His home in every believer, protecting, teaching, and guiding. He isn't simply hanging around – despite all that is going on He is totally focussed on His children. He is completely aware of our thoughts, our feelings, our desires, our weaknesses, and our strengths. He knows it all and is there to uplift and guide, to teach and correct.

DAY 265

September 22

As soon as Jesus heard the word that was spoken, He said to the ruler of the synagogue, "Do not be afraid; Only believe."

Mark 5:36

MARK 5:36

Most of us have confronted fear at some point in our lives. Often, we have allowed that fear to hold us back from moving into areas that could enrich our own life, or the lives of others. However, as Christians, it is prudent to remember that God has promised to go before us, and bring us through victoriously as we obey Him. When God "prepares the way", we can trust that whatever happens will turn out for our good, according to His perfect plan for us.

The words "fear not" could simply mean "don't run". Rather than giving in to it, we should rather stand firm, knowing that God has gone before us and prepared the way. Even if our mouth is dry and our knees are shaking, we must carry on asking God to strengthen us. We need to determine that our lives are not going to be ruled by fear, but, by the Word of God.

Giving in to fear alters God's best plan for our life. So, use the power of His Word to do what He wants you to do - even if you have to do it afraid.

DAY 266

September 23

That through death He might destroy him who had the power of death and release those who through fear of death were all their lifetime subject to bondage

Hebrews 2:14-15

ALMOST THERE

HEBREWS 2:14-15

Sin certainly can bring death and destruction into our lives. However, people regularly reject obedience to God because they consider it too restrictive. In fact, the opposite is actually true – sin enslaves us, while submission to God's will sets us free.

The particular form of slavery the Devil wields, in this verse, is the fear of death. Most of us are afraid to die, and this can cause us to make all sorts of immoral and irrational decisions. Christians are not necessarily immune to this fear. Our faith, however, does provide a different perspective on life and death.

Instead of fearing death above all else, and living as a slave to that fear, the believer can take advantage of a "more abundant" life, through Christ. Jesus isn't merely a detached spirit giving us orders. He took on suffering and hardship that other people also experience. This not only allows Him to comfort us with compassion, it makes His sacrifice and victory applicable to our lives. Exactly because He has experienced human pain and suffering, we can be assured that He understands ours and will not leave us destitute.

DAY 267

September 24

But in every nation whoever fears Him and works righteousness is accepted by Him

Acts 10:35

ALMOST THERE

ACTS 10:35

God has no favourites. Because we are all sinners, we all need Jesus. The journey to salvation starts at the foot of the cross for everyone. There is no way around it. There are no shortcuts, no favourites. But, at the same time, everyone is welcome.

"And remember that the heavenly Father to whom you pray has no favourites. He will judge or reward you according to what you do. So you must live in reverent fear of Him during your time here as "temporary" residents." (1 Peter 1:17)

Our Christian life not only starts at the cross – it is also lived out at the cross. Salvation is not a one - time event, but a daily renewal. Even as God's children we are still responsible for our actions. God is ever ready to pour out His grace if we ask. But we can't use it in vain.

God has no favourites, but, this quote from St Augustine holds true – "God loves each of us as if there were only one of us." God would have sent Jesus to die on the cross just for one soul – that's how much He loves us.

DAY 268

September 25

The fear of the Lord is to hate evil;
Pride and arrogance and the evil
way and the perverse mouth, I hate

Proverbs 8:13

PROVERBS 8:13

According to the Bible, the fear of God is the beginning of wisdom, and wisdom is "to depart from evil." This means we must avoid evil, or anything that lures us into wickedness. As children of God we must stay away from all forms of sin – lies, cheating, murder, envy, stealing, adultery, fornication, child abuse etc. "There is no peace for the wicked: They are like the troubled sea which cast out mire and dirt. There is no peace sayeth the Lord to the wicked."
(Isaiah 57: 20-21)

But what does it mean to "fear the Lord"? The Hebrew word used in Proverbs has the meaning of "reverencing the Lord". It means to be reverent, with humility, towards God- because we acknowledge His great power and authority. It is the same sort of reverence and respect we show towards our parents. If our father warns us against the danger of drinking or smoking, we will not go against what he tells us, if we respect his words. Instead, we will fear the consequences of disregarding the advice and concern shown for our wellbeing. This is a healthy fear, keeping us from harm -
not a debilitating, tormenting fear.

When we fear God's words, we will not go against them. Instead, we will apply them to our lives.

DAY 269

September 26

He who has the Son has life:
He who does not have the Son of
God does not have life

1 John 5:12

1 JOHN 5:12

If we want the life that is in Jesus to become our life, we need to be obedient to His words of life – we have to keep His commandments. When we follow His commandments, we become conformed to His image. That was the intention from the very beginning – that the life He lived, and the words He spoke, should become our way of life as well. We have to take up our cross daily and follow Him.
That leads us to eternal life.

It is our choice to do good. We choose to keep His commandments and be conformed in His image - which ultimately brings us life and blessings.

"Then the life of Christ becomes manifested in us." (2 Corinthians 4:10) "We become ambassadors of His life; we live that He may be glorified, and that when He is revealed, we shall be pure as He is pure – we shall be like Him." (1 John 3:1-3)

DAY 270

September 27

For it is written says the Lord,
"Every knee shall bow to me,
And every tongue shall confess
to God" So then each of us shall
give account of himself to God

Romans 14:11-12

ALMOST THERE

ROMANS 14:11-12

"So then each one of us shall give account of himself to God" This must be one of the most solemn statements made by St Paul in his epistles. He was laying down a principle – hoping to check the rash judgements, common among Christians in Rome, regarding the religious observances of their Christian neighbours. Some of the Roman Christians were vegetarians; others ate anything that came their way. Some observed private anniversaries; to others all the days were the same. The Church had not laid down any rule or laws about these matters. As such, no individual believer had the right to challenge another's liberty, or judge anyone's conduct. "Why" asked Paul, "dost thou judge thy brother? For we shall all stand at the judgement-seat of Christ. For it is written, As I live, saith the Lord, to me every knee shall bow, and every tongue confess to God, so then each one of us shall give account of himself to the Lord."
(Romans 14:10-11)

This truth is as relevant today as it was to the Roman readers. We are expected to rise above the controversies and differences that confront us on a daily basis. We all belong to God – we are part of the same family. Whatever food we do or do not eat, whatever days we do or do not consider holy, one thing remains absolutely certain – we will all one day give account of our actions or omissions (as well as everything else we do or say in our lives). "Each one of us will give account of himself to God." God alone is our judge.

DAY 271

September 28

Therefore judge nothing before the time, until the Lord comes, who will both bring to light the hidden things of darkness and reverse the counsels of the heart. Then each one's praises will come from God.

1 Corinthians 4:5

1 CORINTHIANS 4:5

In "The Church and the Surprising Offense of God's Love", Jonathan Leeman comments on the above verse: "Statistics may have their uses for churches, but the most important things about churches cannot be measured – the difference between fake and real, between flesh and spirit, between the minds of men and the mind of God. Only as we stand before God on the day of judgement will the real measurement of things be revealed."

It is difficult, even as Christians, to live each day knowing whose judgement really matters. There are too many stumbling blocks – we value the opinions of people too much, we think too highly of human courts, or of public opinion outside of the Church. And, we give too much attention to being acceptable to the world.

It is important to remember that feeling okay about what we are doing is not the same as being okay in God's sight. There is a day when everything will come to light, and we will know and see ourselves as God does. That is far more sobering than any comment- positive or negative- we may receive from our fellow human beings. "Do not fear man, buy fear God." (Matthew 10:28)

DAY 272

September 29

For whoever finds me, finds life, and obtains favour from the Lord, but he who sins against me wrongs his own soul; all those who hate me, love death

Proverbs 8:35-36

PROVERBS 8:35-36

In this verse, King Solomon is referring to "wisdom"- whoever finds wisdom, will find life and obtain favour from the Lord. The Bible emphasises that one of the greatest qualities we can possess is wisdom. King Solomon, with all his wealth and possessions understood its value -"How much better to get wisdom than gold!" (Proverbs 16:16)Because wisdom helps us to understand the difference between what is right and wrong in God's sight, acquiring and exercising wisdom will lead to happiness and longevity of life – it is an important quality that God wants to see in us. Isaiah, on the other hand, prophesised to unwise leaders throughout time – Isaiah 30:1 says they are "rebellious children…who take counsel, but not of Me, and who devise plans, but not of My Spirit."

Author David Kupelian speaks out in his book The Marketing of Evil: "Since the 1960's, America-from her government to her schools, and, even to her churches-has steadily fallen away from the Judeo-Christian values that previously illuminated and gave life and strength to the nation's institutions. This is equivalent to turning out the country's lights. Moreover, no longer guided by universal standards of right and wrong, Americans have had nothing more reliable than their own feelings to guide them in the moral realm. And, as modern marketing well knows, when people are operating primarily on the basis of feelings and emotions, they are wide open to every sort of imaginable manipulation."

Have the United States and other Western societies replaced the laws of God-His wisdom-with humanly devised ideas and beliefs? If so, the results will produce dire consequences for the people they lead. We cannot escape the consequences of our actions, and unless we have a change heart, we will find ourselves on the opposite side of God's mercy and compassion.

September 30

Death has been swallowed up in victory. Where, O' death is your victory. Where, O' death, is your sting?

1 Corinthians 15:54-55

1 CORINTHIANS 15:54-55

Among all the facts of mortality, nothing is more certain than its deathly end. Death is the most democratic experience in life - we all participate in it. Most of us would like to think that it only happens to other people. We don't like to grow old, and we certainly don't like the idea of dying. And, when it happens, how tragic, how poignant, is the sorrow of those left behind. The grieving widow, the motherless child, the father, bereft and alone – all speak of the wounds of parting.

"If a man dies, shall he live again?" (Job 14:14) That was the great universal question framed by Job. He spoke what every living man and woman has pondered. The Bible teaches that death is an enemy of man and God. But, it also teaches that this enemy, death, will ultimately be destroyed forever; that, in fact, it has already been defeated at the cross and resurrection of Jesus Christ.

For Christians, death brings permanent freedom from evil. It also means that we finally become like Jesus. So much of self is involved in what we do here on earth. But, one day, through Christ, we will have perfect love. His death sealed the testimony of His love for all mankind. His resurrection opened the gates of salvation to all generations.

DAY 274-304

October

Prayer to the Holy Spirit

Breathe into me, Holy Spirit, that my thoughts may all be holy. Move in me, Holy Spirit, that my work, too, may be holy. Attract my heart, Holy Spirit, that I may love only what is holy. Strengthen me, Holy Spirit, that I may defend all that is holy. Protect me, Holy Spirit, that I may always be holy.

- Saint Augustine

DAY 274

October 01

Trust in the Lord with all thy heart and lean not unto thine own understanding. In all thy ways acknowledge him, and he shall direct thy paths.

Proverbs 3:5-6

PROVERBS 3:5-6

No need to recall the past; No need to think what was done before. See I am doing a new deed even now it comes to light; can you not see it? Yes, I am making a way in the wilderness, paths in the woods it is I, I it is, who must blot out everything and not remember your sins.

- Isaiah 43: 18-19 and 25

DAY 275

October 02

I will lead the blind by ways they have not known,
Along unfamiliar paths I will Guide them;
I will turn the darkness into light before them
and make rough places smooth. These are the
things I will do; I will not forsake them.

Isaiah 42:16

PROVERBS 3:5-6

Most of us have had low points in our lives. Times when we haven't felt particularly spiritual - when praying seemed liked hard work, and it was too painful to cast light into the shadowy corners of our hearts. At those moments we experienced the feeling of being forsaken.

I, for one, have doubted and wrestled with God when I disagreed with His plan for my life. I've become angry when my prayers were "ignored" – not realising that they had been answered, but not in the way I wanted them to be. Fortunately, even during my "prodigal child" stage, God has remained faithful and has never stopped coming to look for me.

At times like these it is pertinent to remember that "at three o'clock, Jesus called out with a loud voice, "Eli, Eli, lema sabachtani?" Which means "My God, my God, why have you abandoned me?" (Matthew 27:46) It is not easy to imagine the pain the crucifixion caused Jesus – it is the perfect tool to bring about the most inhumane of human sufferings. It is even worse to contemplate when we acknowledge that it is our sin that caused Him to suffer – our sins that caused His Father to "forsake" Him at that precise moment in time.

But, it was at that moment when Jesus uttered the words "My God, my God, why has thou forsaken Me," that our own brokenness reached deep within His spirit and bound us to the Father – just like the tiny hand of a new-born curls around his mother's finger.

"My God, my God, why hast though forsaken me?" These words assure us of every struggle, every valley, and every circumstance being vindicated, corrected, and justified on the cross. These are the words of our own heart – these words wrapped within His. Because God had to turn His head away when Jesus suffered, He can look upon our suffering and hold us through it – He has no need to forsake us – Jesus paid the price for our sin and united us, forever, with His almighty Father.

DAY 276

October 03

When I am afraid I will trust in you.
In God, whose word I praise, in God I trust.
I will not be afraid.

Psalm 56:3-4

ALMOST THERE

PSALM 56:3-4

According to the introductory statement to this Psalm, David wrote this when he had been seized by the Philistines in Gath (1 Samuel 21:10-15), and he starts it by expressing his situation and his fear. From this initial fear, he puts his trust in God – which is the only response we should have to any situation.

When we turn to God and read His Word, it brings any situation back into perspective. It makes us realize that if we trust Him, there is no need to be afraid - because He is greater than anything that we could possibly fear. If we really think about it, we will concede that we don't see the fullness of our hope in God until fear arrives and causes us to lean on Him.

David openly acknowledges that he was afraid. Fear is a normal instinct, and a reality that we all have to deal with at one time or another. It is not a weakness and only becomes a problem for a believer when it becomes the most compelling factor in our life – thereby causing us to respond more to the fear than to the Lord's promise that He will take care of and protect us.

DAY 277

October 04

Do not fear, for I am with you;
Do not be dismayed, for I am
your God. I will strengthen you
and help you; I will uphold you
with my righteous right hand.

Isaiah 41:10

ISAIAH 41:10

Isaiah 41:10 reminds us of the promise of God's presence. The first thing God wants to impart to us is that He does not want us to be afraid. God has plans for us, and, they are good plans (Jeremiah 29:11). He knows that while faith in Him and His Word opens the door to His plans and purpose for us, fear unlocks the door to doubt and disbelieve. When adversity hits we need to do everything in our power – including praying, praising, and immersing ourselves in the Word– in order to stay strong in our faith.

"I am with you." This is the best reason of all not to give in to fear – we have the Lord's presence to accompany us at all times, everywhere we go. (Joshua 1:9) Jesus Himself said, "I am with you always, even to the end of the world." (Matthew 28:20) In desperate times our feelings will often tell us that we are all alone in our troubles. We can live by feelings, or we can live by faith – the choice is ours. When we give the Lord His rightful place in our lives, He becomes responsible for our welfare and well-being – "Do not be dismayed, for I am your God." God is our protector and provider. He fights our battles for us, and makes Himself available to us every moment of every day. Sometimes, we may feel that we have been "ambushed" by sudden calamities and hardships, but nothing comes as a surprise to God – He has a solution for all our cares. No matter what happens, we can endure it – we can rely on Him to strengthen and help us – "I will strengthen and help you."

The presence of God is a fact of life. Paul rightly said of God, "In Him we live, and move, and have our being." (Acts 17:28) How precious it is to be grounded in some of the most powerful promises God makes in His word.

DAY 278

October 05

I lift up my eyes to the hills –
where does my help come from?
My help comes from the Lord,
the maker of heaven and earth

Psalm 121:1-2

ALMOST THERE

PSALM 121:1-2

Some people call this Psalm, (Psalm 121), the "traveller's Psalm." In many homes it is read when a member of the family is about to go on a journey. It is not so much a prayer as a meditation on God's providence.

"David Livingstone, the famous missionary and explorer of the continent of Africa, read Psalm 121 and Psalm 135, which praises God for His sovereign rule over all things, as he worshipped with his father and sister before setting out for Africa in 1840. His mother-in-law, Mrs Moffat, wrote him at Linyardt that Psalm 121 was always in her mind as she thought about and prayed for him." (James Montgomery Boice)

Others call it the "soldier's Psalm." Rev. Matthew Henry (1662-1714) explains – "they think it was penned in the camp, when David was hazarding his life in the high places of the field, and thus trusted God to cover his head in the day of battle."

It really doesn't matter how we interpret it. Whether we are at home or travelling, we are exposed to dangers and hardships. This Psalm directs and encourages us to place out trust and confidence in God, and, by faith, to put ourselves under His protection, and to commit ourselves to His care.

DAY 279

October 06

Even though I walk through the valley of the shadow of death, I will fear no evil; For you are with me; Your rod and your staff, they comfort me.

Psalm 23:4

PSALM 23:4

In a homily given by Pope Francis some time ago, He warned the faithful against the deception of life's "alienations"- in other words, "living as though we never had to die." Instead, He urged them to think about "what mark they want to leave on the world." As Christians, we theoretically know that we need not fear death. The Bible paints a beautiful picture of what happens when we die – "For the trumpet will sound, and the dead will be raised incorruptible, and we shall be changed. For this corruptible must put on incorruption and this mortal must put on immortality…..death is swallowed up in victory. Oh death, where is your sting? (1 Corinthians 15:52-55)

There is only one of two ways we can depart from this life. We could go out empty, with nothing to show for our time spent on this earth. If our focus is only on earthly things, with no vision for eternal life, we will have no eternal treasures stored up, no life with Christ, nothing to take to eternity. Or, we can be faithful disciples of Jesus Christ, learning from Him, and building up a storehouse of eternal worth. We can live our life in such a way, that when we die, He will say to us, "Well done good and faithful servant" (Matthew 25:21 and 23). So, it is how we spend our time on this earth that will affect the way we will react when we finally come to meet our maker. If we live a faithful life in obedience to God's Word, we will face death with joy and peace. We will be transformed from fearing death to having God's view about death – which is simply to be reunited with Him.

DAY 280

October 07

Cast all your anxiety on him
Because He cares for you

1 Peter 5:7

1 PETER 5:7

In Matthew 18:3 Jesus says, "Assuredly, I say to you, unless you change and become as little children, you will by no means enter the kingdom of heaven." Little children have almost no anxiety. The trust and confidence they have in their parents is unshakeable. They go to bed at night totally at peace, and secure in the knowledge that they are loved and that all their needs will be taken care of.

In the same way, God loves us more than we love ourselves, and desires only the best for us. He loved us so much that he died for us - so it should be easy to trust him with smaller issues. So why do we struggle to let go and to "cast our anxieties on Him"? Humility is an essential part of our faith, and, when we cast all our anxieties on God, we are humbling ourselves under His mighty hand (1 Peter 5:6).Worry is associated with pride, because being humble is the opposite of pride. When we worry we think we are better than God and our pride makes us think we can handle things on our own.

Jesus promised never to abandon or to forsake us (Hebrews 13:5). This doesn't mean that by casting all our anxieties on him all our problems will disappear. It does mean that through faith and trust in God, we gain peace of mind that enables us to listen for guidance from the Holy Spirit.

DAY 281

October 08

Be strong and courageous.
Do not be terrified; Do not
be discouraged, for the Lord
your God will be with you.

Joshua 1:9

ALMOST THERE

JOSHUA 1:9

In 1 Corinthians 16:13-14, Paul gives an action list of 5 things a Christian should do: "Be on your guard; stand firm in the faith; be men of courage; be strong; do everything in love." Courage is at the centre of these character traits. It is "the ability to do something that you know is difficult or dangerous." Usually, we think of courage as a death-defying act, or a great heroic sacrifice. However, the truth is, it takes a great deal of courage to face some of the ordinary challenges in life. As Christians, we often draw on courage when we stand up for our convictions and principles -simply because it is the right thing to do, even if there is no personal gain or reward. One of the biggest problems facing the Church today is the lack of courage to do what God has called and enables us to do. We can't make a difference in the world by imitating it. If we want to make a difference, we have to be different, and, that takes courage. As Christians, we need to be filled with integrity. We can't be afraid to call sinful behaviour sin, even if others deem it politically incorrect. We must stand up for God and the principles we believe in. Like Joshua, we might be afraid – but God has promised to be with us, always.

"Sometimes we forget too easily that we are not in heaven yet. God promised He would dry away our tears and heal our diseases. But we still have to wait for Jesus to return to us; And that has not happened yet."
- Prof Jan van Der Watt

DAY 282

October 09

You O Lord, keep
my lamp burning;
My God turns my
darkness into light.

Psalm 18:28

ALMOST THERE

PSALM 18:28

In the Bible, light is an image of prosperity, success, happiness, and holiness. A candle (a light), signifies safety, comfort, glory, and well-being. Darkness is the opposite of light. "Walking in the dark", means walking void of all light. It means walking on an unsure footing, with no firm foundation to stand on.

In spite of adversity, David felt assured that God would grant him prosperity, as though his lamp burned constantly in his dwelling. Whenever he felt discouraged, he took his eyes off himself, and remembered his God – "Why, my soul, are you downcast? Why so disturbed within me? Put your hope in God, for I will yet praise Him, my saviour and my God." (Psalm 43:5)

David's soul was anchored in the Lord, so much so, that whenever he felt out of sorts, he would encourage himself by confession: "Lord, thou wilt light my candle; thou wilt revive and comfort my sorrowful spirit; thou wilt guide my way, that I may avoid the snares that are laid for me. Thou wilt light my candle to work by, and give me an opportunity of serving thee."

David's prayer life should encourage us. We should never allow ourselves to be overcome by the vicissitudes of life. As long as God is our Source of Light, there is light at the end of the tunnel. We must remember, and hold onto, the fact that "we have been called out of darkness, into the marvellous light." (1Peter 2:9)

DAY 283

October 10

The Lord is my light and my salvation; whom shall I fear? The Lord is the strength of my life; of whom shall I be afraid?

Psalm 27:1

PSALM 27:1

Being a person of faith doesn't mean that we will never be afraid. Sometimes we are justifiably scared – of an illness, of physical pain, about the unknown, an uncertain future, and, of course, for many of us, public speaking. At other times, it is more about wanting to be conformed to this world, to fit in. Fears like - "what will they think of me? What are they going to say about me? What will they do if I don't do as they want? What if they reject me? What if they don't like me?" No one is immune to fear, and, we will not go through life without facing any troubles.

Fear, according to the dictionary, means: "To put to flight, to flee, be afraid of one, hesitate to do something for fear of harm." The antidote to fear, of course, is faith. Jesus said, "In this godless world you will continue to experience difficulties. But take heart! I have conquered the world" (John 16:33). For a Christian, our faith is in God. He is the object of our faith, and the one on whom it rests (Psalm 91:2). We are called to overcome our fears and live our lives by faith (Mark 4:40).

When our faith is in God and His promises govern our thoughts, we will make choices that honour Him. Acts of obedience will characterize our life because of the trust we place in Him. When our starting point is faith, everything else proceeds from that (Psalm 9:10). However, if fear controls our thoughts, we become ineffective, immobilized, and, even disobedient to God's call on our life. We then make unwise decisions.

Courage is the deliberate decision to trust God and obey Him, no matter what you are feeling. As you do, your fears actually become opportunities, not obstacles -they are a way of putting God's power and strength on display (Psalm 56:3-4).

DAY 284

October 11

You rule over the surging sea, when its waves mount up, you still them.

Psalm 89:9

PSALM 89:9

In one of the most beloved stories in the Bible found in Mark 4:35-41, Jesus and his disciples are crossing the Sea of Galilee when a storm rolls in. The waves threaten to sink the boat. Jesus is asleep. Asleep! How can he be asleep? Terrified, the disciples wake him and ask if he cares that they may be killed. Jesus gets up, tells the wind and the waves to be still, and then asks the disciples why they are so afraid.

Storms threaten to sink our faith. Not the every- day inconveniences like a flat tire or hassles at work, but the difficulties that cause us to question God's goodness. Stuff like a prolonged illness, the death of a loved one, a loss of purpose, a broken marriage – and God seems to be asleep. If He really cared and understood, then surely He would prevent this from happening?

However, in the story, the storm is not the point. The storm is real and terrifying – the disciples believe that they will not survive – but the point is not about surviving the storm. The point is about who is in the boat with them. Jesus can calm the storms of our lives. But, His purpose is not to calm our storms, but to save our souls. Jesus did not come to give us a comfortable life, he came to defeat death.

The storm is not where we face the enemy. The storm is where we meet God. Relief from the storm is not necessarily the best thing that can happen to us. The best thing that can happen, is that is helps us to be conformed to the image of Christ.

Jesus can calm the storm in our life. But even if He does not, we can trust that He will uphold us, we can believe that He will transform us, and we can be assured that He loves us.

DAY 285

October 12

And when the cold is unbearable,
he sends his word to bring the thaw
and warm wind to melt the snow.

Psalm 147:17-18

PSALM 147:17-18

"My God is called Love"

One day Mother Teresa took in a woman off the streets of Calcutta. Her body was a mess of open sores infested with bugs. Mother Teresa patiently bathed her, cleaning and dressing her wounds. The woman never stopped shrieking insults and threats at her. Mother Teresa only smiled. Finally the woman snarled, "Sister, why are you doing this? Not everyone behaves like you. Who taught you?" She replied simply, "My God taught me". When the woman asked who this god was, Mother Teresa kissed her on the forehead and said: "You know my God. My God is called Love." – published by the Franciscan Media.

Mother Teresa taught us that, in the poor, we meet Jesus – not a reminder of Jesus, not a symbol of Jesus, but Jesus himself, face-to-face, hungering for our love, thirsting for our kindness, waiting to be clothed by our compassion. The unwanted, the unloved, the alcoholics, the dying, the destitute and the abandoned, the lonely, the outcasts and untouchables, the leprosy sufferers – all those who are a burden to human society, who have lost all hope and faith in life, who have forgotten how to smile, who have lost the sensibility of the warm hand-touch of love and friendship – they look to us for comfort. If we turn our back on them, we turn it on Jesus. And, at the hour of our death, we will be judged on what we have done for them and to them – and that will depend on whether or not we have recognized Christ in them.

DAY 286

October 13

Then he arose and rebuked the wind, and said to the sea, "Peace, be still." and the wind ceased and there was a great calm.

Mark 4:39

ALMOST THERE

MARK 4:39

As children, the saying "into every life a little rain must fall" may not have meant much, but, it took on a whole new meaning when we grew up and made our way into the world.

We all have to navigate our way through the storms of life. The path we walk on a daily basis, changes constantly. Some days the sun is shining and the sky is blue. Other days, it is cold and windy. Sometimes, a siren warns us of an impending storm. Sometimes, we end up in the middle of a storm without any warning at all. No matter what, we must learn to navigate the storms that come. We must learn how to handle the process of pain, and understand its vitality in our progress as we tread ahead on the pathway of life.

Jesus, too, faced storms in His life – some that we can never imagine the sheer force behind. He could have taken the easy way out – He had the power to do whatever He wanted. But, He chose to face the storm, and, He overcame. "In the world you will have troubles and trials and distress and frustration; but take heart! For I have overcome the world." (John 16:33) Unfortunately, we all have to face these storms – some big, some small. But, through Jesus, we already have hope. When we face a season filled with pain and our heart is breaking, we must remember that pain is a process, and that process takes time. The only way to heal is to let go and let God take over. Allow the past to heal itself so that you can move forward - walking in the authority that Jesus has given you.

DAY 287

October 14

Let not your heart be troubled; you believe in God, believe also in me.

John 14:1

ALMOST THERE

JOHN 14:1

"Do not let your heart be troubled; believe in God, believe also in me. In my Father's house are many dwelling places; if it were not so, I would have told you; for I go to prepare a place for you. If I go and prepare a place for you, I will come again and receive you to myself, that where I am, there you may be also."

Martin Luther called this passage "the best and most comforting sermon that the Lord Christ delivered on earth, a treasure and a jewel not to be purchased with the world's goods." These verses become the foundation for comfort, not only for the disciples, but also for us.

John 14:1-4 is all about trust. Trust and faith go hand in hand. If Jesus had wanted, He could have given the disciples a play by play account of the next 24 hours - arrest, trial, beating, crucifixion and death. He could have laid it out in so much detail that they would not have had so much fear and doubt. But He didn't. He gave them just enough clues to hold on through all the turmoil - but not so many to keep Peter from his denials, and the eleven from fleeing the gardens. He could of told them when and where to run, but he didn't. He let them wrestle with all that was to come, and, either their faith would make it or it would break.

I think that is how God deals with us as well. He doesn't give us a blow by blow account of all the difficulties we will confront in our lifetime. We don't know what sickness, disaster, or deaths, we will have to face the next day, or, the next decade. But, we rest in the fact that Jesus has told us enough to sustain us through the difficult times in our life. And, like Peter, it doesn't mean we will never make a mistake or that our faith won't ever waiver – but, it does mean that in the end everything will get worked out, our faith will grow, and God will make good on His promises.

DAY 288

October 15

"I will not leave you orphans; I will come to you. A little while longer and the world will see me no more, but you will see me. Because I live, you will live also."

John 14:18-19

ALMOST THERE

JOHN 14:18-19

The definition of an orphan is "a child who has lost both parents through death. Or, "a young animal that has been deserted by or has lost its mother."

It is important for parents to consider appointing a legal guardian for their children. This ensures that the child's protection and well-being will be taken care of in the event of their death. This legal guardian will make all the important decisions regarding the child's welfare - decisions about where the child will live, schooling, and general care, until the age of 18.

In the same way, Jesus, when delivering His farewell discourse to his disciples at the last supper, assures them that He will not leave them orphans. He promises that they will see Him - and this does happen in His post-resurrection appearances to them.

But, most importantly, He promises them their own "legal guardian". He will send the Holy Spirit to help them when He is physically gone. Thus, the disciples would not be without a teacher. And, just as the disciples took great comfort in that knowledge, so too, can we. Jesus' promise applies to us as well. We are never left to our own devices. We are never abandoned. As believers, the Holy Spirit resides in our hearts forever. He is our Helper, Comforter, and Guide. Jesus gave the Spirit as "compensation" for His absence.

The Spirit leads us in the way we should go about our spiritual business. "When He, the Spirit of Truth, comes, He will guide you into all truth." (John 16:13)

DAY 289

October 16

For you are my lamp O Lord;
The Lord shall enlighten my darkness.

2 Samuel 22:29

2 SAMUEL 22:29

In our country, South Africa, we are going through a period in our history where power outages are a fairly regular occurrence. As a result, most homes have an adequate supply of good torches and plenty of batteries. From trying to remember not to flip on light switches out of habit, to strategizing which windows to open to get the optimal breeze going, it really makes you appreciate the electricity we usually take for granted. If you've ever stumbled through the darkness in the middle of the night trying to locate a torch, you can appreciate the situation.

Just like a torch is crucial for finding your way through a room full of obstacles, in the middle of the night, during a power outage, the Bible is the all- sufficient guide given to us, by God, for navigating our lives in a dark world. It contains everything we need to know in order to have faith in God, repent, receive salvation, and live a life pleasing to Him. It teaches us right and wrong, shows us the difference between true and false doctrines, and, reveals the character and nature of God.

"All Scripture," as 2 Timothy 3:16-17 says, "is given by inspiration of God, and is profitable for doctrine, for reproof, for correction, for instruction in righteousness, that the man of God may be complete, thoroughly equipped for every good work."

DAY 290

October 17

The name of the Lord is a strong tower;
The righteous run to it and are safe.

Proverbs 18:10

PROVERBS 18:10

"The name of Yahweh is a strong tower; the righteous run to it and are protected. A rich man's wealth is his fortified city; in his imagination it is like a high wall." (Proverbs 18:10-11)

At first glance you may read these consecutive verses as two individual proverbs, each having its own meaning. Upon a closer look, you will see that these two proverbs are like two sides of the same coin – two world views, two ways of life, two realities, two choices for life.

A strong tower was a central place in an ancient city where people could run to when threatened by an enemy – a place of refuge. Yahweh's name implies God's character as the eternal, powerful, faithful, covenant-keeping God. So, God is a place where righteous people can find refuge and safety. People, who have faith in, call on the name of, and, rely on God, are made righteous. Thus they are protected from all enemies, including death, because they are safe inside the strong tower of God's reality.

In stark contrast, a rich man relies on his own wealth for his protection. A person's wealth – things you acquire or accomplish in this world – might seem as if it protects you like a high wall around a fortified city. But, the protection offered by relying on yourself, your wealth, and, your accomplishments, is only imagined safety and security. It is imagined because wealth and success in this world are not real from the eternal perspective of God's reality. They go away. They don't last forever – they have no eternal significance.
And so, we have two choices – we trust in God or we trust ourselves. The decision is really not that complicated.

DAY 291

October 18

I would hurry to my place of shelter,
Far from the tempest and storm

Psalm 55:8

PSALM 55:8

From the Psalms we read, "In God is my salvation and my glory; the rock of my strength, and my refuge, is in God." (Psalm 62:7) The storms of life are painful and hard to endure – a young boy has cancer, a little girl is in need of a new heart, a man needs a kidney transplant, parents battle with a drug- addict child, spouses try to salvage a broken relationship…… There is an old hymn, the text of which was written by Vernon J Charlesworth and later adapted by the gospel singer and composer, Ira Sankey. The verses of this old hymn speak well to the storms…

"The Lord's our rock, in Him we hide, A shelter in the time of storm; Secure whatever may be – tide, A shelter in the time of storm, Mighty rock in a weary land, Cooling shade on a burning sand; Faithful guide for the pilgrim band, a shelter in the time of storm (Refrain)
A shade by day, defense by night,
A shelter in the time of storm;
No fears alarm, no foes affright,
A shelter in the time of storm
O Rock divine, O refuge dear,
A shelter in the time of storm;
Be Thou our helper ever near,
A shelter in the time of storm"

DAY 292

October 19

He stilled the storm to a whisper
The waves of the sea were hushed.

Psalm 107:29

PSALM 107:29

All of us journey through storms and difficult seasons in our lives. Often we feel abandoned when facing these hardships. But God patiently waits for us in the eye of the storm -as well as in every other difficult situation we have to endure. All we have to do is cry out to, and reach out for, Him. We are closest to Him when we are at our weakest – but the truth is that the Lord is a refuge for us, not just in the storm, but in every moment of life.

The Oxford Dictionary defines "refuge" as "a condition of feeling safe or sheltered from, pursuit, danger, or trouble". The Free Dictionary defines it as "a source of help, relief, or comfort in times of trouble" - this one resonates well with King David's use of the word.

King David often referred to the Lord as a refuge, a rock, and a fortress. When we lean on the Lord, as King David did, in our time of need, we will find Him waiting with open arms. If we trust Him and turn to Him in our moments of distress, He will shed His grace, strength, safety, deliverance, provision, joy, restoration, and comfort on us, each and every time.

Psalm 91:2 offers us the comfort we need to face the storms: "I will say of the Lord, He is my refuge and my fortress; my God; in Him will I trust."

DAY 293

October 20

Be still and know
that I am God.

Psalm 46:10

PSALM 46:10

We cannot put ourselves directly in the presence
of God if we do not practice internal
and external silence.

In silence we will find new energy and true unity.
Silence gives us a new outlook on everything.

The essential thing is not what we say but what God
says to us and through us. In that silence, He will
listen to us; there He will speak to our soul, and there
we will hear His voice.

Listen in silence because if your heart is full of other
things you cannot hear the voice of God. But when
you have listened to the voice of God in the stillness
of your heart, then your heart is filled with God.

In nature we find silence – the trees, flowers, and
grass, grow in silence. The stars, the moon,
and the sun, move in silence.

Silence of the heart is necessary so you can hear
God everywhere – in the closing of a door, in the
person who needs you, in the birds that sing,
in the flowers, in the animals.

- Mother Teresa (In the Heart of the World)

DAY 294

October 21

The Lord will sustain him on his sickbed
And restore him from his bed of illness.

Psalm 41:3

PSALM 41:3

It is often said that people in the medical profession make the worst patients. When they get ill they stubbornly refuse to accept it, until they are so sick that they are forced to stop and pay attention. Then, they proceed to tell everyone what to do, or, insist on doing things for themselves that they really cannot do at that moment in time. Grace and patience elude them when they are not in the driving seat. Being a carer makes it very difficult to be the one receiving the care – we are not used to the idea of being dependent on others. It is a lesson in humility (and love) that, I suspect, many of us in the caring profession need to learn. Psalm 41 helps put things in perspective. Verse 3 can be translated: "...all his bed You (O Lord), will turn, change, and transform." In other words, this passage is saying that God will make up and turn our sickbed. Like a parent caring for a sick child, or, like a nurse with their patient, God cares for us and tends to us in our sickness and in our health; He transforms our circumstances - if we allow Him to. We might find it hard to accept help from our colleagues and families, but, we need to let our defences down and let God tend to us. Is your heart broken? Are you over-burdened, stressed and weary? Are you caught up in uncertainty or feel directionless and lost? Take heart – God is always there to tend to you and sustain you throughout the tough times. God "restores us from our bed of illness."

DAY 295

October 22

My grace is sufficient for you, for my strength is made perfect in weakness.

2 Corinthians 12:9

ALMOST THERE

2 CORINTHIANS 12:9

We are often fearful and weak, but we are never alone. We can claim the words of "Amazing Grace" as our own. Although written in the 1700's, they are still relevant today -"Tis grace has brought me safe thus far, and grace will lead me home." As Christians, we have the Holy Spirit within us. We have heavenly hosts above us and Jesus standing up for us. And, we have God's super-powered grace to strengthen and carry us through.

Saint Paul's life revealed this truth - He wrote, "I was given a thorn in my flesh, a messenger from Satan to torment me and keep me from becoming proud. Three times I have begged the Lord to take it away. Each time, He said -"My grace is all you need. My power works best in weakness." (2 Corinthians 12:7-9)

We all have a thorn in the flesh – the sharp end of it pierces the soft skin of our life and lodges beneath the surface. Every step we take is a reminder of that thorn piercing our flesh.

A debilitating illness, a broken heart, a destroyed marriage, a bad report card, tears flowing in the middle of the night – all thorns in the flesh. No matter how hard and how often we pray to the Lord to take it away, the answer is always the same – "My grace is all you need." God's grace wipes out everything on the landscape. It is not puny, but plentiful. Not teeny, but torrential. It is majestic and it meets us right now, at our point of need, and equips us with courage, wisdom and strength.

DAY 296

October 23

The eternal God is your refuge, and underneath are the everlasting arms.

Deuteronomy 33:27

DEUTERONOMY 33:27

As Christians we are urged to be Disciples of Christ – to be active in His Church, to be of service to those in need, and to help spread the Gospel. This involves spending time enriching our own spiritual life, and trying to make a difference in the lives of others.

But the other side to our Christian life - being "underneath the everlasting arms", depends more on faith than action. It entails placing our trust in God and being confident in His ability to take care of us.

"Everlasting Arms", as applied to God, symbolises a number of things. It can mean protection – a father puts his arm around a child when he is in danger. It can be a demonstration of affection - it is a token of love when we embrace someone. It can be a symbol of strength – an arm we can lean on with confidence – "in the Lord Jehovah is everlasting strength" (Isaiah 26:4). And finally, it can denote endurance – the arms of God are "everlasting" – they never grow weary of supporting us.

At the two extremes of life, God comes with special assurance. "He shall gather the lambs in His arms, and carry them in His bosom" (Isaiah 40:11), is for the children. "Even in your old age and grey hairs I am he, I am he who will sustain you" (Isaiah 46:4), brings comfort to the aged. And so, throughout the course of our life, we can take refuge underneath the wings of Gods love. Whether we are happy or sad, God is there to share in our joy, or to wipe away our tears. And as He has promised, He "never slumbers nor sleeps" (Psalm 121:4).

DAY 297

October 24

I sought the Lord, and he
answered me and he delivered
me from all my fears.

Psalm 34:4

PSALM 34:4

How many of us, as young children, went in search of our parents in the middle of the night when we got sick or had a bad dream. Nothing felt safer, or was more comforting, than crawling into their bed and snuggling up to them. The thought that they may refuse us love and attention, didn't even enter our heads. We knew, without a shadow of doubt that they would take care of us.

Why then, do we hesitate to, or sometimes, even forget to, seek the Lord when confronted with illness or other hardships. We are so reluctant to entrust God with our lives, and yet, He is ever present to comfort us and to liberate us from all our fears. He is our Heavenly Father and, like our earthly parents, He will never fail to draw us into His loving arms when we ask Him to. God is love. He created us and He knows us. He waits, in love, for us to look to Him for deliverance.

DAY 298

October 25

In the world you will have trouble,
But take courage,
I have conquered the world.

John 16:33

ALMOST THERE

JOHN 16:33

As Christians, we believe that Jesus broke, and defeated, the power of sin and death by accepting his Father's will to go to the cross. And, in so doing, He brought life and immortality to light. Because of it, even in the midst of sorrows and trials, we can take heart and have peace. The hard things in life are only temporary. Our peace is not in the absence of strife and trouble, but in the knowledge that they prepare us for eternal glory. Jesus insured that death will not have the final say.

DAY 299

October 26

Do not let your hearts be troubled.
You have faith in God;
Have faith also in me.

John 14:1

ALMOST THERE

JOHN 14:1

What does it mean to have faith? Our world is a beautiful place because of its diversity - in culture, lifestyle, as well as in faith. The meaning of faith is different for each of us, but one thing is universal – being a person of faith gives you peace of mind and a purpose in life.

Having faith means recognizing that you have no control – that, what will be, will be. It entails letting go of your worries, believing that your life has a reason, and, that all will be OK in the end.

There will always be difficult life decisions to make, and hard situations to face and take care of. Sometimes these things might seem a bit overwhelming – life will never be plain sailing. But faith gives you someone, or something, to lean on during these times when you feel incapable of making it on your own.

Faith makes you realise that nothing in this life is permanent. It does not ensure that life will be easy and free of sadness and strive – it will, however, give you the extra push to make it through those bad patches when you start to question it all.

It is important to have faith in your own abilities, but, it is more important to know and believe that God is in control and has paved the path for your journey through this life. Walking on that path ensures a homecoming in His Kingdom when your earthly life is done.

DAY 300

October 27

Your Father knows what you
need before you ask him.

Matthew 6:8

MATTHEW 6:8

If God already knows what our needs are, why do we need to ask him for anything at all? Why doesn't He simply provide us with our wants and desires?

Perhaps it is because we have been born with a free will, and our expectations may not always be in alignment with His divine plan for our life. As parents, we often have to say no to our children's wants and demands. We have the ability to see ahead and to inherently know what is best for them. Sometimes, the decisions are tough to make, and our children fail to understand that we are acting out of love for them. Anger and resentment often follow.

Our only way of communicating with God is through prayer - He wants us to remember that we can bring our needs, dreams, desires, and, even our fears, to Him. Ultimately, God will provide for us. He is our Father and will always do what is best for us.

DAY 301

October 28

The Lord is with me,
Like a mighty champion.

Jeremiah 20:11

JEREMIAH 20:11

Jeremiah was being rejected for delivering the prophecies of God to the people. He was on an emotional roller coaster – unhappy with life and cursing his birth the one moment, and, full of hope the next. Sometimes, he was almost rebelling against God.

This pattern seems to repeat itself in the life of most Christians. It is easy to acknowledge our faith when the going is good. However, it is when the going gets tough and hardships abound, that the Lord becomes "our mighty champion." Although it may seem as if God has deserted us and left us to our own devices, He is ever present. We too rebel against God when we cannot make sense of life. But God understands our human frailness and stays loyal to us. Like Jeremiah, we must continue crying out to God and trust that He is in control of our life.

DAY 302

October 29

The Lord is my light and my salvation;
Whom shall I fear?

Psalm 27:1

PSALM 27:1

There is a lot to be afraid of in this life – cancer, our loved ones suffering and dying, losing our job, mental illness, terrorism, and even global warming. However, one fear stands out from the rest. Human beings are social animals and being part of a group, having a sense of belonging and being loved, is paramount for our wellbeing and self-worth. Loneliness was long thought of as a shadow following old people, but, a survey conducted in London in 2014, showed that young people were more likely to become depressed because of loneliness, than people over 55 years of age. Young people are increasingly scared of never finding love that leads to a lasting relationship and family life.

When we face these storms of fear and uncertainty, it is a great blessing and comfort to know that the Lord has promised to be our refuge. Jesus is our rock and, through faith and prayer, we will always find shelter and security in His arms. "I will pray the Father, and He will give you another Helper, that He may abide with you forever-the Spirit of truth.....I will not leave you orphans; I will come to you." (John 14:16-18) We never need to feel abandoned and alone – Jesus promises to be with us – and even be, through His Spirit, in us.

DAY 303

October 30

Come to me, all you who labour and are burdened, and I will give you rest

Matthew 11:28

MATTHEW 11:28

One night I dreamed a dream. As I was walking along the beach with My Lord, across the dark sky flashed scenes from my life. For each scene, I noticed two sets of footprints in the sand- one belonging to me, and one to my Lord.

After the last scene of my life flashed before me, I looked back at the footprints in the sand. I noticed that at many times along the path of my life, especially at the very lowest and saddest times, there was only one set of footprints.

This really troubled me, so I asked the Lord about it. "Lord, you said once I decided to follow you, you'd walk with me all the way. But I noticed that during the saddest and most troublesome times of my life, there was only one set of footprints. I don't understand why, when I needed you the most, you would leave me."

He whispered, "My precious child, I love you and will never leave you- never ever during you trials and testings. When you saw only one set of footprints, it was then that I carried you." - Mary Fishback Powers

Afflictions are but the shadows of Gods' protecting wings - George MacDonald

DAY 304

October 31

Hide me in the
shadow of your wings

Psalm 17:8

PSALM 17:8

In this Psalm, David is praying to God and asking Him to defend him and keep him safe from his enemies.

It is a beautiful analogy. Imagine a parent bird completely shielding her brood from evil and danger. Cherishing them with the warmth of her own heart by covering them with her wings, she demonstrates a parent's love in perfection. (Spurgeon) In the shadow of her wings they are protected from predators, the elements, and any other danger surrounding them.

God is our Father, we are His offspring, and His love for us is unfailing. He will never desert us in times of trouble or need. He will shield us, and protect us, from our enemies. All we have to do is to pray and ask for His help. And, like David, we must be steadfast in our faith, and have a calm confidence that God will hear us when we cry out to him in distress.

We can forgive a child for fearing the dark;
The real tragedy of life is people
Who fear the light
- Plato

DAY 305-334

November

A Prayer of Saint Anselm

Lord Jesus Christ; Let me seek you by desiring you,
And let me desire you by seeking you;
Let me find you by loving you, and love you in finding you.
I confess, Lord, with thanksgiving, that you
have made me in your image.
So that I can remember you, think of you, and love you.
But that image is so worn and blotted out by faults,
And darkened by the smoke of sin,
That it cannot do that for which it was made,
Unless you renew and refashion it
Lord, I am not trying to make my way to your height,
For my understanding is in no way equal to that,
But I do desire to understand a little of your truth
Which my heart already believes and loves
I do not seek to understand so that I can believe,
But I believe so that I may understand;
And what more, I believe that unless I do believe,
I shall not understand

— St Anselm

DAY 305

November 01

You will keep in perfect peace
Him whose mind is steadfast,
Because he trusts in you

Isaiah 26:3

ALMOST THERE

ISAIAH 26:3

This verse is ideal to commit to memory. In this time of turmoil, political instability, racial tensions, violence against women and children, genocide, and all sorts of other atrocities, it is difficult to believe that God is in control. Our faith also threatens to fail when we face pain and hardships in our personal life. Watching a loved one suffering and fading away from cancer, or, being unable to provide for your family due to financial strain, is a sure way of losing our "perfect peace."

But Isaiah wrote, "Thou wilt keep him in perfect peace, whose mind is stayed on thee: because he trusteth in thee." This wonderful promise, given to Israel in the darkest period of their history, should prove to be of special help to us today, just as it was to them. But our mind must be "stayed" on Christ – then we are trusting in Him.

In order for us to have peace, all we need to do is to focus our minds on God. When we truly focus our minds on the Lord, along with that focus will come trust in Him, and in His power.

Peace is a condition of freedom from disturbance within our soul; it is perfect harmony reigning within us. St Paul captures this fully when he communicates with the Philippians – "And the peace of God, which transcends all understanding, will guard your hearts and your minds in Christ Jesus." (Philippians 4:7)

DAY 306

November 02

When Jesus spoke again to the people,
He said "I am the light of the world.
Whoever follows me will never walk in darkness,
But will have the light of life."

John 8:12

JOHN 8:12

Following Jesus means accepting His authority and acting in accordance with His teaching. As true followers of Jesus, we choose not follow the ways of sin, but, rather choose to repent of our sin in order to stay close to the Light of the World.

When we take a candle into a room it dispels darkness. Therefore a light is an illumination bright enough to see with. A light in the darkness, like a candle, gives the ability to see. A light offers someone who is stumbling in the darkness, the opportunity to see where they are going.

Jesus uses the word, "light", metaphorically. He uses it to refer to Himself as being able to illuminate the truth. His teachings guide us back to God. Believing in the Light of His Word, gives us the Light of Eternal Life. And, just as physical light is necessary for physical life, spiritual light is necessary for spiritual life. And, just as plants will never move away from the light, the believer will always lean towards spiritual things – fellowship, prayer, and studying the Word of God.

Jesus came to be the Light of the World, and, as His representatives on earth, He commands us to be "lights" too. Our lives need to reflect the Light of Christ, so that all who see it can follow the light and find everlasting life.

DAY 307

November 03

For with you is the fountain of life;
In your light we see light.

Psalm 36:9

PSALM 36:9

These words of King David seem to be paving the way for Jesus. Water is the source of all life. Without water we cannot survive. Jesus, the Source of Living Water, extends an invitation of eternal life to all who thirst. "If anyone is thirsty, let him come to me and drink." (John 7:37)

The words of Jesus' invitation echo in our ears. Jesus stands at the door of our hearts and speaks to each person, offering the water of eternal life. However, the first requirement is thirst. Everyone has spiritual thirst – it is part of our human condition. Sin, is our seeking relief from this thirst, in something other than God.

Jesus invites those who recognize their need, those who are poor in spirit (Matthew 5:3), to come to him and drink. Drinking from the fountain of life means to believe in him, to trust him, to receive his teachings, and obey his commands. When we believe, we open our hearts to receive his grace and the gift of the Spirit.

DAY 308

November 04

Blessed are all those
Who put their trust in Him

Psalm 2:12

PSALM 2:12

Trusting in God does not simply mean believing in Him - it is much more than that. It involves our actions, our thoughts, our words, and our motives. It means not worrying about tomorrow. It means trusting Him with our health, our finances, our home, our work, our relationships, and all our tomorrows.

There will always be times in our life when things seem too hard to bear or to handle- times when our world seems to be falling apart and feelings of despair fill our hearts and minds. It is then that we must take refuge, and draw strength, from the knowledge that God knows our tomorrow. Jesus commands us not to worry – "therefore I tell you, do not worry about your life, what you will eat or drink; or about your body, what you will wear." (Matthew 6:25)

It is easy to forget the truth that God loves us, fights for us, and takes care of our every need. We should strive to remain close to God's word every day. When we constantly remind ourselves of his good works, his saving power, and his great love for us, we become "like a weaned child with its mother; like a weaned child I am content." (Psalm 131:2)

DAY 309

November 05

The Lord will keep you from all harm He will watch over your life. The Lord will watch over your coming and going both now and for evermore

Psalm 121:7-8

PSALM 121:7-8

"The Lord will keep you from all harm"

When confronted with things like human need, hunger, depravation, evil, and even death, these words of the Psalmist seem far removed from the reality of the suffering we often have to endure.

We may suffer terribly in this life. But no matter what the specifics of our life are, we all have plenty of assurance of God's goodness, and care, throughout our life and death. We may sink in the storms of life, but Jesus always reaches out as we flounder. The answer to our prayers may not always be as quick as we would like them to be. They may not even be clearly visible or understood. But, when we look back on our life, we will see God's power, and guidance, over the long haul.

God loves us, and our suffering does not go unnoticed by him. It is true that bad things may happen to us. But when we affirm and believe in God's ultimate power, our life takes on a new meaning and a new purpose.

DAY 310

November 06

The Lord himself will fight for you;
You have only to keep still.

Exodus 14:14

EXODUS 14:14

Those of us who grew up in a house with an older brother will recall how they teased us, and drove us crazy. However, they always protected us, loved us unconditionally, and played a huge role in our early life. The pranks and silly games boys played, taught us not to get angry or frustrated too easily. Boys always keep their emotions in check - "suck it up" and move on. We learnt to follow suite, and not carry our emotions on our sleeves – we got tough. And, although he showed us how to stand up for ourselves and not get pushed around, sometimes, we just needed our older brothers' protection. Men, like a lion to its cubs, adopt a very protective nature when it comes to the well-being of their little sisters.

God is greater than even the best older brother. He promises that He will fight for us, protect us, clothe us, and feed us. Getting through this world and this life is not easy for anyone, and, if we rely on our own strength, it is immeasurably harder. All we have to do is be still, ask God for help, and then trust that He has the skills to deliver.

DAY 311

November 07

It is the Lord who marches before you; He will be with you and will never fail you or forsake you.

Deuteronomy 31:6

DEUTERONOMY 31:6

Throughout the history of warfare there has been a divide between the armchair generals and those who charged forwards, pistols drawn. During both the First World War, and the Second, Rommel was often criticised for being so far forward that he worried his staff sick. He dismissed these cautions by declaring that a commander must be forward in order to "read" the battle. But there was another reason. Rommel knew that the presence of a commander can have an extraordinary effect on his troops. Napoleon, too, knew that the sight of a leader could spur the morale of the men. Great men have always dared to serve, and to lead, from the front.

It is no surprise then, that it is Jesus, who marches in front of us. Jesus is present at every battle we encounter during our life. He is there with guidance, support, comfort, and love. His presence lifts our morale and gives us the strength to face our hardships. His wisdom is there for us to draw on, and, His teachings are like a beacon for us to follow. And sometimes, when it all seems too much, He simply enfolds us in His arms, and charges forward on our behalf.

DAY 312

November 08

"Peace I leave with you, My peace I give to you; not as the world gives do I give to you. Let not your hearts be troubled, Neither let it be afraid."

John 14:27

ALMOST THERE

JOHN 14:27

Jesus wants us to have peace. Without it we are missing out on one of the major blessings his death and resurrection has secured for us. Somehow, I think, we make it too hard and complicated for ourselves. We believe that in the midst of a storm only the "super saints", who have "super faith", can maintain peace of mind. However, the Bible assures us that it does not require heroic acts of piety. In fact, the secret to contentment is very simple – "Trust in the Lord with all your heart" (Proverbs 3:5).

Experiencing God's peace is a gift - given freely – to every child of His. In the Old Testament, in the wonderful words of the benediction used by the priests, the promise is: "The Lord lift up His countenance upon you and give you peace" (Numbers 6:26). We cannot hope for a life without pain, but we can, with the help of the Holy Spirit, experience peace amidst the sorrow.

"Thou will keep him in perfect peace whose mind is stayed on Thee" (Isaiah 26:3)

"God hasn't promised skies ever blue, flower strewn pathways always for you God hasn't promised sun without rain, Joy without sorrow, peace without pain But God has promised strength from above, unfailing sympathy, undying love"- Unknown

DAY 313

November 09

But if the Spirit of him who raised Jesus from the dead dwells in you, He who raised Christ from the dead will also give life to your mortal bodies through his Spirit who dwells in you

Romans 8:11

ROMANS 8:11

Near the end of his life, D L Moody said, "Soon you will read in the newspapers that I am dead. Don't believe it for a moment. I will be more alive than ever before."

The apostle Paul wrote, "I have been crucified with Christ; it is no longer I who live, but Christ lives in me" (Galatians 2:20). It is God's desire for us to be "conformed to the image of His Son" (Romans 8:29). The degree to which God, and Jesus, dwell in us as Christians, depends on the degree to which we follow the leading of the Holy Spirit, and use His power to actually become Christ-like - in nature, character, spirit, attitudes, approach and love. We need to "walk as He walked and live as He lived" (1 John 2:6). When we humbly and earnestly strive to be like Jesus, the Holy Spirit will give us the knowledge, understanding, and strength, to change and live righteously.

It is the heart and core of Christianity to want to change and become like Jesus – to have His life formed in us. Without Jesus our life is futile. But if we belong to Him, no matter when we die, we have the certainty that God, who raised Jesus from the dead, will raise us too through His Spirit who dwells in us.

DAY 314

November 10

"Jesus Christ who died.....
Who was raised up to life
Is at the right hand of God.....
Interceding for us"

Romans 8:34

ALMOST THERE

ROMANS 8:34

Intercession, or intercessory prayer, is the act of praying to a deity on behalf of others. In Western Christianity, Intercession forms a distinct form of prayer, alongside Adoration, Confession and Thanksgiving.

A follower of Jesus – a Christian – should strive to be Christ-like. One of the most important ways in which we can achieve this, is in attempting to help carry each other's burdens. In the same way that the Godhead - Father, Son and Holy Spirit- are tied together, three in one, we as human are tied together. We are all part of a greater whole. God calls us to care for each other. He asks us to pray for a stranger, or for someone who has done us harm. When we try to walk in someone else's shoes and feel their pain, when we pray for others and put their interest before our own, or when we willingly forgive those that hurt us, we align ourselves, and our actions, with God's will.

By including intercessory prayer in our daily life – praying for those living on the streets, for countries ravaged by war, for the sick, the elderly, or the lonely – we begin to heal ourselves. With the help of the Holy Spirit we begin to see Christ in the guise of the poor, the stranger, the enemy, and those in need of our help.

Jesus intercedes for us in heaven - it is our role to intercede for each other on this earth.

DAY 315

November 11

I knew that you were a God of tenderness and compassion, slow to anger, rich in graciousness, relenting from evil

Jonah 4:2

JONAH 4:2

It is because of God's compassion, slowness to anger, and willingness to forgive, that we are able to face our life, and death, without fear and trepidation. In Isaiah 49:15 we read, "Can a woman forget her nursing child, that she should not have compassion on the son of her womb? Yes, they may forget, yet I will not forget you." This description underscores the depth of Jesus's compassion for us. The compassion that a mother feels for her child is probably one of the tenderest feelings known to mankind. A small baby needs to be fed, cuddled, and otherwise tended to - and a mother's heart doesn't allow her to ignore those needs. And yet, the tender compassion of our God is infinitely stronger. He is fully aware of our needs and our hardships. He knows when we succeed and are happy, or when failings and disappointments cause despair and sadness.

Psalm 34:18 assures us that when we are "broken at heart", or "crushed in spirit", Jehovah, like a loving parent, "is near" – always compassionate and ready to help and guide us.

DAY 316

November 12

For the wages of sin is death, but
the gift of God is eternal life in
Christ Jesus our Lord

Romans 6:23

ROMANS 6:23

"Do not love the world or the things in the world. If anyone loves the world, the love of the Father is not in him. For all that is in the world – the lust of the flesh, the lust of the eyes, and the pride of life- is not of the Father but is of the world. And the world is passing away, and the lust of it, but he who does the will of God abides forever."
(1 John 2:15)

Jesus died on the cross, and, because of His sacrifice and grace, we have been freed from the attractions of this life, and from the power that sin once held over us. And so, just as Christ was raised from the dead, we too are given the chance to live a new life - a life of holiness, purity, and integrity. In the words of Saint Paul –"You may have been freed from the slavery of sin, but only to become "slaves" of righteousness." (Romans 6:18) We now find our reward in serving and loving others. This reward leads to our sanctification, and ends in eternal life.

DAY 317

November 13

Having come down in a cloud, the Lord stood with him there..... Moses at once bowed down to the ground in worship.

Exodus 34:5 & 8

EXODUS 34:5 & 8

In the same way that Jesus taught us to "First take the log out of your own eye, and then you will see clearly to take the speck out of your brother's eye", Saint Paul cautions all Christians against standing in judgement of their fellow believers. We are called upon to make moral decisions concerning good and bad, right and wrong, being helpful or unhelpful, kindness and cruelty. But we should never be arrogant or critical. Guiding others should always be done with affection, kindness, and understanding.

Finally, we will all stand before the judgement seat of God. Then we will have to give an account of how we fulfilled his purpose for us on earth - to trust him, to love him, to obey him, and to display his greatness to the world. When we show love, kindness, and understanding to others, and recognize our own faults, before standing in judgement of them, we truly confess to all that "Jesus Christ is Lord." God knows our every thought and no sin is hidden from His sight. If we live according to His word, and by faith, we can be sure to face judgement day without fear.

DAY 318

November 14

The eyes of the Lord are upon those who fear him, Upon those who hope for his kindness...

Psalm 33:18

PSALM 33:18

What does it mean to fear God, and why must we fear him? The Hebrew verb, yare, can mean, "to fear, to respect, to reverence", and the Hebrew noun, yirah, usually refers to the fear of God - and is viewed as a positive quality. The Greek noun, phobos, can mean "reverential fear" of God – "not a mere 'fear' of His power and righteous retribution, but a wholesome dread of displeasing Him". (Vine's Complete Expository Dictionary of Old and New Testament Words, 1985, Fear, Fearful, Fearfulness").

So, therefore, the fear of the Lord is an attitude of respect - a response of reverence and wonder. In the words of King David "Come, you children, listen to me; I will teach you the fear of the Lord...... Keep your tongue from evil, and do good; seek peace and pursue it." (Psalm 34: 11, 13-14)

A healthy fear of God includes the fear of the consequences of disobedience. There may be times of temptation or trial, when we forget some of the better reasons for obeying God - that is when we had better think of the consequences. (Exodus 20:20)

DAY 319

November 15

All things are possible with God.

Mark 10:27

MARK 10:27

"For God all things are possible" – this must surely be one of the most powerful verses in scripture. Jesus has just seen the rich young man, eager to "inherit eternal life", go sadly away when told that he would have to relinquish all that he owned. This was a young man who had two things - everything and nothing. He was wealthy and successful, but he turned away from Jesus with nothing. He had everything that money could provide, yet he was searching for something more in life.

"I have run; I have crawled; I have scaled these city walls; Only to be with you. But I still haven't found what I'm looking for." "You broke the bonds; And you loosed the chains; Carried the cross for my shame; Oh my shame, you know I believe it. But I still haven't found what I looking for." These are the words of Bono and the Irish rock group, U2, recorded in 1987. They echo the universal search of millions of people today. What we all seek is a relationship with Jesus. But, just like the rich young man, we also ask - "What shall I do to inherit eternal life"? The answer requires real sensitivity and honesty with regards to our own instincts and values. Wealth is usually a reward of hard work – but work itself can also be an emotional obstacle to following Jesus. Managing careers become more important than making time for family, our spiritual life, or serving others. Wealth and status make us arrogant, selfish, and insensitive to the needs of our neighbour. In trying to find "what we are looking for", we have to follow Jesus – store our treasures in heaven. We cannot simply try harder to be good – we have to accept God's love and his promise. When we trust God for the things we really need in life, we have no need to hold on to our possessions or status. Then, unlike the rich young man, we will not turn sadly away – we will turn towards a new life, and a new relationship, with God, our Father.

DAY 320

November 16

The fear of man lays a
snare. But whoever trusts
in the Lord is safe.

Proverbs 29:25

PROVERBS 29:25

Every Christian at some point has to deal with, and face, the "fear of man". Just when we think we are enjoying spiritual growth and victory, it rears its power over us and hinders us from living in the freedom Christ has called us to. This "fear of man" is a biblical category of fear that entails our preoccupation with what other people think of us. It is a fear that makes us long for people's approval and fear people's rejection. This preoccupation with what others think about us puts people above God in our lives.

Teenagers are particularly vulnerable. They have peer pressure to contend with – they must think, dress, talk, and believe, in a certain way. They are pressured into liking certain things, and into disliking and rejecting others. As adults, the "fear of man" manifests in a variety of ways. We dislike looking foolish, and therefore miss many opportunities -because we shy away from things we are not good at. We often become motivated by pride, and, as a result, our lives and identities get determined by what people think- rather than what God thinks of us. Our need to be the centre of attention, to be well-liked, and seen as successful, represents the snare that separates us from God .The Bible teaches us that the way to overcome the "fear of man" is with a greater fear – "the fear of God". "The fear of the Lord is the fountain of life that allows one to turn away from the snares of death" (Proverbs 14:27). As Christians we believe, and should remember, that on the day we stand before the judgement seat of Christ, all those things we deemed so important, will melt away- and only His approval and acceptance of us will make us welcome in His kingdom.

When God is big, we are small and others are small and life is in the right perspective.

DAY 321

November 17

In the world you will have trouble, but take courage, I have conquered the world

John 16:33

ALMOST THERE

JOHN 16:33

Jesus died for us on the cross, and, in so doing He gave us eternal life, and conquered sin. But we still need to live in this world, and face the hardship and suffering that goes along with it. Jesus warned us of that.

A Christian way to respond to these tribulations could be to "pay forward" the sacrifice Jesus paid for our salvation.

We don't all need to be volunteers in disaster areas, or fire fighters or police, who put their lives in direct danger to protect us. But we can all play a role in feeding the hungry, or taking care of the elderly, the infirm, and the orphans. Simply adding our prayer to the collective voice against evil and cruelty is enough. Jesus conquered the world, but, we are His heirs, and have a joint responsibility to serve on this earth.

DAY 322

November 18

Can any of you by worrying
add a single moment to
your life-span?

Matthew 6:27

MATTHEW 6:27

We all realise that this is a rhetorical question, and, that it is asked so as to provoke thought and action. Instead of living with constant anxiety we are challenged to find ways to take charge of our lives. The cloth of life has not been fairly cut, and some people endure more hardship and suffering than others. However, the more we learn to trust God and to except that He cares for us, the easier it is for us to be proactive and find solutions to the problems we face.

Maturity is the ability to joyfully
live in an imperfect world
- Richard Rohr

DAY 323

November 19

Do not work for food that perishes
But for the food that endures for eternal
life, which the Son of Man will give you

John 6:27

ALMOST THERE

JOHN 6:27

With these words Jesus is not suggesting that we never eat, try to earn a living, watch TV, play sport, socialise, or do any of the things that make us human.

However, He is cautioning us against doing all these things in lieu of looking after our spiritual life. We live in this world and most of us enjoy material pleasures. Jesus did too, and He understands this. He is simply reminding us that material pleasures and possessions will pass away.

We simply cannot afford to neglect the spiritual activities that will bring us to eternal life.

DAY 324

November 20

There shall be one
shepherd for them all.

Ezekiel 37:24

EZEKIEL 37:24

Here we are reminded that we all belong to the same God. No matter what our race, colour, creed, culture, or even our sexual orientation, we are all children of the one divine God.

The prophet Ezekiel was writing during a period of division and exile of God's people. But, it is a sad reality that in our age, there is as much animosity between nations and different religions as there was in his time.

God sent the good shepherd, His son, Jesus, to bring a vision of unity to the flock. Although we resist, we are constantly being drawn back to each other. As Christians, we are expected to lead the way in acceptance, and tolerance, of our neighbours.

"Blessed are the pure in heart,
for they will see God."

"Blessed are the peacemakers, for they will be called children of God." (Matthew 5:8-9)

DAY 325

November 21

I have given you a model to follow, so that as I have done for you, you should also do.

John 13:15

JOHN 13:15

The example that Jesus is referring to, and wants us to emulate, takes place during the last supper with his disciples. Jesus is aware that His time has come, and that soon he will be betrayed by one that he loves. Yet he chooses to spend his last hours giving a demonstration of servant leadership – he washes their feet.

Jesus is trying to teach them, and us, a fundamental lesson of life. We are all equal in God's sight - the master is no greater than the servant, the rich no greater than the poor. Black or white, male or female, we are all here to serve and love one another.

Jesus humbled himself to emphasise that no one is too great, too superior, too rich, or, even too famous, to offer help and comfort to others. God expects us to reach out to those less fortunate than ourselves.

DAY 326

November 22

You will show me
the path to life.....

Psalm 16:11

ALMOST THERE

PSALM 16:11

I cannot recall, with total clarity, all the momentous occasions of my life. I was too young to remember much about my first holy communion, or my confirmation. I have some pleasant, and scary, memories of my first day at school. I can easily relive the feelings of pride, joy, and relief, I felt at my graduation ceremonies.

One thing was constant throughout all these major life events – my parents were at my side, sharing in my accomplishments. If they had not guided, taught, and helped me prepare to make a success of my life, these milestones would have been that much harder to attain.

God promises to show us the path to everlasting life. This path, inevitably, involves our death, and the fear of the unknown that accompanies it. However, God sent Jesus to be with us, to teach and guide us on our spiritual path. Jesus is our spiritual parent, and, like our earthly parents, he will be with us every step of the way.

As long as I am content to know
That he is infinitely greater than I,
And that I cannot know him unless
He shows himself to me,
I will have peace,
And he will be near me and in me,
And I will rest in him.
- Thomas Merton

DAY 327

November 23

My strength and courage is the Lord, and he has been my saviour.

Psalm 118:14

ALMOST THERE

PSALM 118:14

One has to wonder what hardship inspired the author to write this psalm. One school of thought is that the author is King David and that at the time he was rejected by his friends and fellow countrymen, and opposed by his enemies.

Our realities are very different, and, as we struggle to make sense of sickness, addictions, murders, poverty and inequality, it might be difficult to accept that Jesus has conquered suffering and death.

Only through faith in His death and resurrection can we triumph over our pain and face our own death without apprehension. Jesus will walk beside us to calm our anxiety and fear. Jesus himself took comfort from this psalm on His way to Gethsemane, and, finally, Golgotha. Let it be our strength and courage as well.
- Professor Jan van der Watt

DAY 328

November 24

I have set before you life and death, the blessing and the curse choose life.....

Deuteronomy 30:19

DEUTERONOMY 30:19

People have rights, human rights. This is the dominant philosophy of our time. This allows every person the freedom to make their own decisions and grants them the freedom of speech. This philosophy places people at the centre which clashes with our faith. Our religion places God at the centre. If a person decides that God must occupy that spot in his life, he gives up the right to decide what's right and what's wrong. This becomes God's choice.

Fortunately God and people want the same thing – happiness. Both want to achieve love, peace and contentment. However, the route that each one maps out to reach that joy and peace differs.

Jesus gave us the roadmap for our life – it is for that reason that He is known as "the Way, the Truth, and the Life" (John 14:6). Real truth is something we can only get from Jesus. So, if anyone is searching for the truth that will lead him or her to true life, they will have to look to Him to find it - Professor Jan van der Watt

DAY 329

November 25

And he said with a loud voice, "Fear God, and give Him glory, because the hour of judgement has come; worship Him who made the heavens and the earth and sea and springs of waters."

Revelation 14:7

REVELATION 14:7

The Bible teaches us that all men have two unavoidable appointments with God – death and judgement. "It is appointed for men to die once, but after this the judgement" (Hebrews 9:27). Regardless of our hectic, busy schedule, our status or age, we will all one day have to face these predestined meetings with our maker. What we are now, what we do now, and, what we believe now, all have a direct bearing on the outcome of these divine appointments.

None of us can escape the physical death, but God has provided a way for us to escape the second, eternal death. "For God so loved the world, that he gave his only begotten Son, that whoever believes in Him should not perish but have eternal life" (John 3:16).

We have all been born with free will. God grants us the privilege to choose how we live our life. We can choose to live a life addicted to the trappings of this world – one filled with immorality, violence, anger and greed. Or we can choose eternal life – living in accordance to the scriptures, repenting from our sins and loving God above all else, and, loving our neighbours as we love ourselves.

DAY 330

November 26

Neither do I condemn you.

John 8:11

JOHN 8:11

How easily we criticise and condemn our neighbours. How often do we harden our hearts and refuse to forgive someone who has done us harm. It would, therefore, seem natural to expect God to judge and condemn us in the same way. No wonder we are afraid to approach him at times.

Let us take courage in the simplicity of today's gospel message. Jesus refrains from judging the adulterous woman and challenges anyone to claim total freedom from sin.

Jesus recognises our sinful nature and is willing to forgive us if we acknowledge him as our Lord and Saviour. Like the adulterous woman, all we need to do is receive his mercy when he extends it. But, like the would-be stoners, we must accept that we are all sinners, and are all dependent on God's mercy.

DAY 331

November 27

Trust in Yahweh forever,
For Yahweh is the everlasting rock.

Isaiah 26:4

ISAIAH 26:4

Jesus gave us a comparison between a wise man and a foolish man. One built his house on a rock, the other on sand. Both faced fierce storms, but when "the rain descended and the floods came, and the winds blew and burst against the house" (Matthew 7:25), one stood firm and the other fell.

How many times have we behaved as if there is another rock – another place to stand, another unshakeable support? Yet always, we turn back to Jesus. He alone knows our heart, our present circumstances, and our hope for the future. He has a plan for our life that only He can fulfil.

Like the wise man, we must listen for, and hear, God's word – He asks us to come to Him, to follow Him, and to find rest in Him. He promises that the everlasting rock will never crumble. "Come to me all you who labour and are heavy laden, and I will give you rest." (Matthew 11:28-29)

DAY 332

November 28

This is the message we have heard from him and declare to you: God is light; In him there is no darkness at all.

1 John 1:5

ALMOST THERE

1 JOHN 1:5

God is perfect – "God is light and in Him there is no darkness at all." Light points to purity, honesty, transparency, and holiness.

Christians are often called "children of light", and are expected "to walk in the light, as He is in the light." But we are not perfect, and trying to live a holy life – not a perfect life – means constantly exposing ourselves to the light, so that where there is sin, it is willingly acknowledged.

In this world we are faced with violence, corruption, greed, poverty, disease, and selfishness. But God's word provides a light for our feet and a lamp for our path. Studying and believing God's word about death and salvation allows us to walk in the light of truth, and provides us with the peace and joy that Christ gives.

When facing the challenges presented in this life, we must remember to walk in the light of our God-given conscience – that part of our soul that deals with right and wrong. It is the light shining out, dispelling darkness - forcing us to recognise our sins and to deal with them

When we truly walk in the light, we see our sinful nature and our need for forgiveness - which comes from the blood of Jesus purifying us and granting us salvation

DAY 333

November 29

May the favour of the Lord our God rest upon us; establish the work of our hands for us. Yes-establish the work of our hands.

Psalm 90:17

PSALM 90:17

Mother Teresa devoted her entire life to helping the poor, the sick, the needy, and the helpless. In 1946, she experienced what she described as a "call within a call"- or inspiration- to leave the Loreto Convent and devote herself to caring for the sick and poor. She then moved into the slums. Her memory, and the legacy that she left behind, will be immortalised. The "work of her hands" was God's work done through her.

Not all of us can be a "Mother Teresa". But whether we are doctors, teachers, policemen, nurses, lawyers, or even politicians, we need to make sure that our work and daily life is in harmony with God's will. In John 9:4 Jesus says, "I must work the works of him that sent me while it is day." This life is short - it is only as the length of a day. What we do with our time on this earth is directly linked to whether or not we believe that our mortality is linked to eternity.

When we bring our will and our work into harmony with God's will and God's work, we find purpose and meaning in life. Our work will be "established" if it is His work. And then the favour of the Lord our God will rest upon us, and grant us eternal rest.

DAY 334

November 30

O Lord, you have searched me and you know me. You know when I sit and when I rise; You perceive my thoughts from afar.

Psalm 139:1-2

PSALM 139:1-2

Perhaps the closest we can get to really knowing and understanding another human being, is in the sacrament of marriage. When two people live together in that lifelong commitment, they grow to know one another's actions, words, and, depending on the degree that they openly communicate, thoughts and feelings. But, even after years of marriage, we can find ourselves at a loss to understand the behaviour, or actions, of our partner – even the closest human relationships fall short of total knowledge.

God, however, knows all things (is omniscient), and is everywhere (is omnipresent). He has perfect knowledge of us, and all our thoughts and actions are open before him. And yet, knowing us so intimately and recognizing our sinful nature, God still desires to have a relationship with us. There is no escape from God, and there is no place to hide. After all, he formed us even in our mother's womb for His purpose, and ordained all of our days before we ever saw the light of day. And so, like King David before us, we must commit ourselves to a life of holiness, and pray that the God who has searched us will complete the process - so that any sin still remaining can be rooted out, and we can walk in God's everlasting way.

DAY 335-365

December

Peace Prayer

Lord, make me an instrument of your peace;
Where there is hatred, let me sow love;
Where there is injury, pardon;
Where there is doubt, faith;
Where there is despair, hope;
Where there is darkness, light;
And where there is sadness, joy.
O Divine Master, grant that I may not so much seek to be consoled as to console; To be understood, as to understand; To be loved, as to love; For it is in giving that we receive,
It is in pardoning that we are pardoned,
And it is in dying that we are born to Eternal Life.
Amen.

- Saint Francis of Assisi

DAY 335

December 01

Then I saw a new heaven and a new earth, for the first heaven and the first earth had passed away, and there was no longer any sea.

Revelation 21:1

ALMOST THERE

REVELATION 21:1

As Christians we look forward to the Second Coming of Christ – to the time when all things will be made new. We are told that there will be a new heaven and a new earth, and that God will dwell amongst us and we will be his people. "And God will wipe away every tear from their eyes; there shall be no more death, nor sorrow, nor crying. There shall be no more pain, for the former things have passed away" (Revelation 21:4). But, in order to gain eternal life and live with our Father in the new heaven and the new earth, we have to remain faithful to him while we are on this earth. God "will repay each person according to what they have done" (Romans 2:6).

God promises to reward those who do His work and strive to live according to His principles – thereby helping to spread the gospel. Rewards are spoken of in the New Testament under the figure of crowns, which will be gained or lost, according to our faithfulness or otherwise. These are: the incorruptible crown, for those who live a disciplined life (1 Corinthians 9:25); the crown of life, for those who patiently endure trials and tribulations (James 1:12); the crown of glory, for those who faithfully care for the flock (1 Peter 5:2-4); the crown of righteousness, for those who love His appearing (2 Timothy 4:8); the crown of rejoicing, for all who are faithful soul-winners (1 Thessalonians 2:19-20).

And so, as we approach the end of our life on this earth, we can draw strength from knowing that if we have loved God with all our heart and have served him faithfully, we are in line for rewards that are so huge we cannot begin to fathom them.

DAY 336

December 02

Send forth your light and your truth,
let them guide me; let them bring
me to your holy mountain, to the
place where you dwell

Psalm 43:3

PSALM 43:3

Light and truth are not two separate things – they are two aspects of the same thing. Truth is the shining of light. When the light shines on us, we receive the truth. And, when we go to God, in fellowship, we are walking in the light. Therefore, on our end, there is truth, and on God's end, there is light. According to Psalm 43:3, we need both light and truth to guide us to his holy mountain – the house of God.

We need the light of God's word to guide us. "Your word is a lamp for my feet and a light for my pathway" (Psalm 119:105). We must know what the Bible says, but that alone is not enough. We must also understand it, let it "dwell in us richly" (Colossians 3:16), and allow it to guide our lives.

When we walk in the light, we must also refrain from walking where there is no light. "Enter through the narrow gate; for the gate is wide and the way is broad that leads to destruction, and there are many who enter through it. For the gate is small that leads to life, and there are few who find it" (Matthew 7:13-14). Avoiding darkness involves the daily choices of our lives. It includes being careful about what TV shows we choose to watch, what websites we visit, or what books we read. The words we speak, and the thoughts we nourish, what we do and say, both on a daily basis, and, in our spiritual practice, must be based on the word of God. If not, we are walking where the light is not shining.

DAY 337

December 03

For me the reward of
virtue is to see your face

Psalm 17:15

ALMOST THERE

PSALM 17:15

"If you want to be the best, you have to do things that others aren't willing to do" Michael Phelps

In an interview that Michael Phelps and his coach, Bob Bowman, had with 60 Minutes after the Beijing Olympics, the interviewer and Bowman discussed the vigorous training that Phelps had undergone in the lead up to the 2008 Olympics - where he would ultimately win those storied 8 gold medals. To be the best at something is, by its very definition, abnormal. To separate yourself from the crowd and become exceptional requires that you leave your comfort zone and reach out across your self-imposed limitations into the realm of the unknown.

In today's psalm, David was determined not to lose his salvation. He knew that repentance and forgiveness were needed to correct his mistakes. He realised that whatever he might gain here on earth, he could not take with him. The same principle applies to us today – "Do not store up for yourselves treasures on earth, where moths and vermin destroy, and where thieves break in and steal" (Matthew 6:19). What is important to understand is that Jesus was not placing a ban on all possessions, or forbidding us to "save for a rainy day." What he does caution against is - the selfish accumulation of goods; extravagant living; cold-heartedness that does not recognise the colossal need of the underprivileged; and the materialism which tethers our hearts to this earth. When we store our treasures on this earth, we are not being provident, but covetous. On the other hand, laying up treasure in heaven lasts for eternity.

Michael Phelps had to dedicate himself to achieve his gold medals- Christians must dedicate themselves to developing a Christ-like character, and growing in the knowledge of Christ. This leads to an increase in faith, hope, and love. Our "Gold medal" is to "see His face."

DAY 338

December 04

For I claim that love is built to last
forever and your faithfulness
founded firmly in the heavens

Psalm 89:2

ALMOST THERE

PSALM 89:2

When you love, give it everything you have got. And when you reach your limit, give it more and forget the pain of it. Because as you face your death it is only the love you have given and received which will count, and all the rest: the accomplishments, the struggle, the fights will be forgotten in your reflection and if you have loved well, then it will all have been worth it. And the joy of it will last you through the end. But if you have not, death will always come too soon and be too terrible to face.
- Richard Allen

In the twilight of our lives, love will be the measure by which we are judged.
- Maurice Chevalier

DAY 339

December 05

So teach us to number our days,
That we may gain a heart of wisdom

Psalm 90:12

ALMOST THERE

PSALM 90:12

Benjamin Franklin wrote: "Dost thou love life? Then do not squander time, for time is the stuff life is made of." What does it mean to number our days? It's not the ability to count how many days we have lived, or to predict how many days we have left. It means realizing the brevity of life – knowing that we only have so many days on this earth, and that we need to "seize the day" and live each moment to the fullest. The Apostle James describes the brevity of life like this – "It is just a vapour that appears for a little while and then vanishes away" (James 4:14). Think of steam from a boiling pot, and how fast the steam disappears once the lid is lifted from it – that is a metaphor of life.

When we recognize that our time on earth is limited, that truth should make us seriously consider how we spend that time. That, in turn, should help us grow in wisdom. Instead of chasing after the next promotion, a salary increase, a new car, or a bigger home, we should rather learn to "love the time." We should cherish the chance to watch the sunrise, or the moments spent driving our children to school. Waiting in line at the grocery store and making an effort to talk to an elderly person, goes a long way to help spread God's love and reveal His glory. Some might choose to build their life around self-gratification, without any regard for the consequences of their actions, or the way of life God has ordained – "Let us eat and drink, for tomorrow we die" (1 Corinthians 15:32). The Christian, however, uses his time to prepare for eternity. He takes these words of scripture to heart – "So teach us to number our days that we may gain a heart of wisdom."

DAY 340

December 06

Return to your resting place, my soul,
Yahweh has treated you kindly.

Psalm 116:7

PSALM 116:7

"I feel thin, sort of stretched, like butter scraped over too much bread" - Bilbo Baggins

It is challenging to be a Christian in this modern world – we are too busy, too connected, and too afraid of silence. For most of us, our jobs may very well be our "new" religion. Circumstances call for 10-hour days during the week, with periodic working over the weekends. And, with smart phones and wireless lap tops, we are virtually able to be "on the job" 24/7. In between, we have to find time to be a family man or woman – often watching our children grow up far too quickly, and wondering if we are being the parents we are truly meant to be. As a result, we feel physically exhausted, mentally worn down, emotionally volatile and, sadly, spiritually thin. This in turn leads to conflict, emotional strife, stress and, ultimately, separation from God.

Jesus said, "Come to me, all you who labour and are heavy laden and I will give you rest. Take my yoke upon you and learn from me…and you will find rest for your souls" (Matthew 11:28-29).

We cannot allow the choices we make to distract us from God and cause us to focus on the things of this world. The key is to make a move towards God. This means re-evaluating and prioritising our schedule, eliminating distractions as much as possible, but mostly, making room and time for God's word. Then he will bathe our soul in a salve of encouragement and healing, restoring the presence of His life-giving Spirit.

DAY 341

December 07

Again, the kingdom of heaven is like a dragnet that was cast into the sea and gathered some of every kind, which when it was full, they drew to the shore; and they sat down and gathered the good into vessels, but threw the bad away

Matthew 13:47-48

MATTHEW 13:47-48

The dragnet is a weighted net that is dragged along the bottom of a body of water to collect an assortment of fish. The net gathers all types of fish, regardless of their value. As a result, after the catch, fishermen need to sort the fish into "good" and "bad". Those worth keeping are gathered into containers, but the rest get tossed away.

In the same way, the gospel message is widely spread across the world, and most people get the opportunity to embrace it. But, just as there are many different types of fish, the gospel message is heard by all, but acted upon in a variety of ways. Jesus taught us that a day of reckoning will come when God will lay open the dragnet and look at each person's life in detail. It is in repenting from our sin, and in desiring to do the will of God, that we become "good" fish – thereby being placed in the Kingdom of God.

DAY 342

December 08

"For nothing is secret that will not be revealed, nor anything hidden that will not be known and come to light."

Luke 8:17

LUKE 8:17

A voice of one calling in the desert: "Prepare the way for the Lord; Make straight in the wilderness a highway for our God every valley shall be raised up, every mountain and hill made low; the rough ground shall become level, the rugged places a plain. And the glory of the Lord will be revealed, and all mankind together will see it. For the mouth of the Lord has spoken."

Isaiah 40:3-5

DAY 343

December 09

Himself bears witness with our spirit that we are children of God, and if children, then heirs – heirs of God and joint heirs with Christ, if indeed we suffer with Him, that we may also be glorified together

Romans 8:16-17

ROMANS 8:16-17

What is the witness of the Holy Spirit? The Holy Spirit wants us to be acceptable in the eyes of God. "As obedient children, do not be conformed to the former lusts which were yours in your ignorance, but like the Holy One that called you, be holy yourselves also in all your behaviour; because it is written, "For you shall be holy, for I am holy" (1 Peter 1:16). The Holy Spirit tells us to "gird" our minds for action, and to "fix" our hope on the grace to come when Jesus returns. He tells us to be "holy and to conduct ourselves with fear or reverence" during our time on earth.

We therefore have determined to live in a way that our Father approves, putting away such things as malice, hypocrisy and envy, and to replace them with the good characteristics we find in the word.

When we read and obey, we become children of the word. It is then that the Holy Spirit bears witness that we are children of God. When we hear and obey, He assures our hearts of our acceptability unto God.

DAY 344

December 10

The fear of the Lord is the beginning of wisdom all those who practise it have a good understanding. His praise endures forever!

Psalm 111:10

PSALM 111:10

The bible mentions two specific types of fear. The first is beneficial, and is to be encouraged. The second is detrimental, and is to be overcome.

The fear of God is beneficial. This type of fear does not necessarily mean to be afraid of something. Rather, it is a reverential awe of God; a reverence for His power and glory; But, also a respect for His wrath and anger. In fearing God, we acknowledge all that He is. Fear of the Lord brings with it many blessings and benefits.

However, the second type of fear mentioned, is not beneficial at all. This is the "spirit of fear" mentioned in 2 Timothy 1:7 -"For God has not given us a spirit of fear, but of power and of love and of a sound mind."

Sometimes this "spirit of fear" overcomes us and, if we want to overcome it, we must trust and love God, completely. "Perfect love drives out fear, because fear has to do with punishment. The one who fears is not made perfect in love." (1 John 4:18)

God knows no one is perfect and He reminds us to "fear not".

DAY 345

December 11

When Simon Peter heard that it was the Lord, He tucked in his garment, for he was lightly clad, and jumped into the sea

John 21:7

JOHN 21:7

How often in our busy lives are we so eager to be in the presence of the Lord that we will literally "jump into the sea and swim towards him"?

Simon Peter swam towards the resurrected Jesus. His love for the Lord was so great that he couldn't wait a moment longer to get to him. Fortunately, we don't have to go to such lengths to spend time with Jesus. In the Adoration of the Blessed Sacrament, we are in the presence of the Lord. When partaking in Holy Communion, we remember His sacrifice, and are spiritually enriched by His presence at the celebration. As children of God we should always be as eager as Simon Peter to get close to Jesus. By uncluttering and prioritising our time, we can make space in our busy schedules to spend loving and serving Him.

DAY 346

December 12

Though I thought I had toiled in vain, and for nothing, uselessly, spent my strength, yet my reward is with the Lord......

Isaiah 49:4

ISAIAH 49:4

It is so easy to forget that our reward is in heaven. As a medical doctor, I spend my days helping and serving others. It is a rare occurrence for anybody to acknowledge and thank me for the time invested in caring for them. No doubt, people in other serving professions experience the same feelings of "giving without appreciation." At times, you wonder if it is all worthwhile.

Isaiah reminds us that our focus is on the Lord, and that we live our lives in service to Him. He suffered in order to save us. Now He asks us to serve and love our neighbour in order to spread His message of kindness. Jesus promises us everlasting life if we follow His example of sacrifice. That is worth more than any earthly reward or praise.

DAY 347

December 13

Unless one is born of water and Spirit
He cannot enter the kingdom of God.
What is born of flesh is flesh
And what is born of Spirit is Spirit.

John 3:5-6

JOHN 3:5-6

In the Old Testament, Water and Spirit often refer symbolically to spiritual renewal and cleansing.

"For I will take you from the nations, gather you from all the lands and bring you into your own land. Then I will sprinkle clean water on you, and you will be clean; I will cleanse you from all your filthiness and from all your idols; Moreover, I will give you a new heart and put a new spirit within you; and I will remove the heart of stone from your flesh and give you a heart of flesh. I will put My Spirit within you and cause you to walk in My statutes, and you will be careful to observe My ordinances." (Ezekiel 36:24-27)

This passage describes Israel's restoration to the Lord by the new covenant.

Against this backdrop, Christ's point in John's gospel is unmistakeable. Without the spiritual washing of the soul, a cleansing accomplished only by the Holy Spirit (Titus 3:5), through the Word of God (Ephesians 5:26), no one can enter God's kingdom.

DAY 348

December 14

Whoever lives the truth comes to the light, so that his works may be clearly seen as done in God

John 3:21

JOHN 3:21

"For God so loved the world, that he gave his only begotten Son, that whosoever believeth in him should not perish, but have everlasting life" (John 3:16). Jesus is the light, sent by God, to show us the way to truthful living.

What is this truth? It is life filled with the fruits of the spirit – love, joy, peace, forbearance, kindness, goodness, faithfulness, gentleness and self-control. It is a life that abhors evil, and speaks out against discrimination and inequality. It is a life spent in quiet communion with God and being part of the Body of Christ.

Living the truth is not easy, but the more we focus on living it and asking God's help in our dark moments, the closer we come to the loving light.

DAY 349

December 15

And this is eternal life,
That they may know you,
The only true God, and Jesus
Christ whom you have sent

John 17:3

JOHN 17:3

This verse is the only place in the scriptures that Jesus defines "eternal life", and it refers to the personal, heart to heart, relationship the Christian is expected to have with God, the Father, and with Jesus himself.

What is the key to truly knowing God? All of us have a strong desire to be loved and known by others. Often we define ourselves by the relationships we form, and by the wealth and possessions we accumulate. We try to find happiness in the empty promises that come from this world, and in living a hedonistic lifestyle.

All of us have sinned and fall short of the glory of God. This sinfulness prevents us from knowing God. Jesus makes it clear that He alone is the way to eternal life and to a personal knowledge of God: "I am the way, the truth, and the life; no one comes to the Father, but through me." (John 14:6)

Once we understand and accept this truth, we can start our journey towards knowing God in a personal way. A key ingredient on this journey is realising that the Bible is God's word and his revelation of himself, his promises, and his will. According to Timothy, all scripture is "God-breathed and useful for teaching, rebuking, correcting, and training in righteousness, so that the man of God may be thoroughly equipped for every good work" (2 Timothy 3:16-17). But we cannot simply read and understand the word. We must apply it in our lives and remain faithful to it. Regular prayer, devotion, fellowship and worship, are also means to bring us closer to God. But, in the end, it is accepting that we, on our own, cannot truly know God – it is the faith we have in Jesus, and his victory on the cross, that allows us to experience an intimate and personal relationship with God, and, that ultimately, will bring us to eternal life.

DAY 350

December 16

Therefore if you bring your gift to the altar, and there remember that your brother has something against you, leave your gift there before the altar, and go your way. First be reconciled to your brother, and then come and offer your gift.

Matthew 5:23-24

MATTHEW 5:23-24

Discover forgiveness that gives you a chance to start over again – this is one of the ten life changing truths described by Prof Jan van der Watt in his book "The Bible in 40 days." Forgiveness is God's special medicine for people who make mistakes. Forgiveness is Godly. It fixes relationships, and it builds bridges so people can start over with God.

Jesus clearly warned that God will not forgive our sins if we do not forgive those who sin against us (Matthew 6:14-15; Mark 11:25). Yet forgiveness is very different from reconciliation. It is possible to forgive someone without offering immediate reconciliation. Forgiveness can occur in the context of one's relationship with God apart from contact with the offender. Reconciliation, on the other hand, is focussed on restoring broken relationships. And where trust is deeply broken, restoration can be a lengthy process.

Differing from forgiveness, reconciliation is conditioned on the attitude and actions of the offender. If they are genuinely repentant, they will recognize, and accept, that the harm they have caused may require time to heal. Even when God forgives our sins, he does not promise to remove all consequences created by our actions. In today's verse, Jesus speaks urgently about reconciliation. Those of us who have been seriously hurt are, rightfully, hesitant about reconciling with the one that did us harm. However, if they are genuinely repentant, it is important to be open to the possibility of restoration.

"Only Christ brings lasting peace – peace with God – peace amongst people and nations and peace in our hearts"
- Billy Graham

DAY 351

December 17

Think of what is above, not of what is on earth.
For you have died, and your life is hidden with
Christ in God. When Christ your life appears,
Then you too will appear with him in glory.

Colossians 3:2-4

ALMOST THERE

COLOSSIANS 3:2-4

St John said that we are in the world but not of the world.

Being "in" the world means being able to enjoy the beauty that God created, without being caught up in worldly pleasures, or succumbing to worldly values.

We are in this world to bring light to those in spiritual darkness. Our lives should show that we are not ruled by sin, or bound by the principles of this world.

"By their fruits you shall know them." (Matthew 7:16) It is our responsibility, as God's children on earth, to exhibit the fruits of the Spirit in our daily lives.

DAY 352

December 18

My sheep hear my voice;
I know them, and they follow me.
I give them eternal life, and they shall never perish.
No one can take them out of my hand.
My Father, who has given them to me,
Is greater than all.......

John 10:27-29

JOHN 10:27-29

As parents, we realise we cannot shield our children from all the danger, hardship, and hurt, they will face during their lifetime. In so much as we cannot avoid our own suffering, we cannot prevent theirs. They will be subjected to illness, peer pressure, criminal intent, and countless other tribulations. Adding this to their own weaknesses and limitations, it becomes easy to understand why so many go astray.

Yet Jesus assures us that as His children, we will never go astray. He is the Good Shepherd, guiding and protecting us. As long as we recognise His voice, He will lead us into everlasting life. He does not promise a life free from suffering, but promises to guide and comfort us during times of hardship. Above all, He promises us eternal life, with God the Father- if we hear and listen to His voice.

DAY 353

December 19

You have faith in God; have faith also in me. In my Father's house there are many dwelling places... and if I go and prepare a place for you, I will come back again and take you to myself.....

John 14:1-3

ALMOST THERE

JOHN 14:1-3

Christians are "future people",
because we have a future with
God. Death is not the end
it is merely a doorway to
a new beginning.
- The Bible in 40 days by
Professor Jan van der Watt

Jesus became man and
sacrificed himself on the cross
in order to save us from sin, and
secure eternal life for us. This is
the foundation of our Christian
faith. If we truly believe that He
has secured a place for us in
God's house, we ought not to
lay our anchor too deeply
in this world.

DAY 354

December 20

One thing I ask of the Lord; This I seek:
To dwell in the house of the Lord all the
days of my life, that I may gaze on the
loveliness of the Lord.....

Psalm 27:4

PSALM 27:4

"Let us live, then, in the light of eternity. If we do not, we are weighting the scales against our eternal welfare. We must understand that "what-so-ever a man soweth" must be taken in its widest meaning, and that every thought and intent of the heart will come under the scrutiny of the Lord at His coming. We can be sure that at the Judgement Seat of Christ there will be a marked difference between the Christian who has lived his life before the Lord, clearly discerning what was for the glory of God, and another Christian who was saved in a rescue mission at the tag end of a depraved and vicious life, or a nominal Christian saved on his deathbed after a life of self-pride, self-righteousness, self-love, and self-sufficiency. All will be in heaven, but the differences will be eternal. We may be sure that the consequences of our character will survive the grave and that we shall face those consequences at the Judgement Seat of Christ."

- Donald Gray Barnhouse (Pastor, Preacher, Radio Pioneer, Theologian, Christian Author)

DAY 355

December 21

The city had no need of sun or moon to shine on it, for the glory of God gave it light, and its lamp was the Lamb.

Revelation 21:23

ALMOST THERE

REVELATION 21:23

The Holy City has no need for the sun and the moon to illume it. The glory of God in the midst of it radiates light to all the surrounding regions. Light is the emblem of knowledge and holiness. "God is light, and in Him is no darkness at all." (1 John 1:5) Jesus is the lamb, and He came as the Light of the World.

As Christians, we also have no need to depend on the sun and the moon to provide our light. Jesus promised to be the sun and the moon for His people. Through His holy church on earth, He leads us towards everlasting life. Through the Holy Spirit, we receive knowledge, and become holy. When we follow the light, we become bearers of the light. And as bearers of light, we lead others to the love and forgiveness of God.

DAY 356

December 22

He will send out the angels and gather his elect..... from the end of the earth to the end of the sky

Mark 13:27

MARK 13:27

"There are no CROWN-WEARERS in Heaven who were not CROSS-BEARERS here below"- Charles Spurgeon (1834-1892).

Yet, as Mark Buchanan so rightly says, "If we are going to become heavenly-minded, we need a vision of heaven worthy of the effort…" So, what keeps motivating Christians around the world to give their lives in service to God? It is God's promise of amazing rewards – the bible is filled with them. God made these promises to keep us from giving up hope, to inspire us to persist in the face of troubles and hardships.

St Paul sums up the subject of a believer being motivated by rewards with this statement: "Therefore, my dear brothers, stand firm. Let nothing move you. Always give yourself fully to the work of the Lord, because you know that your labour in the Lord is not in vain." (1 Corinthians 15:58)

God promises His elect more than we can ever ask for or imagine – "No eye has seen, no ear has heard, no mind has conceived what God has prepared for those who love him." (1 Corinthians 2:9)

DAY 357

December 23

So we fix ours eyes not on what is seen, but on what is unseen. For what is seen is temporary, but what is unseen is eternal.

2 Corinthians 4:18

ALMOST THERE

2 CORINTHIANS 4:18

Now faith is being sure of what we hope for and certain of what we do not see" (Hebrews 11:1)

Faith is the means by which we can see that which is unseen.

It is so easy to get caught up in trappings of this life – riches, honours, carnal pleasures, profits. To "look" at these things is to desire them, and to make them the main focus and purpose of our life. And often, for the believer, as we lose sight of our discipleship, we also lose sight of our Christian values and principles.

Jesus urged us to "be in this world, but not of the world." (John 15:19)

As followers of Christ, sin has no power over us, and we don't have to be slaves to the principles and values of this world. The objects of faith - immortality, eternal life, the searching for holiness, and producing the fruits of the spirit, are the things that are unseen. They are the things that are eternal. They are the things that Jesus died for and that the Holy Spirit keeps alive in our hearts. When we die to the pleasures of this earth, we inherit eternal life and the peace that passes all understanding.

DAY 358

December 24

But in keeping with His promise we are looking forward to a new heaven and a new earth, the home of righteousness

2 Peter 3:13

2 PETER 3:13

On Christmas Day Jesus Christ was born, and His journey on this earth began. He was sent by God, his Father, to establish his church on earth and to choose the custodians of God's message. Finally, He would sacrifice himself on the cross as atonement for our sins - thereby paving a way forward for us.

It is easy to forget that Jesus has already taken care of our future. In times of crisis, and when faced with the corruption, failures, pain and problems, encountered on a daily basis, we lose all hope and courage. But, Jesus promised a life of abundance, and this promise encompasses the here and now, as well as all eternity. The Holy Spirit is ever present to assist in dealing with feelings of despair and coping with life's circumstances. We are never alone – "if God is for us, who can be against us?" (Romans 8:31)

When we grow weary of life's battles, let us take refuge in the knowledge that we are promised a new heaven and a new earth – in which righteousness, peace, and harmony, reigns.

DAY 359

December 25

For unto us a Child is born, unto us a Son is given; and the government will be upon His shoulder. And his name will be called Wonderful, Counsellor, Mighty God, Prince of Peace.

Isaiah 9:6-7

ALMOST THERE

ISAIAH 9:6-7

If Jesus was to be called by all these names – Wonderful, Counsellor, Mighty God, Prince of Peace- why was he born in a stable? Was it purely coincidence or was it a significant part of the Christmas story?

"And this shall be a sign unto you; Ye shall find the babe wrapped in swaddling clothes, lying in a manger" (Luke 2:12). Father Michael van Sloun believes that Jesus was not laid in a manger by accident. He believes that it is a major spiritual symbol. Animals go to the manger for physical food, but with Jesus lying on the hay, we can go there for spiritual food. Jesus feeds us with Word and Sacrament- His gospel, and the Eucharist. Jesus wants us to devour his word (Jeremiah 15:16, Revelation 10:9-10), chew on it, ruminate on its meaning, swallow and digest it, and then make it part of the fabric of our being. Jesus' word has the power to save our souls, and the infant in the feeding trough is the Bread of Life (John 6:35), and whoever eats this bread will live forever (John 6:51).

Jesus, born in a stable and lying in a manger, could also signify the kind of God he is. Why would the God who is worthy to "receive glory and honour and power" (Revelation 5:12), have such a lowly birth? Perhaps it means that, just like in a stable, no matter how smelly, dirty, noisy, and crowded our lives are, Jesus wants to be a part of it. No matter how much we mess up, regardless of how bad we believe we are, or how much guilt we carry with us, Jesus wants us to invite him in.

"Christ's character was more wonderful than his greatest miracle" Alfred Lord Tennyson

DAY 360

December 26

Therefore be merciful, just as your Father also is merciful. "Judge not, and you shall not be judged. Condemn not, and you shall not be condemned. Forgive, and you shall be forgiven. Give and it will be given to you: good measure, passed down, shaken together and running over, will be put into your bosom. For with the same measure that you use, it will be measured back to you"

Luke 6:36-38

LUKE 6:36-38

For Jesus, forgiveness is paramount. He often spoke about forgiveness, forgave those who sinned against others, and forgave those who sinned against him.

Jesus taught, "If you forgive others their transgressions, your heavenly Father will forgive you." (Matthew 6:14) When Peter asked how often it is necessary to forgive, he replied, "Seventy-seven times" (Matthew 18:22). This number is to be taken symbolically, not literally, to illustrate the never-ending way we are expected to forgive. Forgiveness requires compassion – remembering the humanity in each person. Jesus demonstrates this in the kind and merciful way he forgave those who had lost their way. When the sinful woman bathed his feet with her tears, and wiped them with her hair, Jesus said, "Your sins are forgiven" (Luke 7:48); when a woman caught in adultery was brought before him, he said, "I do not condemn you" (John 8:11); and as he hung on the cross he told the repentant criminal, "Today you will be with me in paradise" (Luke 23:43).

Jesus wants us to forgive those who directly hurt or betray us, just as he did. He prayed for the soldiers that had scourged and nailed him. And, after the resurrection, in the Upper Room, even though Peter had denied him, and the others had deserted him, instead of being angry, he chose to show compassion and says to them "Peace be with you" (John 20:19). Forgiveness refuses to seek vengeance, fosters an inner attitude of grace, and necessitates that we pray for those who do us harm.

DAY 361

December 27

And so we have the prophetic word confirmed, which you do well to heed as a light that shines in a dark place, until the day dawns and the morning star rises in your hearts

2 Peter 1:19

2 PETER 1:19

Just as surely as a calendar year ends and a new one begins, our earthly life will come to an end and we will enter a new life in the presence of God our Father.

As we approach the end of our life, the words of scripture should encourage us, lead us, and educate us. 2 Peter 1:16-21, focuses on Old Testament prophecies about Christ that have been fulfilled. The birth, life, death, and resurrection, of Jesus, were all prophesied in the Old Testament. The Apostle Peter, near death, insisted that his eyewitness of the transfiguration confirms that the prophecies about the Messiah are true, and that it vindicates everything which had been written about the Messiah by the prophets of old. The "Transfiguration" was the moment witnessed by Peter, James and John, when Christ was revealed in His bright and shining glory (Luke 9:28-36), and a voice from heaven declared that Jesus is His Son (2 Peter 1:16-18).

We live in a world of darkness, sin, hardship, and disease. Yet, for most of us, the realities of this life are easier to face than the uncertainty surrounding death, and life thereafter. But, the Apostle Peter describes Jesus as the Morningstar (a name also given to him in Revelation 22:16). Jesus will bring light to the world and to our hearts. And so, as our time on this earth draws to a close, we can look forward to those prophecies that are not yet fulfilled – especially the one pointing to Jesus' return as judge and king. But we cannot be idle while we wait – we must work hard to add to our faith the goodness and qualities of Jesus.

DAY 362

December 28

So the last shall be first, and the first last: for many shall be called, but few chosen

Matthew 20:16

MATTHEW 20:16

What Jesus is teaching in today's verse, (that comes from the parable of the landowner who hires workers for his vineyard), is that heaven's value system is far different from earth's value system. Those who are esteemed and respected in this world may be frowned upon by God. The opposite is also true: those who are despised and rejected in this world may, in fact, be rewarded by God. More often than not we view the world, ourselves, and others, through the lens of fairness rather than grace – the exact opposite of how God views the world and our lives. Fairness is based on what we deserve, how hard we work, what we achieve, how we behave. We live in, and promote, a wage based society in which you earn what you get. You deserve the consequences, good or bad, of your actions. However, in God's value system, grace trumps human fairness. In God's world, grace is the rule, not the exception. Grace looks beyond our productivity, our appearance, our race or ethnicity, our accomplishments, our failures. Earning our way makes distinctions and separates. Grace seeks unity and inclusion. It reminds us that we are not nearly as self-sufficient, deserving, or independent, as we would like to believe. Grace does not justify, or excuse, discrimination, unfairness, or oppression – rather it reveals the goodness of God.

When we accept and understand God's grace, we will refuse to compete in such a way that someone must lose in order for us to win. When we stop comparing ourselves, and our lives, to others, we create room for grace to emerge. When we let go of comparison, competition, expectation, and judgement, we find the way of grace – the way of God.

DAY 363

December 29

I heard a loud voice from the throne saying, "Now the dwelling of God is with men, and He will live with them. They will be His people, and God himself will be with them and be their God. He will wipe every tear from their eyes. There will be no more death or mourning or crying or pain, for the old order of things has passed away."

Revelation 21:3-4

REVELATION 21:3-4

Tears are part and parcel of the human condition. In Ecclesiastes 3:4, Solomon tells us that there "is a time to weep, and a time to mourn, and a time to dance." Since the time of Eden, the history of humanity has been a "trail of tears" – a constant treadmill of hunger, pain, sorrow and abuse. But, although the Bible calls this earth "the Valley of Tears", we are never truly alone when we cry. The Psalmist, David, wrote, "You keep track of all my sorrows. You have collected all my tears in your bottle. You have recorded each one in your book." (Psalm 56:8)

Most of us have wiped tears from someone else's eyes, or had our own tears of pain or sorrow, wiped from our face. As children it is easy to be on the receiving end of such affection. But, as we get older, crying becomes something we tend to do more privately. It is an incredibly intimate thing to cry in front of someone else and have them reach out and comfort us in our moment of distress. The wiping away of tears is a gesture that both acknowledges pain, and shows compassion. In this world of sadness it is our Christian duty to give lifesaving smiles, hugs, and kisses. Mother Teresa believed that the poor and destitute don't need our tears of guilt and feelings of inadequacy - because we cannot change their plight. They need a sense of belonging and acknowledgement – they want to experience love and compassion. By performing small acts of kindness - a simple smile, or a "hello" – we can make a person's day brighter. At the orphanage, Shishu Bavhan, every morning, volunteers go from crib to crib, picking up each baby, and giving them a loving hug. Mother Teresa believed that these babies could get medicine and food, but if they were not hugged, they would die. We are promised a time when there will be no more crying or pain. But we have to heed the words of Jesus – "truly I tell you, whatever you did for the least of these brothers and sisters of mine you did for me." (Matthew 25:40)

"Death belongs to life as birth does. The walk is in the raising of the foot as it is in the laying down of it"

DAY 364

December 30

The Lord bless you and keep you; The Lord make His face shine upon you, and be gracious to you; The Lord turn his face towards you, and give you peace.

Numbers 6:24-26

ALMOST THERE

NUMBERS 6:24-26

As Christians, we often call ourselves "blessed". Unfortunately, we are usually referring to material gain and prestige – "this new car is such blessing; feeling really blessed today – finally got the promotion I was hoping for; my child got the gold medal for achievement in sport – God certainly heaps his blessings on our family".

Thinking we are "blessed" because of fame and fortune, goes against the grain of everything that Jesus taught. If we want to define "blessing", Jesus spells it out quite clearly: "Blessed are the poor in spirit, for theirs is the kingdom of heaven. Blessed are those who mourn, for they will be comforted. Blessed are the meek, for they will inherit the earth. Blessed are they who hunger and thirst after righteousness, for they will be filled. Blessed are the merciful, for they shall be shown mercy. Blessed are the poor in heart, for they will see God. Blessed are the peacemakers, for they will be called the sons of God. Blessed are those who are persecuted because of righteousness, for theirs is the kingdom of heaven."
(Matthew 5:1-12)

We belong to a God who gives hope to the hopeless, who loves the unlovable, who comforts the sorrowful. He has planted that same power within us. We are meant to emulate his example - then his face will shine upon us, then he will be gracious unto us, and then he will grant us peace.

"Watching a peaceful death of a human being reminds us of a falling star - One of a million lights in a vast sky that flares up for a brief moment only to disappear into the endless night forever"- Elizabeth Kubler-Ross

DAY 365

December 31

May the grace of the Lord Jesus Christ, and the love of God, and the fellowship of the Holy Spirit be with you all.

2 Corinthians 13:14

ALMOST THERE

2 CORINTHIANS 13:14

This blessing, often referred to as "the benediction" or "the grace", is used by St Paul to end his letter to the Corinthian Church. It is also, possibly, the only blessing we need in our life.

The "grace of Christ" that he showed when he died to save us. The "love of God" that he constantly shows by the way he cares for us. The "fellowship of the Holy Spirit" that is ever present to guide and help us.

"May he support us all the day long till the shades lengthen and the evening comes and the busy world is hushed and the fever of life is over and our work is done. Then in his mercy may he give us a safe lodging and a holy rest and peace at the last"
- John Henry Newman

Heaven is not a place and it is not a time. Heaven is being perfect.
- Jonathan Livingstone Seagull

May the road rise up
to meet you.
May the wind be
always at your back.
May the sun shine
warm upon your face;
The rain fall soft
upon your fields.
And until we meet
again, May God hold
you in the palm of
his hand.

www.ingramcontent.com/pod-product-compliance
Lightning Source LLC
Chambersburg PA
CBHW040409010526
44108CB00046B/2771